Arabic

lonely planet

phrasebooks

and

Siona Jenkins

Egyptian Arabic phrasebook
3rd edition – May 2008

Published by
Lonely Planet Publications Pty Ltd ABN 36 005 607 983
90 Maribyrnong St, Footscray, Victoria 3011, Australia

Lonely Planet Offices
Australia Locked Bag 1, Footscray, Victoria 3011
USA 150 Linden St, Oakland CA 94607
UK 2nd floor, 186 City Rd, London, EC1V 2NT

Cover illustration
Fiery Sky by Mick Ruff

ISBN 978 1 74059 391 5

10 9 8 7 6 5 4 3 2

Printed through Colorcraft Ltd, Hong Kong
Printed in China

about the authors

Siona Jenkins went to Cairo for six months of Arabic language study in 1989 and stayed for fourteen years. She has long ago given up the rigours of the classical language for the far more useful, and easier, 'aamiya. Her language skills have been useful in ways she could never have imagined, whether for finding locals in remote oases to dress up as Romans for National Geographic television, or when appearing on the small screen as a guide and translator for wandering American magicians and Australian chefs. Now based in London, she works as a freelance journalist and travel writer. She has also penned guidebooks to Egypt and Lebanon for Lonely Planet.

from the authors

Writing a phrasebook sounded like an easy assignment – until I started doing it. The sheer volume of words and phrases sorely tested (but ultimately improved) my knowledge of Egyptian Arabic and meant that I had to find friends who were willing (or at least coercible) to double-check my work. Ghada Tantawi was a patient helper who put up with some blush-inducing questions about sexual vocabulary that were eventually ditched for propriety's sake. Ahmed Emad did not blush so easily and was also a great source of slang and football talk. Karima Khalil and Butros Wagih Boutros were incredibly helpful for medical terminology that I have thankfully never had to employ. My old teacher, Peter Daniel, checked through my presentation of grammar and made some extremely useful suggestions. Haya Husseini was a patient editor who bore this author's crazy schedule and late answers to queries with good humour. And finally, Leo was as sanguine as ever with his mother's long hours at the computer, for which he deserves a large kiss as well as a big thank you.

from the publisher

As innumerable as grains of desert sand, so too are the contributors to this book. It originated with Sally Steward and Peter D'Onghia, then spent time under the supervision of Karin Vidstrup Monk before coming under the skillful reign of Ingrid Seebus. Haya Husseini thoroughly edited the manuscript before it was passed into the hands of Vicki Webb, who proofread, further edited and sweated over the demons of the Arabic script, and Sophie Putman had the pleasure of applying her editorial talents to the final stages of its creation. Quentin Frayne keyed in part of the Arabic script and acted as Arabic consultant throughout the project. Camilia Saad took over from sister Diana Saad, checking the Arabic script and mastering the disobedient Arabic software to key in corrections. Sarah Curry helped with editing and layout checking and all were superbly supervised by Karina Coates. On the creative side, our favourite Frenchman, Fabrice Rocher, oversaw the exquisite layout provided by Yukiyoshi Kamimura, who also produced the inspirational inside illustrations. Last, but never least, Natasha Velleley applied her mapping talents to ensure we all know the region in which to use this book.

Special thanks to Dr Boyo G Ockinga, Senior Lecturer in Egyptology, Department of Ancient History, Macquarie University, for providing the section on ancient Egyptian and hieroglyphs.

Many thanks to Scott Wayne, who, with Harry Sabongy and Diana Saad, wrote the first edition of the Lonely Planet Egyptian Arabic phrasebook, from which this edition developed.

Finally, thanks to Siona Jenkins for the creation of the Sustainable Travel section for this new edition.

CONTENTS

INTRODUCTION

With around 65 million people, Egypt has one of the largest single country populations in the Arab world. Even so, Egypt's cultural and linguistic influence far outweighs its size. Because Cairo has been the centre of Arab broadcasting and film for most of this century, the city has an unrivalled cultural domination in the Arab world, and also, more significantly, within Egypt. Cairo (often referred to by the same word in Arabic as Egypt, Maṣr) is a city synonomous with a country, a reflection of the effect the Cairene metropolis has had at both regional and local levels.

In the rest of the Arab world, rare is the community that has never heard Cairene (Egyptian) Arabic dialect in a soap opera or radio broadcast. As a result of this cultural saturation, Cairene Arabic is the closest Arabs have to a colloquial lingua franca. Although there are regional variations within Egyptian Arabic, primarily between the north and the south, Cairene Arabic is spoken throughout the country and understood throughout the Arab world.

The ancient Egyptians were a Hamito-Semitic race, which meant that their language was related to the Semitic language family, including Arabic, Hebrew and Aramaic, as well as the languages of East Africa (Amharic and Galla). Christianity became the official religion of Egypt in 312 AD, along with the rest of the Roman Empire. Coptic, the language of Christian Egyptians, was an amalgam of Greek and ancient Pharaonic languages. A few words survive from this earlier time, mostly in the form of placenames and in the Coptic calendar, which is still used by farmers throughout the country. But apart from these few exceptions, Coptic was almost entirely supplanted by Arabic after the Muslim conquest of Egypt in 639 AD.

As in all other Arab countries, the written and spoken word may differ in Egypt. Roughly speaking, written Arabic is divided into two categories: Classical Arabic is the language of the Qurān (Koran) and of ritual; while Modern Standard Arabic mixes the classical form with contemporary words and usage. It is the language of the media and is used throughout the Arab world. But try to speak either of these on the street and you're likely to be met with blank stares, curiosity or laughter. Colloquial Arabic, or 'amiyya, is the variety people speak. Although 'amiyya is not, strictly speaking, a written language, it's often used in political cartoons in newspapers and magazines, as well as in popular music. It's also the language of some protest poetry and literature, an effective device in a country where almost half the population is illiterate.

A rough written version of Egyptian 'amiyya has evolved, based on Modern Standard Arabic, but with sentence structure and spelling adjusted to reflect the spoken word. This is the style used with the Arabic script that accompanies the transliteration of the language in this phrasebook. This should be useful for those with some background in Arabic, or for those who want to learn the script. And it can be pointed to as a last resort for those who've failed to make themselves understood.

The Arabic script in this book, unlike in the transliterations, shows only the masculine form. Don't forget that Arabic is, of course, read and written from right to left.

ARTHUR OR MARTHA?

All Arabic nouns are either masculine or feminine. Many feminine nouns end in the suffix -a, or -ya, while masculine nouns may end in any letter. (See Grammar, page 19.)

In this phrasebook, the feminine ending of a word is separated from the masculine form by a slash:

engineer	muhandis/a (m/f)	مهندس
journalist	ṣaHafi/ya (m/f)	صحفى

Do you speak English?
bititkallim/ee ingileezi? (m/f) بتتكلم إنجليزى؟

When the difference between masculine and feminine forms is more complex, both forms of a word are given in full:

What's your name? ismak/ismik ey? (m/f)

ABBREVIATIONS USED IN THIS BOOK

adj	adjective
f	feminine
lit	literally
m	masculine
n	noun
pl	plural
sg	singular

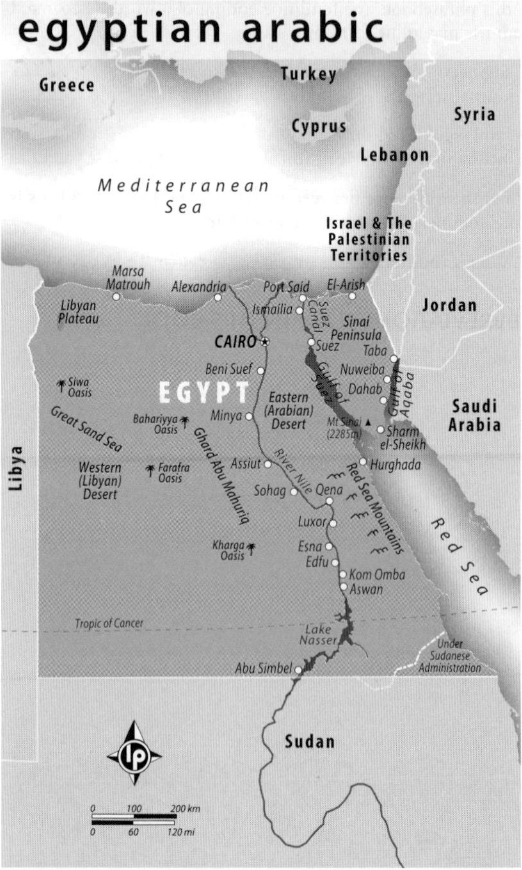
egyptian arabic
Greece
Turkey
Syria
Cyprus
Lebanon
Mediterranean Sea
Israel & The Palestinian Territories
Marsa Matrouh
Alexandria
Port Said
El-Arish
Jordan
Libyan Plateau
Ismailia
Suez Canal
Sinai Peninsula
CAIRO
Suez
Taba
Beni Suef
Nuweiba
Gulf of Suez
Gulf of Aqaba
Siwa Oasis
EGYPT
Dahab
Eastern (Arabian) Desert
Saudi Arabia
Great Sand Sea
Bahariyya Oasis
Minya
Mt Sinai (2285m)
Sharm el-Sheikh
Ghard Abu Mahuriq
Libya
Western (Libyan) Desert
Farafra Oasis
Assiut
River Nile
Hurghada
Red Sea Mountains
Sohag
Qena
Red Sea
Luxor
Kharga Oasis
Esna
Edfu
Kom Omba
Aswan
Tropic of Cancer
Lake Nasser
Under Sudanese Administration
Abu Simbel
Sudan
0
100
200 km
0
60
120 mi

PRONUNCIATION

For many speakers of English, pronouncing Arabic can seem like an exercise in tongue-twisting. A number of Arabic sounds don't exist in English, so trying to fit the language into easily-pronounceable Roman characters isn't easy (which is why you can see so many different spellings of English-word signs in Egypt and other Arab countries.)

But mastering the basic sounds isn't as difficult as you might think. This phrasebook uses a simplified system of transliteration that makes these sounds pronounceable for those who haven't studied linguistics or spent hours in a classroom learning the finer points of Arabic grammar. Try to pronounce the transliterated sounds and words slowly and clearly. And keep in mind that Egyptians are aware that Arabic isn't an easy language and are very forgiving of mispronunciation.

VOWELS

Vowels can be divided into two groups: short and long. Short vowels are rarely printed in Arabic script (one of the reasons the written language is so difficult to master) but are simple for English speakers to pronounce. Long vowels have only three forms but have five variations in pronunciation. Again, their pronunciation is straightforward.

Short Vowels

a as the 'a' in 'had'
e as the 'e' in 'bet'
i as the 'i' in 'hit'
u as the 'u' in 'put'

Long Vowels

aa as the 'a' in 'bad', but lengthened
ā as the 'a' in 'father'
ee as the 'ee' in 'fee'
ō as the 'o' in 'for'
oo as the 'oo' in 'boo'

Vowel Sounds (Diphthongs)

ow as the 'ow' in 'how'
ey as the 'y' in 'why'
ay as the 'ay' in 'day'

CONSONANTS

Most Arabic consonants are similar to their English counterparts (see Transliteration System on page 16). When consonants are doubled in the transliteration, both should be pronounced: Hammam, 'bathroom', is pronounced Ham-mam. Several Arabic consonants have no English equivalents, but the two characters that give non-Arabic speakers the worst nightmares are the 'ayn and the glottal stop which is called the hamza.

The 'ayn has no English equivalent and is best tried by saying 'ah' and then constricting your throat muscles as if gagging. Egyptian Arabic, particularly in and around Cairo, has a much softer 'ayn than most other Arabic dialects so people will usually understand you if you don't constrict your throat perfectly. We've transliterated it as an apostrophe (').

The glottal stop or the hamza has been transliterated as (ᶜ). It can best be described as a break in the voice, rather like the sudden stop between the words 'uh-oh', or as in the Cockney English pronunciation of the 'tt' in 'bottle'. It can occur at the beginning, middle or end of a word.

'ayn	'	a constriction of the throat
hamza (glottal stop)	ᶜ	as the vocal break in 'uh-oh'

The 'q' sound of the letter ق in the Arabic alphabet is often pronounced as a glottal stop in Egyptian Arabic.

Other Consonants

Arabic has a number of other sounds that present varying degrees of difficulty for non-native speakers. They include:

gh	a roll in the back of the throat that sounds like the Parisian 'r'
H	a strongly whispered 'h', almost like a sigh of exasperation
q	a 'k' sound pronounced at the very back of the mouth
kh	as the 'ch' in the Scottish 'loch'
r	trilled
s	as the 's' in 'sin'
sh	as the 'sh' in 'ship'. Where the 's' and the 'h' are pronounced separately, the two letters are separated by a hyphen to avoid confusion, as in as-hal, 'easier'.
zh	as in the 's' in pleasure; rarely used in Egyptian Arabic

EMPHATIC CONSONANTS

There are four emphatic consonants in Arabic: ḍ, ṣ, ṭ and ẓ. They are 'heavier' than their non-emphatic counterparts, and are pronounced with the back of the tongue raised high up in the back of the mouth. An example that could approximate the sound of an emphatic 'd' is the double 'd' in puddle.

STRESS

In Egyptian Arabic, stress is usually placed on the second-last syllable:

six	*sit*ta
bookshop/library	mak*ta*ba

If a word ends in a long vowel or in a double consonant, stress falls on the final syllable:

cupboard	dul*aab*
important	muh*imm*

In general, the stress falls on the third or last syllable if the word has three or more consonants interspersed with vowels:

she hit	ḍara*bit*

TRANSLITERATION SYSTEM

Following is a complete list of the Modern Standard Arabic alphabet. Each letter's transliterated symbol(s), as spoken in Egyptian Arabic, appears in the right column. Note that in Arabic, a letter can have up to four representations, dictated by its position in a word. Eg, the letter 'b' is quite different on its own compared to when it appears at the beginning, in the middle, or at the end of a word.

Final	Medial	Initial	Alone	Transliteration
ﺎ			أ	a/aa/ā
ﺐ	ﺒ	ﺑ	ب	b
ﺖ	ﺘ	ﺗ	ت	t
ﺚ	ﺜ	ﺛ	ث	th - transliterated as t or s in this book
ﺞ	ﺠ	ﺟ	ج	g/zh
ﺢ	ﺤ	ﺣ	ح	H
ﺦ	ﺨ	ﺧ	خ	kh
ﺪ			د	d or z
ﺬ			ذ	dh - not in Egyptian Arabic
ﺮ			ر	r
ﺰ			ز	z
ﺲ	ﺴ	ﺳ	س	s

Final	Medial	Initial	Alone	Transliteration
ـش	ـشـ	شـ	ش	sh
ـص	ـصـ	صـ	ص	ṣ
ـض	ـضـ	ضـ	ض	ḍ
ـط	ـطـ	طـ	ط	ṭ
ـظ	ـظـ	ظـ	ظ	ẓ
ـع	ـعـ	عـ	ع	the 'ayn
ـغ	ـغـ	غـ	غ	gh
ـف	ـفـ	فـ	ف	f
ـق	ـقـ	قـ	ق	q (often pronounced as a glottal stop)
ـك	ـكـ	كـ	ك	k
ـل	ـلـ	لـ	ل	l
ـم	ـمـ	مـ	م	m
ـن	ـنـ	نـ	ن	n
ـه	ـهـ	هـ	ه	h
ـو			و	oo/ō/ow
ـي	ـيـ	يـ	ي	y/ee/ay/ey

In Egyptian Arabic, the sounds of the spoken word don't always correspond to those of the written Arabic script. For this reason, we've given the colloquial pronunciation where there is a difference. For example, the letter 'th' is pronounced like the 'th' in 'thin' in classical Arabic, but is usually pronounced as a 't' or 's' in spoken Egyptian Arabic.

But the best advice to anyone trying to master the pronunciation is to simply plunge in, test the reactions and, above all, listen to native speakers and learn.

ROOTS & PATTERNS

Arabic words are based on a system of roots and patterns. While knowledge of their formation isn't crucial to being understood in Egypt, becoming familiar with the concept will give you a deeper understanding of the language.

A root is a core group of letters which is associated with a particular meaning. Usually a root will consist of three consonants, but can sometimes be made up of four or, occasionally, two.

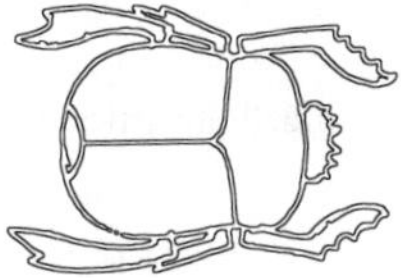

Adding various combinations (or patterns) of vowels and consonants to the root gives words that relate to the basic root meaning. For example, words based on the root ktb are related to writing:

Root: ktb

katab	he wrote
kitaab	book
maktaba	bookshop/library

Words that are based on the root drs are related to information and learning:

Root: drs

darasa	he studied
madrasa	school
mudarris	teacher (m)
dirāsa	a study

WORD ORDER

Word order in Egyptian Arabic usually follows the pattern subject-verb-object. Less frequently used, but still correct, is the standard word order in Classical Arabic: verb-subject-object.

The boy speaks English.
  il walad biyitkallim ingileezee
  (lit: the boy speaks English)
The bus arrived late.
  wiṣil il utubees mitʿakhir
  (lit: arrived the bus late)

ARTICLES

Egyptian Arabic has no indefinite article (a, an). The definite article 'the' is il:

book	kitaab	the book	il kitaab
girl	bint	the girl	il bint

When il precedes a noun that starts with d, ḍ, n, r, s, ṣ, sh, t, ṭ, z, or ẓ (and usually g and k), the l is dropped and the first consonant of the word is doubled:

sun	shams	the sun	ish shams
back	ḍahr	the back	iḍ ḍahr
dog	kalb	the dog	ik kalb

GRAMMAR

EMPHATIC TIP!

Don't let the emphatic consonants, ṣ, ḍ, ṭ and ẓ put you off. Even if you pronounce them in exactly the same way you'd normally pronounce these consonants, you'll still be clearly understood.

NOUNS

Gender

Arabic nouns are either masculine or feminine. Most feminine nouns end in the suffix -a or -ya , while masculine nouns may end with any letter:

MASCULINE		FEMININE	
book	kitaab	table	tarabeeza
morning	ṣabāH	year	sana

Some feminine nouns do not end in -a, such as the names for certain countries, cities and parts of the body:

Egypt	maṣr	mother	umm
hand	eed	sister	ukht
sun	shams		

Some masculine nouns end in -a, for instance:

air	hawa

Plurals

There are three basic forms of the plural: the dual, the standard and the collective.

1. As its name suggests, the dual is used when referring to two of something. In words that end in -a, it's formed by removing the -a and adding the suffix -tayn. For words that don't end in -a, the suffix -ayn is added.

library	maktaba	two libraries	maktabtayn
book	kitaab	two books	kitaabayn

2. Standard plurals aren't so straightforward. Regular masculine nouns take the ending -een, while regular feminine nouns substitute their -a ending with -aat.

engineer (m)	muhandis	engineers (m)	muhandiseen
engineer (f)	muhandisa	engineers (f)	muhandisaat

However, many nouns have irregular plurals that simply have to be learned:

house	bayt	houses	buyoot
school	madrassa	schools	madaaris
day	yōm	days	ayaam

3. Collective plurals are used to describe a group or class of items, particularly fruit and vegetables. In this case, the collective form is used, except when talking about a specific number, in which case you add -a to the collective form.

eggplants	bitingaan	an eggplant	bitingana
apples	tufaaH	an apple	tufaaHa
trees	shagar	a tree	shagara

ADJECTIVES

Adjectives come after the noun they describe and have to agree with the noun in both number and gender. If a noun is preceded by a definite article, then so must the adjective:

the big dog	ik kalb ik kabeer (m) (lit: the dog the big)

but:

the dog is big	ik kalb kabeer (m) (lit: the dog big)

The feminine form of the adjective is made by adding the suffix -a:

the popular girl	il bint il maHbooba (f) (lit: the girl the popular)

but:

the girl is popular	il bint maHbooba (f) (lit: the girl popular)

Plurals of adjectives vary in the same way as nouns, which means there is no set pattern. However, there are several generalisations:

1. When the plural noun refers to people, the most common form is the addition of the suffix -een to the singular form of the adjective.

the happy teacher	il mudarris il mabsooṭ (lit: the teacher the happy (sg))
the happy teachers	il mudarriseen il mabsooṭeen (lit: the teachers the happy (pl))
the angry tourist	il sāyiH il za'laan (lit: the tourist the angry (sg))
the angry tourists	il suwwāH il za'laneen (lit: the tourists the angry (pl))

2. A common irregular form of the plural adjective is the replacing of the long vowel sound in the middle of the adjective with the long vowel ā.

the big girl	il bint ik kabeera (lit: the girl the big (sg))
the big girls	il banāt ik kubār (lit: the girls the big (pl))

3. All plurals referring to inanimate objects use the feminine singular form of the adjective, regardless of the gender of the noun.

the big house	il bayt ik kibeer (lit: the house (m) the big (m, sg))
the big houses	il buyoot ik kibeera (lit: the houses the big (f, sg))
the small bus	il utubees iṣ ṣughayyar (lit: the bus (m) the small (m, sg))
the small buses	il utubeesaat iṣ ṣughayyara (lit: the buses the small (f, sg))

Comparatives & Superlatives

The comparative and superlative share the same form in Arabic and do not change according to gender. They're most commonly formed by removing the vowels from the adjective. So, kibeer, meaning 'big', becomes kbr, the root form. Then 'a' is added before the root and another 'a' before the last consonant to form akbar.

	Adjective	Root	Comparative/Superlative	
big	kibeer	kbr	akbar	bigger/biggest
cheap	rakhees	rkhs	arkhas	cheap/cheapest
many	kiteer	ktr	aktar	more/most

When used for comparison between two nouns, the word min, 'than', is added to the comparative form:

bigger than	akbar min
The girl is bigger than the boy.	il bint akbar min il walad (lit: the girl bigger than the boy)

DEMONSTRATIVES

Like adjectives, demonstratives agree with the number and gender of the noun they refer to.

this (one); that (one) (m)	da	
this (one); that (one) (f)	dee	(to refer to animals & objects, also in the plural)
these/those	dōl	(to refer to people)

this house	il bayt da (lit: the house this)
those animals	il Hayawanaat dee (lit: the animals those)

PRONOUNS

Subject Pronouns

Subject pronouns can be omitted if the subject is clear from the verb or context.

SUBJECT PRONOUNS			
SG		PL	
I	ana	we	iHna
you (m)	inta	you	intu
you (f)	inti	they	humma
he	huwa		
she	hiyya		

Object Pronouns

Object pronouns take the form of suffixes (see box below):

I saw them.	(ana) shuftuhum (lit: (I) I-saw-them)
I like it.	baHibbu (lit: I-like-him/it)

OBJECT PRONOUNS			
DIRECT OBJECTS		INDIRECT OBJECTS	
me	-ee	to me	-nee/-lee
you (m)	-ak	to you (m)	-lak
you (f)	-ik	to you (f)	-lik
him/it	-u	to him	-lu
her/it	-ha	to her	-laha
us	-na	to us	-lina
you (pl)	-ku	to you (pl)	-luku
them	-hum	to them	-luhum

Direct object pronouns can also be used with prepositions (see page 36):

This letter is from her. il maktoob da minha
(lit: the letter this from-her)

When both a direct and an indirect object pronoun occur in a sentence, the word order follows the same structure as in English: verb + direct object + indirect object.

Write it for me.
iktibhaalee

iktib	you-write
ha	it (f)
lee	for-me

Send them to us.
iba'at-humlina

iba'at	you send
hum	them
lina	to us

VERBS

Arabic has only two true tenses, which function differently to tenses in English: the imperfect tense represents incomplete action in the present or future, and the perfect (past) tense represents completed action.

Imperfect

The imperfect is formed by adding the prefixes and suffixes below to the root form of the verb. From the root form ktb (to write), the basic conjugation is derived as shown:

	Prefixes & suffixes	Imperfect	
I	a-	aktib	I write
you (m)	ti-	tiktib	you (m) write
you (f)	ti- ... -ee	tiktibee	you (f) write
he	yi-	yiktib	he writes
she	ti-	tiktib	she writes
we	ni-	niktib	we write
you (pl)	ti- ... -u	tiktibu	you (pl) write
they	yi- ... -u	yiktibu	they write

Present and future forms of a verb are formed by adding different sets of prefixes to the imperfect form of the verb.

Imperfect – Present

To form the simple present tense, the prefix bi- is added to the basic conjugation of the verb.

I write	baktib	we write	biniktib
you (m) write	bitiktib	you (pl) write	bitiktibu
you (f) write	bitiktibee		
he writes	biyiktib	they write	biyiktibu
she writes	bitiktib		

Present and continuous action is denoted by the active participle of the verb. The participle – corresponding to the -ing ending of the English verb – is treated like an adjective and must agree in number and gender.

I (m) am writing	ana kaatib
I (f) am writing	ana kaatba
you (m) are writing	inta kaatib
you (f) are writing	inti kaatba
we are writing	iHna kaatbeen
you are writing	intu kaatbeen
they are writing	huma kaatbeen

Imperfect – Future

The future is formed by adding the prefix Ha- to the imperfect form of the verb (see previous page).

I will write	Haktib	we will write	Haniktib
you (m) will write	Hatiktib	you (pl) will write	Hatiktibu
you (f) will write	Hatiktibee		
he will write	Hayiktib	they will write	Hayiktibu
she will write	Hatiktib		

Perfect (Past)

The perfect (past) tense, used for actions that have been completed, is created by adding suffixes to the root form of a verb (see page 19 for an explanation of verb roots). The third person singular (he) does not take a suffix in the perfect tense.

Root form: ktb (to write)

	SUFFIX	PERFECT	
I	-t	katabt	I wrote/have written
you (m)	-t	katabt	you (m) wrote/have written
you (f)	-tee	katabtee	you (f) wrote/have written
he	-	katab	he wrote/has written
she	-it	katabit	she wrote/has written
we	-na	katabna	we wrote/have written
you (pl)	-tu	katabtu	you wrote/have written
they	-u	katabu	they wrote/have written

TO BE

- Arabic has no present tense of the verb 'to be'.

She is from Aswan.	hiyya min aswan (lit: she from Aswan)

Subject pronouns are optional if the verb already contains the subject pronoun.

He is tired.	(huwa) ta'baan (lit: (he) he-tired)

- The perfect tense of the verb 'to be' is formed with the word kaan, 'was'. The perfect tense of kaan is formed by adding the suffixes used in the perfect tense (see above). Subject pronouns, as usual, are optional, and are shown here in brackets.

I was	(ana) kunt	we were	(iHna) kunna
you (m) were	(inta) kunt	you (pl) were	(intu) kuntu
you (f) were	(inti) kuntee		
he was	(huwa) kaan	they were	(humma) kaanu
she was	(hiyya) kaanit		

GRAMMAR

- The future tense of 'to be' is formed by adding the prefix Ha- to the imperfect form of kān (see page 26 for how to form the imperfect).

I will be	Hakoon	we will be	Hankoon
you (m) will be	Hatkoon	you (pl) will be	Hatkoonu
you (f) will be	Hatkoonee		
he will be	Haykoon	they will be	Haykoonu
she will be	Hatkoon		

- Keep in mind that 'there is' has its own construction:

there is	fee
there isn't/aren't	mafeesh
there were	kaan fee
there wasn't/weren't	makaansh fee

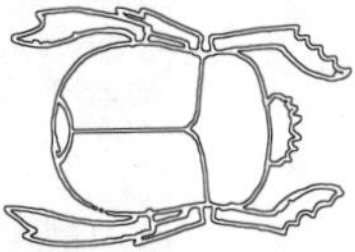

TO HAVE

- The present form of the verb 'to have' is formed by the word 'and, followed by the possessive suffix (see page 33 for possessive suffixes).

I have	'andee	we have	'andina
you (m) have	'andak	you (pl) have	'anduku
you (f) have	'andik		
he has	'andu	they have	'anduhum
she has	'andaha		

- The past of 'to have' is formed by adding the word kaan to 'and in its present form.

I had	kaan 'andee
she had	kaan 'andaha
we had	kaan 'andina

- The future of 'to have' is formed by adding Haykoon to 'and in its present form.

I will have	Haykoon 'andee
she will have	Haykoon 'andaha
we will have	Haykoon 'andina

The box below shows some key verbs. They are displayed in the first person singular present tense (except for 'be', which doesn't exist in the present tense and therefore has to be in the perfect tense; see page 28).

KEY VERBS			
be	kunt	live	a'eesh
bring	ageeb	make	a'mal
arrive/come	awṣal	meet	at^{c}aabal
depart/leave	amshi	need	aHtaag
do	a'mal	prefer	afaḍḍil
go	arooH	return	arga^c
have	andee	say	a^{c}ool
know	a'rif	stay	a^c'ud
like/love	aHib	take	aakhud

MODALS

When a verb is used as a modal with another verb, both must agree with the subject of the sentence.

Can/Could

- The imperfect form of the verb dar, 'can', is used to express 'can'.

I can	a^{c}dar	we can	ni^{c}dar
you can (m)	ti^{c}dar	you can (pl)	ti^{c}daru
you can (f)	ti^{c}daree		
he can	yi^{c}dar	they can	yi^{c}daru
she can	ti^{c}dar		

• 'Could' is expressed by placing the word kaan, 'was', before the imperfect form of dar. (See page 28 for conjugations of kaan.)

I could write.	kunt a^{c}dar aktib (lit: I-was I-can I-write)

Want

You'll be using this verb a lot. Fortunately, it's one of the easiest verbs to use.

I (f) want	'ayza	we want	'ayzeen
I (m) want	'aayiz		
you (m) want	'aayiz	you (pl) want	'ayzeen
you (f) want	'ayza		
he/it wants	'aayiz	they want	'ayzeen
she wants	'ayza		

• To use 'want' as a modal verb, its imperfect form ayiz is used together with the imperfect form of the second verb.

In the following examples, 'go' is represented by its imperfect form rooH with its prefixes ti- for the third person singular and ni- for the first person plural.

She wants to go.	'ayza tirooH (lit: she-wants she-goes)
We want to go.	'ayzeen nirooH (lit: we-want we-go)

• 'Wanted' is expressed by placing the perfect tense of kaan, 'was', before the imperfect form of 'want', ayiz.

We wanted to go.	kunna 'ayzeen nirooH (lit: we-were we-want we-go)

Must/Have To/Need To

To indicate need, Egyptian Arabic uses the word miHtaag. In its modal form, this verb behaves in the same way as 'can' and 'want'.

I (f) need a coffee.	miHtaaga ahwa (lit: I-need coffee)
We need to travel.	miHtageen nisaafir (lit: we-need we-travel)

To Like

The word yiHibb, 'to like', is used in the same way as the previous modal forms, but with the addition of the prefix bi-.

He likes to travel.	biHibb yisaafir (lit: he-likes he-travels)
They like to travel.	biHibbu yisaafiru (lit: they-like they-travel)

POSSESSION

Possessive Adjectives

The simplest way of forming the possessive is by adding a suffix to the noun.

Masculine nouns simply take a possessive suffix:

book	kitāb	my book	kitāb-ee
house	bayt	their house	bayt-hum

When a feminine noun ends in -a, replace the -a ending with -it and add then a possessive suffix (see box on next page):

ticket	tazkara	your ticket	tazkarit-ik
bag	shanṭa	our bag	shantit-na

POSSESSIVE SUFFIXES

SG		PL	
my	-ee	our	-na
your (m)	-ak	your	-ku
your (f)	-ik		
his/its	-u	their	-hum
her/its	-ha		

Bitaa'

Another way of expressing possession is through the word bitaa', which roughly translates as 'belonging to'. Bitaa' can be used as a possessive adjective (my, your) as well as on its own as a possessive pronoun (mine, yours, etc). However, when used as a possessive pronoun, it should be used only for objects and never for people. The possessive pronoun also has to agree with the gender of the noun.

	(M)	(F)
my/mine	bitaa'ee	bitaa'tee
your/yours (m)	bitaa'ak	bitaa'tak
your/yours (f)	bitaa'ik	bitaa'tik
his	bitaa'u	bitaa'tu
hers	bitaa'ha	bitaa'itha
our/ours	bitaa'na	bitaa'itna
your/yours (pl)	bitaa'ku	bitaa'itku
their/theirs	bitaa'hum	bitaa'it-hum

her book (m); the book is hers	il kitāb bitaa'ha (lit: the book belong-her)
their bag (f); the bag is theirs (f)	ish shanṭa bitaa'it-hum (lit: the bag belong-their)

QUESTIONS

Questions can be formed simply by changing the intonation of a statement from a flat tone to a rising tone, just as in English.

He brought the food.	(huwa) gaab il akl (lit: (he) brought the food)
Did he bring the food?	(huwa) gaab il akl?

Interrogatives usually come at the end of a sentence, but can be placed at the beginning of a sentence for particular emphasis. Here's an example using fayn, 'where'.

Where's the hotel?	if fundu[c] fayn? (lit: the hotel where?) fayn if fundu[c]? (lit: where the hotel?)

QUESTION WORDS			
how?	izzay?	which?	ayy?
what?	ey?	who?	meen?
when?	imta?	why?	lay?
where?	fayn?		

NEGATIVES

There are two forms of negative in Egyptian Arabic.

1. The prefix-suffix combination of ma-...-sh can be added to verbs.

He went.	huwa rāH (lit: he he-went)
He didn't go.	huwa marāHsh (lit: he he-didn't-go)

2. The negative can also be expressed with the word mish, which is similar to English 'not'. Mish is used before verbs in the future tense, as well as before adjectives and nouns.

I will not write.	mish Haktib (lit: not I'll-write)
This is not good.	da mish kuwayyis (lit: this not good)
I'm not an engineer. (m)	ana mish muhandis (lit: I (m) not engineer)

BEYOND THE VEIL

At heart, Egypt is a traditional society, and nowhere is the difference between Egyptian culture and the secular culture of industrialised countries more evident or misunderstood than in regard to women.

Cliches abound on both sides, with outsiders seeing Egyptian women as oppressed victims and Egyptians seeing Western women as immoral. For Western visitors, the veil is confirmation of all their preconceptions but, in fact, this too is a complex issue.

Egypt has experienced a wave of conservatism in recent years which has resulted in many women dressing more conservatively and, in many cases, donning the headscarf, or Higaab. This is at its most extreme (and is often a political statement) in the case of women who cover their faces and even wear gloves. For some it is an expedient: it allows them to wander around more freely, their dress stating to the world that they are 'decent'. For others, it means thumbing the nose at fashion; for others still, it *is* the fashion (check out the different ways to wear a headscarf).

Higaab	headscarf	حجاب
muHagabba	woman who wears Higaab	محجبة
niqāb	fabric covering face	نقاب
munaqqaba	woman who covers her face	منقبة

GRAMMAR

PREPOSITIONS

Most prepositions in Egyptian Arabic are straightforward and are given in the dictionary at the back of this book. However, you should be aware that object pronouns in the form of suffixes (see page 25) can be added to the following words:

against	'ala
from	min
like	zay
on	'ala
for	'ashaan
with	ma'
from me	min-nee
like you (pl)	zay-ku
for them	'ashaan-hum

COLOUR THE SKY

The preposition 'of' can be expressed through word order and the use of *one* definite article (the). As in English, the possessed noun is placed before the possessor.

the name of the city	**ism il medina** (lit: name the city)
the woman's bag	**shantit is sitt** (lit: bag the woman)

If the phrase is indefinite (a sky), the definite article is dropped (colour sky).

a name of a city	**ism medina** (lit: name city)
a woman's bag	**shantit sitt** (lit: bag woman)

CONJUNCTIONS

Conjunctions are used in exactly the same way as in English, but are more heavily stressed.

and	wa
but	bas
or	ow
if	low
until	lighaayat
since/than	min
because	'ashaan

She likes to eat and sleep.	bitHibb taakul wa tinam (lit: she-likes she-eats and she-sleeps)
We want this or these.	'ayzeen dee ow dōl (lit: we-want this or those)

FINALLY, AN INVARIABLE!

A meaning closer to the English word 'must' is expressed by the word **laazim**. This doesn't vary and appears before the imperfect form of the verb.

He must travel.	**laazim yisaafir** (lit: must he-travels)
You must go.	**laazim tirooH** (lit: must you-go)

DID YOU KNOW ...

'To like' and 'to love' are one and the same verb in Arabic, including Egyptian Arabic, and are differentiated by context only. So if you hear someone telling you that they 'love' you, all they probably mean is that they like you and are happy to tolerate you for a while.

التعارف MEETING PEOPLE

Egyptians are famous among other Arabs for their friendliness and humour. But despite their generally easy-going attitude, there are certain formalities that are always followed when meeting people. Even if simply calling a close friend on the phone, enquiries are made into their health or their family before getting down to business. Many greetings involve set responses, and these can vary depending on the gender or number of people involved, so even the simplest 'hello' is not straightforward.

YOU SHOULD KNOW مهمّ المعرفة

The word aywa is exclusive to the Egyptian dialect. Nā'am is more formal and is also used for answering when one's name is called.

Yes.	^{c}aywa/na'am	أيوه/نعم.
No.	la^{c}	لأ.
May I?; Do you mind?	mumkin?	ممكن؟
Sorry.	aasif/a (m/f)	آسف.
Never mind.	ma'lish	معليش.
You're welcome.	'afwan; il 'afu	عفواً.

Excuse me.
'an iznak/iznik/izniku (m/f/pl) — عن إذنك.

Please.
low samaHt/i/u (m/f/pl) — لو سمحت.

Thank you (very much).
shukran (gazeelan) — شكراً جزيلاً.

GREETINGS & GOODBYES اللقاء والوداع

Good morning.	ṣabaH il khayr	صباح الخير.
Response:	ṣabaH in noor	صباح النور.
Good afternoon/evening.	misa^c il khayr	مساء الخير.
Response:	misa^{c}in noor	مساء النور.

There are a number of ways of saying 'hello' in Egypt. The most formal, salaam 'alaykum, is used throughout the Arab and Islamic world. Occasionally, if you initiate the greeting, you'll also hear wa raHmat allāhi wa barakaatu (lit: and the mercy of God and his blessings) tagged onto the end. The words ahlan wa sahlan or simply ahlan are less formal.

Hi.	ahlan	أهلاً.
Goodbye.	ma'is salaama	مع السّلامة.
Bye.	bai	باي.

Hello./ Welcome.	ahlan wa sahlan	أهلاً وسهلاً.
Response:	ahlan beek/beeki/ bikum (m/f/pl)	أهلاً بيك.
Hello.	is salaam 'alaykum (lit: peace be upon you)	ألسّلام عليكم.
Response:	wa 'alaykum is salaam (lit: upon you be peace)	وعليكم السّلام.
Good night.	tiṣbaH/i/u 'ala khayr (m/f/pl)	تصبح علي خير.
Response:	winta/i/u min ahla (m/f/pl)	وأنت من أهله.

CIVILITIES آداب التعارف

Many thanks.
mut shakkreen — متشكّرين.

You're welcome.
'afwan; il 'afu — عفواً.

Excuse me. (to get attention)
low samaHt/ee/tu (m/f/pl) — لو سمحت.

Excuse me. (to get past)
'an iznak/iznik/iznuku (m/f/pl) — عن إذنك.

Excuse me. (apology)	ma'lish	معلش.
Pardon.	effendim	أفندم.

FORMS OF ADDRESS المخاطبة

Egyptians use a bewildering number of terms to address one another. There's no rule for using these titles and it takes time to learn what's appropriate. Some common titles include:

'aam	uncle	a labourer or working-class man
sheikh/Hagg	pilgrim	an old man
Hagga	pilgrim	an old woman
ustaaz/a	professor	an educated man/woman
duktōr/a	doctor	an educated man/woman
bay/hānim		a wealthy man/woman

The following are the basic forms of address that can be used as polite references or as forms of address. When used to address someone, they're usually preceded by ya.

Sir	effendim/Hadritak	أفندم
Madam	madaam/Hadritik	مدام
Mr	sayyid	سيّد
Mrs	sayyida	سيّدة
Miss	aanisa	آنسة
Excuse me, miss.	an iznik, ya aanisa	عن إذنك، يا آنسة.

BODY LANGUAGE لغة الجسم

Egyptians usually shake hands when meeting someone for the first time, but the hand is shaken loosely, not firmly. When greeting someone they know, the handshake becomes almost a slap on the palms, followed by a brief clasp.

Between women, and men who know each other well, kisses on the cheek are often exchanged. Although physical contact between the sexes isn't accepted behaviour in public, walking hand in hand is not a problem. Anything more should be kept out of the public eye.

> **TIP**
>
> The 'ayn sound (') is made by constricting the throat.
>
> The glottal stop (ᶜ) is made by a break in the voice, like the sound made between the words in 'uh-oh'.

FIRST ENCOUNTERS أول لقاء

How are you?
izayyak/izayyik/izayyuku? (m/f/pl) — إزيّك؟

Fine. And you?
kwayyis/a, al hamdulillah. — كويّس، الحمدلله.
wa inta/i? (m/f) — وأنت؟

How's it going?
'aamil/'amla/'amleen ey? (m/f/pl) — عامل إيه؟

What's your name?
ismak/ismik ey? (m/f) — إسمك إيه؟

My name is ...
ismee ... — إسمي ...

I'd like to introduce you to ...
mumkin 'arrafak/'arrafik bi ... (m/f) — ممكن أعرّفك ب ...

I'm pleased to meet you.
tasharrafna — تشرّفنا.

It was nice meeting you.
furṣa sa'eeda — فرصة سعيدة.

MEETING PEOPLE

MAKING CONVERSATION المحادثة

Do you live here?
inta 'aysh/inti 'aysha hina? (m/f) — إنت عايش هنا؟

Where are you going?
rāyiH/rayHa fayn? (m/f) — رايح فين؟

What are you doing?
bit'amal/ee ey? (m/f) — بتعمل إيه؟

This is my boyfriend/girlfriend.
da/di ṣadiqee/adiqtee (m/f) — ده صديقي.

This is my husband.
da gōzee — ده جوزي.

This is my wife.
di mirātee — دي مراتي.

What do you think (about) ...?
ey rayyak/rayyik fee ...? (m/f) — إيه رايك في ...؟

Can I take a photo (of you)?
mumkin aṣawwarak/aṣawwarik? (m/f) — ممكن أصوّرك؟

What's this called?
ismuh/ismaha ey? (m/f) — إسمه إيه؟

It's great here.
il makaan da gameel — المكان ده جميل.

We love it here.
iHna mabsooṭeen giddan hina — إحنا مبسوطين جداً هنا.

Are you waiting, too?
inta/inti kamaan mistanni/ye? (m/f) — إنت كمان مستنّي؟

That's strange!
da ghareeb! — ده غريب!

That's funny. (amusing)
da laṭeef — ده لطيف.

Are you here on holiday?
inta/inti fee agaaza? (m/f) — أنت في أجازة؟

I'm here ...	ana hina ...	أنا هنا ...
for a holiday	fi agaaza	في أجازة
on business	fi shughl	في شغل
to study	lid dirāsa	للدّراسة

How long are you here for?
Hatu'ud hina addi ey? حتقعد هنا قدّ إيه؟
I'm here for ... days/weeks.
ana/Ha'ad/Hana'd ... أنا حاقعد هنا ...
ayaam/asaabi' أيّام/أسابيع.
Do you like it here?
inta/inti mabsooṭ/a hina? (m/f) أنت مبسوط هنا؟
I like it here very much.
ana mabsooṭ/a giddan (m/f) أنا مبسوط جداً.
We're here with our family.
iHna hina ma' il 'eyla إحنا هنا مع العيلة.
I'm here with my boyfriend/girlfriend.
ana hina ma'a ṣadeeqee/ṣadeeqtee أنا هنا مع صديقي/صديقتي.
I'm here with my husband/wife.
ana hina ma'a gōzee/mirātee أنا هنا مع جوزي/مراتي.

USEFUL PHRASES كلمات مفيدة

Sure.	akeed	أكيد.
Just a minute.	da^c^ee^c^a waHida	دقيقة واحدة.
OK.	maashi	ماشي.
It's OK.	mish mushkila	مش مشكلة.
It's important.	di Haaga muhimma	دي حاجة مهمّة.
It's not important.	mish muhimm	مش مهم.
It's (not) possible.	(mish) mumkin	(مش) ممكن.
Look!	buṣ/buṣee! (m/f)	بصّ!
Listen (to this)!	isma'/buṣee! (m/f)	إسمع!
I'm ready.	ana gaahiz/gahza (m/f)	أنا جاهز.
Are you ready?	inta/i gaahiz/gahza? (m/f)	أنت جاهز؟
Let's go!	yalla beena!	يالاّ بنا!
See you later!	ashufak ba'dayn!	أشوفك بعدين!
See you tomorrow!	ashoofak bukra!	أشوفك بكره!
Good luck!	Haẓ sa'eed!	حظ سعيد!
Just a second!	sanya waHida!	ثانية واحدة!

NATIONALITIES جنسيّات

You'll find that many country names in Egyptian Arabic are similar to English. Remember though – even if a word looks like the English equivalent, it will have an Arabic pronunciation (for example, ustrālya for Australia). If you still can't explain, try pointing to the map.

Where are you from?
inta/inti minayn? (m/f) إنت منين؟

I'm from ...	ana min ...	أنا من ...
We're from ...	iHna min ...	إحنا من ...
Australia	ustrālya	أستراليا
Canada	kanada	كندا
England	ingiltera	إنجلترا
Europe	urooba	أوروبا
France	faransa	فرنسا
Ireland	eerlanda	إيرلندا
Israel	isrā'eel	إسرائيل
Japan	il yabaan	أليابان
New Zealand	nyu zeelanda	نيو زيلاندا
Scotland	iskutlanda	إسكتلندا
the USA	amreeka	أمريكا
Wales	weylz	ويلز
the Middle East	il sharq il awsaṭ	الشرق الأوسط
the Arab world	il 'aalim il 'arabi	العالم العربي
We come from a/the ...	iHna min ...	إحنا من ...
I live in a/the ...	ana 'ayesh/a fee ... (m/f)	أنا عايش في ...
city	il medina	المدينة
countryside	ir reef	الريف
mountains	ig gibaal	الجبال
seaside	gamb il baHr	جمب البحر
suburbs of ...	fee ḍawāHi ...	في ضواحي ...
village	qarya	قرية

CULTURAL DIFFERENCES إختلافات ثقافيّة

How do you do this in your country?
bit'amal kida izzay fee baladak? بتعمل كدا إزّاي في بلدك؟

Is this a local or national custom?
il 'aada di bitit'amal fil balad kullaha walla hina bas? العادة دي بتتعمل في البلد كلّها ولاّ هنا بس؟

everybody	kulli naas	كلّ الناس
local	maHalli	محلّي
national	waṭani	وطني

I don't want to offend you.
ana mish 'aayiz/'ayza aḍayᶜak (m/f) أنا مش عايز أضايقك.

I'm sorry, it's not the custom in my country.
aasif/a, mish bin'amal kida fee baladna (m/f) آسف، مش بنعمل كدا في بلدنا.

I'm not accustomed to this.
ana mish mit'awwid 'ala da أنا مش متعوّد على ده.

I don't mind watching, but I'd prefer not to participate.
mumkin atfarrag lākin mish Haᶜdar ashaarik ممكن أتفرّج لكن مش حاقدر أشارك.

I'm sorry, it's against my ...	aasif/a, da ḍidd ... bitaa'i (m/f)	آسف ده ضدّ ... بتاعي.
beliefs	il mu'taqidaat	المعتقدات
culture	it taqaleed	التقليد
religion	id deen	الدّين

(But) I'll give it a go.
(laakin) Hagarrab (لكن) حجرّب.

MEETING PEOPLE

AGE السنّ

How old are you?
'andak/'andik kam sana? (m/f) عندك كم سنة ؟

How old is your ...?	... 'anduh/'andaha kam sana? (m/f)	... عنده كم سنة ؟
daughter	bintak	إبنتك
son	ibnak	إبنك

I'm ... years old.
'andi ... sineen (younger than ten years) عندي ... سنين.
'andi ... sana (older than ten years) عندي ... سنة.

(See Numbers & Amounts, page 201, for your age.)

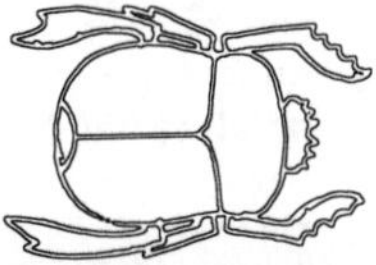

HIM, HER AND ALL

When addressing others in stock phrases, even with a simple 'hello', Arabic differentiates between not only the singular masculine and feminine forms, but also between the plural.

Generally, the feminine form ends with an -i:

hello ahlan beeki

The plural form ends with -u or -um:

hello ahlan bikum

The male form has no set ending.

OCCUPATIONS المهن

What (work) do you do?
inta/inti bitishtaghal/ee ey? (m/f) إنت بتشتغل إيه؟

I'm a/an ...	ana ...	أنا ...
archaeologist	'aalim Hafriyaat	عالم حفريّات
architect	muhandis/a Hafriyaat (m/f)	مهندس معماري
artist	fannaan/a (m/f)	فنّان
businessman	ragil a'maal	رجل أعمال
businesswoman	sayyidat a'maal	سيّدة أعمال
chef	ṭabākh/a (m/f)	طبّاخ
doctor	duktōr/a (m/f)	دكتور
engineer	muhandiṣ/a (m/f)	مهندس
farmer	muzāri'	مزارع
homemaker	sitt bayt	ست بيت
journalist	ṣaHafi/ya (m/f)	صحفي
labourer	'aamil	عامل
lawyer	muHaami	محامي
mechanic	mekaneeki	مكانيكي
nurse	mumarriḍ/a (m/f)	ممرّضة
photographer	muṣawwar/a (m/f)	مصوّر
secretary	sikriteera	سكرتيرة
scientist	'aalim/a (m/f)	عالم
student	ṭālib/a (m/f)	طالب
teacher	mudarris/a (m/f)	مدرّس
tourist guide	murshid/a siyaHi/ya (m/f)	مرشد سياحي
university professor	brofissoor (m/f)	بروفيسور
waiter	garson/a (m/f)	جرسون
writer	muᶜallif/a (m/f)	مؤلّف

I'm unemployed.
m'aandeesh shughl ما عنديش شغل.

What are you studying?
bitudrus/bitudrusee ey? (m/f) بتدرس إيه؟

I'm studying ...	ana badrus ...	أنا بدرس...
Arabic	'arabi	عربي
art	funoon	فنون
arts/humanities	'uloom insaniyya	علوم إنسانيّة
business adminstration	idārit a'maal	إدارة أعمال
teaching	tarbiyya	تربية
Egyptology	'ilm il maṣriyaat	علم المصريّات
engineering	handasa	هندسة
English	ingileezi	إنجليزي
history	tareekh	تاريخ
languages	lughaat	لغّات
law	qanoon	قانون
medicine	ṭib	طبّ
science	'ilm	علم

FEELINGS — الإحساسات

I'm ...	ana ...	أنا ...
Are you ...?	inta ...	إنت ...؟
afraid	khāyif/khayfa (m/f)	خايف
angry	za'lān/a (m/f)	زعلان
cold	bardān/a (m/f)	بردان
depressed	mukta'ib/a (m/f)	مكتئب
grateful	mutshakkir	متشكّر
happy	mabsooṭ/a (m/f)	مبسوط
hot	Harrān/a (m/f)	حرّان
hungry	ga'ān/a (m/f)	جعان
in a hurry	mista'gil/a (m/f)	مستعجل
right (correct)	saH	صح
sad	Hazeen/a (m/f)	حزين
sleepy	'aayiz/'ayza anaam (m/f)	عايز أنام
sorry (apology)	aasif/a (m/f)	آسف
sorry (condolence)	ma'lish	معلش
sorry (regret)	nadmaan/a (m/f)	ندمان
thirsty	'aṭshān/a (m/f)	عطشان
tired	ta'baan/a (m/f)	تعبان
well	bi khayr	بخير
worried	al'aan/a (m/f)	قلقان

POLITELY YOURS

Egyptians have a polite form of saying 'you' to men and women. It can also be used on its own as 'sir' or 'madam'.

to a man:	Haḍriṭak	حضرتك
to a woman:	Haḍritik	حضرتك

BREAKING THE LANGUAGE BARRIER

تخطّي حاجز اللغة

Do you speak English?
bititkallim/ee ingileezi? (m/f) — بتتكلّم إنجليزي؟

Yes, I do. — aywa — أيوه.
No, I don't. — laᶜ — لأ.

Does anyone speak English?
fee Hadd biyitkallim ingileezi? — فيه حدّ بيتكلّم إنجليزي؟
I speak a little.
ana batkallim shuwayya — أنا بتكلّم شويّة.
Do you understand?
faahim/fahma? (m/f) — فاهم؟
I (don't) understand.
ana (mish) faahim/fahma (m/f) — أنا مش فاهم.
Could you speak more slowly?
mumkin titkallim/ee bi rāHa? (m/f) — ممكن تتكلّم بالرّاحة؟

PLEASE. PLEASE? PLEASE!

There are three ways of saying 'please' in Egyptian Arabic:

- min fạdlak/fạdlik/fạdluku (m/f/pl) informal — من فضلك
- low samaHt slightly more formal; can also be used to get somebody's attention — لو سمحت
- itfạdal/i/u (m/f/pl) used when offering something to somebody — إتفضّل

Could you repeat that?
mumkin ti^{c}ool/ee taani? (m/f) — ممكن تقول ثاني؟

Please write it down.
mumkin tiktibuh/tiktibeeh? (m/f) — ممكن تكتبه؟

How do you say ...?
izzay a^{c}ool ...? — إزّاي أقول ...؟

What does ... mean?
ya'ni ... ey? — يعني ... أيه؟

BIJO BLEASE

The letters 'p' and 'v' don't exist in Arabic. The usual pronunciation for the letter 'p' is 'b'. So, for 'please', you may hear blease.

For those ubiquitous Peugeot taxis, you may hear Bijo. A common misconception among Western travellers is that the taxis are so called because they truly are ancient 'gems'. (The word sounds like bijoux, 'jewels' in French.)

العائلة FAMILY

Egypt is a traditional society and the family is the centre of social life, as well as an insurance policy in case things go wrong.

Most Egyptians frown on sex between unmarried partners and although many realise that foreigners may have different views on the subject, they don't appreciate you flaunting this. So if you're travelling with your girlfriend or boyfriend, it's often best to say you're married. Likewise, if you're a woman travelling alone and want to fend off unwanted advances, a mythical husband and a ring can help.

QUESTIONS أسئلة

Are you married?	
inta/inti mitgawwiz/mitgawwiza? (m/f)	انت متجوّز ؟
Do you have a boyfriend/girlfriend?	
'andak ṣadeeq/a?	عندك صديق ؟
How many children do you have?	
'andak/'andik kam 'ayyil? (m/f)	عندك كم عيل ؟
How many brothers/sisters do you have?	
'andak/'andik kam akhwaat? (m/f)	عندك كم أخوات ؟
How old are they?	
'anduhum kam sana?	عندهم كم سنة ؟
Do you live with your family?	
inta/inti 'aysh/'aysha ma' ahlak/ahlik? (m/f)	إنت عايش مع أهلك ؟

REPLIES أجوبة

I'm ...	ana ...	أنا ...
single	'aazib/'azba (m/f)	عازب
married	mitgawwiz/a (m/f)	متجوّز
separated	munfaṣil/a (m/f)	منفصل
divorced	muṭala'/a (m/f)	مطلّق
a widower/widow	armal/a	أرمل

I don't have any children.
ma'andeesh atfal — معنديش أطفال.

I have a daughter/son.
'andi bint/walad — عندي بنت/ولد.

I live with my family.
ana 'aysh/'aysha ma' ahli (m/f) — أنا عايش مع أهلي.

FAMILY MEMBERS أعضاء العائلة

baby	baybi	بيبي
boy	walad	ولد
brother	akh	أخ
my brother	akhooya	أخويا
children	atfāl	أطفال
Christian name	il ism il awwil	الإسم الأوّل
dad	bāba	بابا
daughter	bint	بنت
family	'ayla	عيلة
father	abb	أب
father-in-law	Hama	حما
girl	bint	بنت
grandfather	gidd	جدّ
grandmother	gidda	جدّة
husband	gōz	جوز
mother	umm	أم
mother-in-law	Hamaa	حماة
mum	māma	ماما
nickname	ism id dela'	إسم الدّلع
sister	ukht	أخت
son	ibn	إبن
wife	mirāt	مراة

TALKING WITH PARENTS

الكلام مع الوالدين

In the countryside, be careful not to compliment a child or baby too much; folklore has it that this will cause the 'evil eye' to fall upon a child.

When's the baby due?
  Hatiwlid imta? حتولد امتى؟

What are you going to call the baby?
  Hatsamoo ey? حتسمّوه أيه؟

Is this your first child?
  da awwil 'ayil? ده أوّل عيل؟

How many children do you have?
  'andak kam 'ayil? عندك كم عيل؟

How old are your children?
  sinn wilaadak/ik addi ey? (m/f) سن ولادك قد أيه؟

I can't believe it! You look too young.
  mish ma' ᶜool! مش معقول!
  shaklik sughayyara شكلك صغيّرة.

Does he/she attend school?
  huwa biyrooH/hiyya هو بيروح
  bitrooH madrasa? المدرسة؟

Is it a private or state school?
  madrasa khāṣa walla مدرسة خاصة ولاّ
  Hukumiyya? حكوميّة؟

Who looks after the children?
  meen biyaᶜd ma' il aṭfāl? مين بيقعد مع الأطفال؟

Do you have grandchildren?
  'andak/'andik aHafād? (m/f) عندك أحفاد؟

What's the baby's name?
  il baybi ismuh/ismaha ey? (m/f) البيبى إسمه ايه؟

Is it a boy or a girl?
  walad walla bint? ولد ولاّ بنت؟

Is he/she well-behaved?
  huwa/hiyya muᶜaddab/a? هو مؤدّب؟

Does he/she let you sleep at night?
  biykhalik/i tinaam/i bil layl? بيخلّيك تنام بالليل؟

He/She is very big for his/her age!
ṣaHitu/ṣaHit-ha kuwayyisa, māshā^c allah! صحته كويسة ما شاء الله!

What a beautiful child!
tifl gameel/a! (m/f) طفل جميل!

He/She looks like you.
hiyya/huwa bitishbahk هي بتشبهك.

He/She has your eyes.
'ayneyha/'ayneyh zayy 'eyneyk/i عينيها زي عينيك.

Who does he/she look like, Mum or Dad?
shabah mama walla baba? شبه ماما ولا بابا؟

SOAPED, STUFFED AND SOAKED IN SLEEP

- After stepping out of the shower, the bath, or the hairdresser's, you may hear:

  na'eeman!
  (heavenly) probably refers to the refreshed state that a good wash or a clean haircut/ hairdo may bring on

- After eating everything on the table or menu, you may hear:

  saHtein!
  (double health) an expression of appreciation for a good appetite

- After waking from a long and deep sleep, you may hear:

  saH el nōm!
  (roused/healthy sleep – saH meaning both 'to rouse' and 'health') either way, the message is: 'Get up, lazybones!'

TALKING WITH CHILDREN الكلام مع الأولاد

What's your name?
ismak/ismik ey? (m/f) إسمك إيه ؟

How old are you?
'andak/'andik kam sana? (m/f) عندك كم سنة ؟

When's your birthday?
'eed milaadak/milaadik imta? (m/f) عيد ميلادك إمتى ؟

Have you got brothers and sisters?
'andak/'andik akhwaat? (m/f) عندك أخوات ؟

Do you go to school or kindergarten?
bitrooH/i madrasa walla Hadāna? (m/f) بتروح مدرسة ولاّ حضانة ؟

Is your teacher nice?
il mudarris/a lateef/a? (m/f) المدرّس لطيف ؟

Do you like school?
bitHibb/i il madrasa? (m/f) بتحب المدرسة ؟

Do you play sport?
bitila'b riyāda? بتلعب رياضة ؟

What sport do you play?
bitila'b anhi riyāda? بتلعب أنهي رياضة ؟

What do you do after school?
bita'mil/i ey ba'd il madrasa? (m/f) بتعمل إيه بعد المدرسة ؟

Do you learn English?
bitita'llim/i ingileezi? (m/f) بتتعلّم إنجليزي؟

We speak a different language in my country, so I don't understand you very well. binitkallim lugha tanya fee baladna, fa ana mish fahimak/fahmak kwayyis (m/f)		بنتكلّم لغة تانية في بلدنا، فأنا مش فاهمك كويّس.
I come from very far away. baladi ba'eeda giddan		بلدي بعيدة جدا.
Do you want to play a game? 'aayiz/'ayza tila'b/i la'ba? (m/f)		عايز تلعب لعبة؟
What shall we play? nila'b ey?		نلعب أيه؟
Have you lost your parents? ḍa't/i min ahlak/ik? (m/f)		ضعت من أهلك؟

WHEN POP REALLY MEANS POP

Waldi and walditi literally mean 'the ones who gave birth to me', and are a polite way of referring to parents.

my father	waldi	والدي
my mother	walditi	والدتي
your father	waldak	والدك
your mother	walditak	والدتك

التنقّل GETTING AROUND

There are reasonably priced transport links throughout Egypt. The densely-populated Nile Valley and Delta have good paved roads as well as an extensive railway network. Rail travel is also the best way to get from Cairo to Upper Egypt and Alexandria. Station wagon service (servees) taxis are a popular form of transport between provincial towns as well as inside the city.

FINDING YOUR WAY معرفة الطّريق

Where's the ...?	fayn il ...?	فين ال...؟
bus station	maw^{c}if il utubees	موقف الأوتوبيس
train station	maHaṭit il aṭr	محطّة القطر
road to (Aswan)	iṭ ṭari^c li (aswān)	الطّريق ل (أسوان)

What time does the ... leave/arrive?	il ... biyimshi is saa'a kam?	ال... بيمشى السّاعة كم؟
aeroplane	tayyāra	طيّارة
boat	markib	مركب
bus	utubees	أوتوبيس
train	aṭr	قطر

How do we get to ...?
nirooH ... izzay? — نروح ... إزّاي؟

Is it far/close by?
hiyya ^{c}urayyiba/ba'eeda min hina? — هي قريّبة/بعيدة من هنا؟

Can we walk there?
mumkin nirooH mashee? — ممكن نروح مشي؟

Can you show me (on the map)?
mumkin tiwarreeni ('alal khareeṭa)? — ممكن تورّيني (على الخريطة)؟

Are there other means of getting there?
fee muwaṣla taanya? — فيه مواصلة تانية؟

What ... is this?	da/dee ... ay? (m/f)	ده/دي ... إيه ؟
city	medina	مدينة
street	shaari'	شارع
village	qarya	قرية

Directions الإتجاهات

Turn ...	Hawid ...	حود ...
right/left	yimeen/shimaal	اليمين/الشّمال
at the next corner	'alal naṣya illi gayya	على الناصية اللي جاية
at the traffic lights	'and il ishāra	عند الإشارة
Straight ahead.	'ala ṭool	على طول.
To the right.	'ala il yimeen	على اليمين.
To the left.	'ala ish shimaal	على الشمال.

behind	wara	ورا
in front of	^{c}uddaam	قدام
far	ba'eed	بعيد
near	^{c}urayib	قريب
opposite	'uṣād	قصاد
here	hina	هنا
there	hinaak	هناك
north	shimaal	شمال
south	ganoob	جنوب
east	shar^{c}	شرق
west	gharb	غرب

TAXI تاكسي

Taxis in cities will pick up as many fares as their car can hold, usually stopping at five. They follow a specific route. To hail a taxi, just flag one down and yell your destination. If the driver's not going there, he'll shake his finger – if he is, he'll stop.

Payment is more complicated. Meters are calibrated for when petrol was far cheaper, and nobody pays any attention to them. The fare is therefore a discretionary sum that's gauged from distance and the amount of time spent in traffic. If you get it wrong, the taxi driver will let you know in no uncertain terms. On the other hand, he will try and to get as much money as he can. It's best to ask around to familiarise yourself with prices.

Taxi! taksi! تاكسي!

Please take me to ...
ana raayiH/rayHa ... (m/f) أنا رايح ...

How much is it to go to ...?
bikam lil ...? بكم لل ...؟

How much is the fare?
bikam? بكم؟

Do we pay extra for luggage?
nidfa' ziyaada lil shanaṭ? ندفع زيادة للشّنط؟

Instructions إرشادات

The next street to the left/right.
ish shaari' illi gayy 'alal shimaal/yimeen الشارع اللي جاي على الشمال/اليمين.

Please slow down.
haddi is sur'a min faḍlak هدّي السّرعة من فضلك.

Please wait here.
istanna hina, min faḍlak إستنّى هنا من فضلك.

Stop at the corner. waᶜif 'alal naṣya وقّف على الناصية.

Stop here! waᶜif hina! وقّف هنا!

Continue! khaleek maashi! خلّيك ماشي!

BUYING TICKETS شراء التذاكر

Where can I buy a ticket?
ashtiri tazkara minayn? أشتري تذكرة منين ؟

We want to go to ...
'ayzeen nirooH ... عايزين نروح ...

Do I need to book?
laazim aHgiz? لازم أحجز ؟

I'd like to book a seat to ...
'aayiz/'ayza aHgiz tazkara li ... عايز أحجز تذكرة لـ...

I'd like ...	'aayiz/'ayza ... (m/f)	عايز ...
a one-way ticket	tazkarit zihaab	تذكرة ذهاب
a return ticket	tazkarit 'awda	تذكرة عودة
two tickets	tazkartayn	تذكرتين
a student's fare	tazkarit lil ṭalba	تذكرة للطلبة
a child's fare	tazkarit lil aṭfāl	تذكرة للأطفال
1st class	daraga oola	درجة أولى
2nd class	daraga tanya	درجة ثانية
3rd class	daraga talta	درجة ثالثة

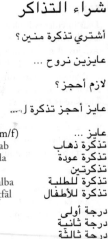

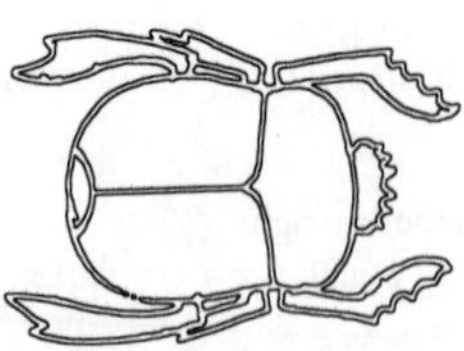

THEY MAY SAY ...

huwa/hiyya malyaan/a (m/f)
It's full.

il riHla ta^{c}akharit
The trip has been delayed.

AIR

الطيران

Is there a flight to ...?
fee tayāra li ...?
في طيّارة ل ...؟

When's the next flight to ...?
il riHla illi gayya imta ...?
الرحلة اللي جايّة إمتى ...؟

How long does the flight take?
il riHla kam saa'a?
الرحلة كم ساعة؟

What time do I have to check in at the airport?
il mafrood awsil il matār imta?
المفروض أوصل المطار إمتى؟

Where's the baggage claim?
fayn il akhd il Haqā^cib?
فين ال أخد الحقائب؟

AT CUSTOMS

في الجمرك

I have nothing to declare.
mish ma'aya Haaga asbit-ha
مش معايا حاجة أثبتها.

I have something to declare.
ma'aya Haaga asbit-ha
معايا حاجة أثبتها.

Do I have to declare this?
laazim asbit da?
لازم أثبت ده؟

This is all my luggage.
kulli ish shunat di bitaa'ti
كل الشّنط دي بتاعتي.

That's not mine.
da mish bitaa'i
ده مش بتاعي.

I didn't know I had to declare it.
ma kuntish 'arif inni kaan laazim asbit da
مكنتش أعرف إنّي كان لازم أثبت ده.

SIGNS

وصول	WUSOOL	ARRIVALS
جمرك	GUMRUK	CUSTOMS
مغادرة	MUGHADARA	DEPARTURES
بوّابة	BAWWAABA	GATE
صالة	SĀLA	TERMINAL

BUS الأوتوبيس

Where's the bus stop?
fayn maHaṭit il utubees? فين محطّة الأوتوبيس؟

Which bus goes to ...?
anhi utubees rayiH ...? أنهي أوتوبيس رايح ...؟

Does this bus go to ...?
huwa il utubees da rayiH ...? هو الأوتوبيس ده رايح ...؟

How often do buses come?
ey mi'aad il utubeesaat? أيه معاد الأوتوبيسات؟

What time is the ... bus?	il utubees ... ma'aaduh imta?	الأوتوبيس ... معاده إمتى؟
first	il awwil/oola (m/f)	الأوّل/الأولى
last	il aakhir	الآخر
next	illi gayy	اللي جاي

Could you let me know when we get to ...?
mumkin tiballaghni lamma nuwsil ...? ممكن تبلّغني لمّا نوصل ...؟

Where do I get the bus for ...?
akhud il utubees li ... minayn? آخد الأوتوبيس ل ... منين؟

TRAIN القطار

What station is this?
di maHaṭit ey? دي محطّة إيه؟

What's the next station?
ay il maHatta illi gayya? إيه المحطّة اللي جايّة؟

Does this train stop at Luxor?
il 'aṭr da biyuᶜaf fee luᶜṣur? القطر ده بيوقف في الأقصر؟

How long will it be delayed?
Hayitakhkhar addi ey? حايتأخّر قد إيه؟

How long does the trip take?
il riHla addi ey? الرحلة قد إيه؟

Is it a direct route?
fee ṭareeᶜ mubaashir? فيه طريق مباشر؟

GETTING AROUND

Is that seat taken?
il kursi da fāḍi? الكرسي ده فا ضي؟
I want to get off at ...
'aayiz/'ayza anzil 'and ... (m/f) عايز أنزل عند ...

> **THEY MAY SAY ...**
> il aṭr it'akhkhar/itlagha
> The train is delayed/cancelled.

BOAT النقل البحري

Where does the boat leave from?
il markib biyiṭla' minayn? المركب بيطلع منين؟
What time does the boat arrive?
il markib Hayiwṣil imta? المركب حيوصل إمتى؟

ferry	ma'ddiyya	معدّيّة
car ferry	'abāra	عبّارة

Feluccas الفلايك

The Nile is the lifeblood of Egypt, and sailing in one of the hundreds of feluccas that ply its waters is the best way of experiencing it up close.

Trips range from hourly jaunts to cruises lasting several days, most commonly from Aswan or Luxor, and are usually arranged with the captain of the boat.

The cost is negotiable, and depends on the number of passengers, whether food is served or permits are required (for overnight trips) and, most importantly, your bargaining skills.

captain	rayyis	ريّس
blanket	baṭaniyya	بطّانية
island	gizeera	جزيرة
oars	migdaaf	مجداف
permit	taṣreeH	تصريح
sail	shirā'	شراع

How many people will be on the boat?
Haykoon fee kam nafar fil felooka? — حيكون في كم نفر في الفلوكة؟
What time do we sail?
HanibHar imta? — حنبحر إمتى؟
How much do you charge per day?
il yōm bikam? — اليوم بكم؟
Does that include food?
da shaamil il akl? — ده شامل الأكل؟
Do we need sleeping bags?
miHtageen sleebinbaagaat? — محتاجين سليبنباجات؟
Do you have lifejackets?
'anduku sutraat inqāz? — عندكوا سترات إنقاذ؟

CAR العربة

Most road signs in Egypt use international symbols. The few written signs are usually in both English and Arabic.

Where can I rent a car?
mumkin a'aggar 'arabiyya minayn? — ممكن أأجّر عربية منين؟
How much is it daily/weekly?
il yōm/il usboo' bikam? — اليوم/الأسبوع بكم؟
Does that include insurance/mileage?
da shaamil it ta'meen/il kilumitrāt? — ده شامل التأمين/الكيلومترات؟
Where's the next petrol station?
fayn maHatit ib benzeen illi gayya? — فين محطة البنزين اللي جاية؟
Please fill the tank.
fawwilha, low samaHt — فوّلها لو سمحت.
I'd like ... litres.
'aayiz/'ayza ... litr (m/f) — عايز ... لتر.

Please check the ...	iṭṭamin 'ala ... low samaHt	إطّمن على ... لو سمحت
oil	zayt	زيت
tyre pressure	ḍaghṭ il'agal	ضغط العجل
water	mayya	ميّة

Can I park here?
mumkin arkin hina? ممكن أركن هنا؟

How long can we park here?
mumkin nirkin hina addi ay? ممكن نركن هنا قد أيه؟

Does this road lead to ...?
iṭaree^c da yiwaddi li ...? الطّريق ده يودّي ل ...؟

air	hawa	هوا
battery	baṭāriyya	بطّارية
brakes	farāmil	فرامل
clutch	debriyaazh	دبرياج
drivers licence	rukhṣit siwa^c^a	رخصة سواقة
engine	mutoor	موتور
garage	garāzh	جراج
indicator	ishāra	إشارة
lights	noor	نور
main road	iṭṭaree^c^ ir rayeesi	الطّريق الرئيسي
oil	zayt	زيت
petrol	benzeen	بنزين
high-octane	tisa'een	تسعين
regular	tamaneen	تمنين
unleaded	min ghayr ruṣāṣ; khamsa wa tisa'een	من غير رصاص/ خمسة و تسعين
petrol station	maHaṭit ib benzeen	محطّة البنزين
puncture	khurm	خرم
radiator	radyateer	رادياتير
road map	khareeṭit ṭuru^c^	خريطة طرق
seatbelt	Hizaam	حزام
speed limit	Hadd is sura'a	حدّ السرعة
tyres	kawitshaat	كاوتشات
windscreen	barbireez	بربريز

TIP

Don't let the emphatic consonants, ṣ, ḍ, ṭ and ẓ put you off. Even if you pronounce them in exactly the same way you'd normally pronounce these consonants, you'll still be clearly understood.

CAR PROBLEMS مشاكل العربيّات

We need a mechanic.
miHtageen mekaneeki محتاجين ميكانيكي.

What make is the car?
il 'arabiyya nu'aha ay? العربيّة نوعها إيه؟

The car broke down at ...
il 'arabiyya it'aṭalit 'and ... العربيّة إتعطّلت عند ...

The battery's flat.
il baṭāriyya nayma البطّارية نايمة.

The radiator's leaking.
ir radyateer makhroom الرادياتير مخروم.

I have a flat tyre.
il kawitsh naayim الكاوتش نايم.

I've lost my car keys.
ḍā'it mafateeHi ضاعت مفاتيحي.

I've run out of petrol.
il benzeen khiliṣ البنزين خلص.

It's overheating.	bitsakhkhan	بتسخن.
It's not working.	mish shaghaala	مش شغّالة.

BICYCLE الدرّاجة

Is it within cycling distance?
mumkin arooH bil'agala? ممكن أروح بالعجلة؟

Where can I hire a bicycle?
a'aggar 'agala minayn? أأجّر عجلة منين؟

How much is it for ...?	... bikam?	... بكم؟
an hour	is saa'a	السّاعة
the day	il yōm	اليوم
the morning	iṣ ṣubH	الصبح
the afternoon	iḍ ḍuhr	الضّهر

bike	'agala	عجلة
brakes	farāmil	فرامل
to cycle	rakib 'agala	ركب عجلة
gears	trōs	تروس
handlebars	gadōn	جدون
helmet	khōza	خوذة
inner tube	shambur	شمبر
lights	noor	نور
padlock	afl	قفل
pump	ṭurunba	طرنبة
puncture	khorm	خرم
saddle	sarg	سرج
wheel	'agala	عجلة

الإقامة ACCOMMODATION

As a major tourist destination, Egypt has a huge variety of accommodation on offer. At the top end of the scale, almost all major international hotel chains are represented in Cairo and resorts on the Red Sea. There are also a large number of excellent two and three-star hotels. In the middle range, there are small, cheap and clean hotels aimed at the foreign traveller. Along the coast, small bamboo huts are also available.

FINDING ACCOMMODATION الحصول على اقامة

I'm looking for a ...	ana badawwar 'ala ...	أنا بدوّر على ...
camping ground	mu'askar	معسكر
hotel	fundu[c]	فندق
pension	pansyōn	بنسيون
youth hostel	bayt shabaab	بيت شباب
Where can I find a ... hotel?	ala[c]ee fundu[c] ... fayn?	ألاقي فندق ... فين ؟
clean	naḍeef	نضيف
good	kuwayyis	كويّس
nearby	urayyib min hina	قريّب من هنا
Where's the ... hotel?	fayn il ... fundu[c]	فين ال ... فندق ؟
best	aHsan	أحسن
cheapest	arkhas	أرخص

What's the address?
il 'unwaan ey? العنوان إيه ؟

Could you write the address, please?
mumkin tiktibee il' unwaan min faḍlak? ممكن تكتب العنوان من فضلك ؟

3-star	talat nugoom	تلات نجوم
4-star	arba' nugoom	أربع نجوم
5-star	khamas nugoom	خمس نجوم

BOOKING AHEAD الحجز مقدماً

I'd like to book a room, please.
'aayiz/'ayza ghurfa low samaHt/ee (m/f) — عايز غرفة لو سمحت.

double room	ghurfa lil itnayn	غرفة للإتنين
single room	ghurfa li waaHid	غرفة لواحد
How much for ...?	bikam li ...?	بكم ل ...؟
one night	layla waHida	ليلة واحدة
a week	usbu'	أسبوع
two people	fardayn	فردين
For (three) nights.	li (talat) layaali	ل (تلات) ليالي.
We'll be arriving at ...	Hanuwṣil ...	حنوصل ...
My name is ...	ismi ...	إسمي ...

Can we pay by credit card?
mumkin nidfa' bi kredit kard? — ممكن ندفع بكريدت كارد؟

CHECKING IN دخول الفندق

Do you have any rooms/beds available?
'andak/'andik ghuraf fadya? (m/f) — عندك غرف فاضية؟

Do you have a room with two beds?
'andak/'andik ghurfa bi sirirayn? (m/f) — عندك غرفة بسريرين؟

Do you have a room with a double bed?
'andak/'andik ghurfa bi sirir muzdawag? (m/f) — عندك غرفة بسرير مزدوج؟

I'd like ...	ana 'aayiz/'ayza ... (m/f)	أنا عايز ...
to share a room	ghurfa mushtarika	غرفة مشتركة
a single room	ghurfa li waaHid	غرفة لواحد

We want a room with (a/an) ...	'ayzeen ghurfa bi ...	عايزين غرفة ب ...
air-conditioner	takyeef	تكييف
bathroom	Hammaam khās	حمّام خاص
hot water	mayya sukhna	ميّة سخنة
shower	dush	دش
TV	tilivisyōn	تليفزيون
window	shibaak	شبّاك

Can I see it?
mumkin ashufha? ممكن أشوفها؟
Are there any others?
fee taani? فيه تاني؟
Where's the bathroom?
fayn il Hammaam? فين الحمّام؟
Is there hot water all day?
fee mayya sukhna ṭool il yōm? فيه ميّة سخنة طول االيوم؟
Is there a discount for children/students?
fee takhfeeḍ lil aṭfāl/ṭalba? في تخفيض لل أطفال/طلبة؟
It's fine. I'll take it.
tamaam. ʿakhudha تمام.اَخدها.

THEY MAY SAY ...

aasif/a, iHna kumpley (m/f) — Sorry, we're full.

REQUESTS & QUERIES طلبات و أسئلة

Where's the bathroom?
fayn il Hammaam? فين الحمّام؟
Where's breakfast served?
il fiṭār biyitʿaddim fayn? الفطار بيتقدّم فين؟
Is there somewhere to wash clothes?
fee makaan li ghaseel il hudoom? فيه مكان لغسيل الهدوم؟
Can we use the kitchen?
mumkin nistakhdim il maṭbakh? ممكن نستخدم المطبخ؟

ACCOMMODATION

Can we use the telephone?
mumkin atkallim fee tilifōn? ممكن أتكلّم في التليفون؟
I need a (another) ...
ana miHtaag/a (kamaan) ... (m/f) أنا محتاج (كمان) ...
Do you have a safe where I can leave my valuables?
fee khazna mumkin aHuṭ feeha hagaat qayyima? في خزنة ممكن أحطّ فيها حاجات قيّمة؟
Could I have a receipt for them?
mumkin tideeni waṣl? ممكن تدّيني وصل؟
Do you change money here?
bitghayyaru filoos hina? بتغيّروا فلوس هنا؟
Do you arrange tours?
bitnazzam gawalaat? بتنظّم جولات؟
Is there a message board?
fee message board? فيه ما سيج بورد؟
Can I leave a message?
mumkin aseeb risaala? ممكن أسيب رسالة؟
Is there a message for me?
fee risaala liyya? فيه رسالة ليّا؟
Please wake us at (seven).
min faḍlak, ṣaHeena is saa'a (sab'a) من فضلك صحّينا الساعة (سابعة).
Please change the sheets.
ghayyar il milayaat, low samaHt/i (m/f) غيّر الملاّيات لو سمحت.
The room needs to be cleaned.
il ghurfa 'ayza titnaḍaf الغرفة عايزة تتنضّف.
Could we have an extra blanket?
mumkin tidieena baṭaniyya ziyaada? ممكن تدّينا بطّانيّة زيادة؟

TIP

Remember the capital H is pronounced as a strongly whispered 'h', rather like a loud sigh of exasperation, all the way from the back of the throat.

ACCOMMODATION

Could we have a mosquito net?
mumkin tideena namusiyya? — ممكن تدّينا ناموسيّة؟

I've locked myself out of my room.
niseet il miftaaH guwwa — نسيت المفتاح جوّه.

No, we left the key at reception.
la^c, sibna il miftaaH 'and il isti^{c}baal — لأ، سيبنا المفتاح عند الإستقبال.

COMPLAINTS — شكاوى

I can't open/close the window.
ish shibaak mish biyitfitiH/biyit'ifil — الشّباك مش بيتفتح/بيتقفل.

I don't like this room.
il ghurfa dee mish kuwayyisa — الغرفة دي مش كويّسة.

The toilet won't flush.
is seefōn mish shaghaal — السيفون مش شغّال.

Can I change to another?
mumkin aghayyar ha? — ممكن أغيّرها؟

It's too ...	huwa/hiyya ... ^{c}awi (m/f)	هو/هي ... قوي
cold	bard	برد
dark	ghaami^c	غامق
expensive	ghaali	غالي
light/bright	zaahi	زاهي
noisy	dawsha	دوشة
small	ṣughayyar	صغيّر

This ... isn't clean.	il ... mish naḍeef/a (m/f)	ال ... مش نضيف.
blanket	baṭaniyya dee	بطّانيّة دي
pillow	makhadda dee	مخدّة دي
pillowcase	kees makhadda da	كيس مخدّة ده
sheet	mileyya dee	ملاّية دي

CHECKING OUT — الخروج من الفندق

What time do we have to check out by?
mafrooḍ niHasib imta? — مفروض نحاسب إمتى؟

I'm/We're leaving now.
ana Hamshi/iHna Hanimshi dilwa'ti — أنا حامشي دلوقتي.

I'd like to pay the bill.
'aayiz/'ayza adfa' il Hisaab (m/f) — عايز أدفع الحساب.

Can I pay with a travellers cheque?
mumkin adfa' bisheek siyaaHi? — ممكن أدفع بشيك سياحي؟

Can I pay by credit card?
mumkin adfa' bi kredit kard? — ممكن أدفع بكريدت كارد؟

Could I have the bill, please?
'aayiz/'ayza il Hisaab, low samaHt (m/f) — عايز الحساب لو سمحت.

There's a mistake in the bill.
fee ghalṭa fil Hisaab — فيه غلطة في الحساب.

Can I leave my backpack here until tonight?
mumkin aseeb shanṭit iḍ ḍahr bitaa'ti hina lighayit innaharda bil layl? — ممكن أسيب شنطة الضهر بتاعتي هنا لغايت النهارده بالليل؟

We'll be back in (three) days.
Hanirga' ba'd (talat) ayaam — حنرجع بعد (تلات) أيام.

Can you call a taxi for me?
mumkin tigeebli taksi? — ممكن تجيبلي تاكسي؟

RENTING
الإيجار

I'm here about your ad for a room to rent. ana hina 'ashaan i'laan ish sha^c^a		أنا هنا عشان إعلان الشقّة.
Do you have any flats to rent? fee sha^c^a lil igār?		فيه شقّة للإيجار ؟
I'm looking for a flat to rent for two months. badawwar 'ala sha'a lil igār li muddit shahrayn		بدوّر على شقّة للإيجار لمدّة شهرين.
I'm looking for something close to the ...	badawwar 'ala Haaga urayyiba min ...	بدوّر على حاجة قريبة من ...
beach	il bilaazh	البلاج
city centre	wusṭ il balad	وسط البلد
railway station	maHaṭit il ^c^aṭr	محطّة القطر
Is there anything cheaper? fee Haaga arkhaṣ?		فيه حاجة أرخص؟
Could I see it? mumkin ashoofha?		ممكن أشوفها؟
How much is it per ... ?	bikam ...?	بكم ...؟
week	il usboo^c^	الأسبوع
month	ish shahr	الشهر

ACCOMMODATION

TIP

Don't let the emphatic consonants, ṣ, ḍ, ṭ and ẓ put you off. Even if you pronounce them in exactly the same way you would normally pronounce these letters, your Arabic will still be clearly understood.

Do you require a deposit?
inta/inti 'aayiz/'ayza mu[c]addam? (m/f) — إنت عايز مقدّم؟

I'd like to rent it for (one) month.
'aayiz/'ayza a[c]aggarha li shahr (waaHid) (m/f) — عايز أأجّرها لشهر (واحد).

I'd like to rent it for (four) months.
'aayiz/'ayza a[c]aggarha li middit (arba') shuhoor (m/f) — عايز أأجّرها لمدّة (أربع) شهور.

apartment	sha[c]a	شقّة
house	bayt/villa	بيت/فيلا
room	ghurfa	غرفة
furnished	mafroosh/a (m/f)	مفروش
unfurnished	mish mafroosh/a (m/f)	مش مفروش

في المدينة AROUND TOWN

LOOKING FOR ... البحث عن ...

Where's a/an/the ...?	fayn ...?	فين...؟
art gallery	ṣālit 'arḍ il funoon	صالة عرض الفنون
bank	bank	بنك
cinema	sinima	سينما
city centre (downtown)	wusṭ il balad	وسط البلد
... consulate	unṣuliyya ...	قنصليّة
... embassy	sifāra(t) ...	سفارة ...
hotel	fundu'	فندق
market	is soo'	السوق
museum	il matHaf	المتحف
police	ish shurṭa	الشّرطة
post office	il busṭa	البوستة
public telephone	tilifōn 'aam	تليفون عام
public toilet	doorit mayya/ hammaam	دورة ميّة/حمّام
telephone centre	is sintrāl	السّنترال
tourist information office	maktab is siyaaHa	مكتب السّياحة

AT THE BANK في البنك

I want to change ...	'aayiz/'ayza aghayyar ... (m/f)	عايز أغيّر ...
cash/money	filoos	فلوس
a cheque	sheek	شيك
travellers cheques	shikaat siyaHiyya	شيكّات سياحيّة

Can I use my credit card to withdraw money?
mumkin asHab filoos bil kredit kard?
ممكن أسحب فلوس بالكريدت كارد؟

Can I exchange money here?		
mumkin aghayyar filoos hina?		ممكن أغيّر فلوس هنا؟
What's the exchange rate?		
nisbit it taHweel ey?		نسبة التحويل إيه؟
buying rate	taman ish sherāᶜ	تمن الشراء
selling rate	taman il bee'a	تمن البيع
What's your commission?		
'umooltak kam?		عمولتك كم؟
How many Egyptian pounds per dollar?		
il dulār bikam?		الدولار بكم؟
Can I have smaller notes?		
iddeeni fakka min faḍlak		إدّيني فكّة من فضلك.
What time does the bank open/close?		
il bank biyiftaH/ biyi'fil imta?		البنك بيفتح/ بيقفل إمتى؟
Where can I cash a travellers cheque?		
mumkin asraf sheek siyaaHi fayn?		ممكن أصرف شيك سياحي فين؟
Can I transfer money here from my bank?		
mumkin aHawwil filoos min il bank bitaa'ee?		ممكن أحوّل فلوس من البنك بتاعي؟
How long will it take to arrive?		
Hatiwṣil imta?		حتوصل إمتى؟
Has my money arrived yet?		
filoosi waṣalit?		فلوسي وصلت؟
Can I transfer money overseas?		
mumkin aHawwil filoos barra?		ممكن أحوّل فلوس برّه؟
The automatic teller machine (ATM) swallowed my card.		
il bank ish shakhsi akhad il-kart bita'tee		البنك الشخصي أخد الكارت بتاعتي.
Please write it down.		
iktibu/iktibi min faḍlak/ik (m/f)		إكتبه من فضلك.
Where do I sign?		
amḍi fayn?		أمضي فين؟

AT THE POST OFFICE في مكتب البريد

Despite the often chaotic appearance of Egyptian post offices, the international post works surprisingly well – as long as you stick to airmail. Domestic post tends to be more erratic. Faxes can be sent from the telephone office.

I want to buy stamps.
'aayiz/'ayza ishtiri ṭawābi' (m/f) — عايز أشتري طوابع.

I want to send a ...	'aayiz/'ayza aba'at ... (m/f)	عايز أبعت ...
letter	gawaab	جواب
parcel	ṭard	طرد
postcard	kart bustāl	كرت بستال

Please send it by air/surface.
iba'at da bil bareed ig gawwi/ 'aadi, min faḍlak/faḍlik (m/f) — ابعت ده بالبريد الجوّي/ العادي من فضلك.

How much does it cost to send this to ...?
adfa' kam 'ashaan ab'at da li ...? — أدفع كم علشان أبعت ده ل ...؟

Where's the poste restante section?
fayn qism il boost restānt? — فين قسم البوست ريستانت؟

Is there any mail for me?
fee ayya gawabaat liyya? — فيه أي جوابات ليّا؟

airmail	bareed gawwi	بريد جوّي
envelope	ẓarf	ظرف
express mail	gawaab mista'gil	جواب مستعجل
mail box	ṣandooᶜ busta	صندوق بوستة
pen	alam	قلم
postcode	raqam bareedi	رقم بريدي
post office	il busta	البوستة
registered mail	gawaab musaggil	جواب مسجّل
surface mail	bareed 'aadi	بريد عادي

TELECOMMUNICATIONS الإتصال بالتليفون

The sintrāl is the place to go to make phone calls and send faxes. International calls are usually paid for in three-minute blocks and are paid for in advance.

Could I please use the telephone?
mumkin atkallim fit tilifoon? — ممكن أتكلّم في التليفون؟

I want to call ...
'aayiz/'ayza ittaṣal bi ... (m/f) — عايز أتّصل ب ...

I want to speak for (three) minutes.
'aayiz/'ayza atkallim (talat) da^{c}aayi^c (m/f) — عايز أتكلّم (تلات) دقايق.

How much does a three-minute call cost?
mukalma talaat da^{c}aayi^c bikam? — مكالمة تلات دقايق بكم؟

How much does each extra minute cost?
da^{c}ee^{c}a ziyaada bikam? — دقيقة زيادة بكم؟

What's the area code for ...?
ey raqam ik kood bita' ...? — إيه رقم الكود بتاع ...؟

I want to make a long-distance (collect) call to (Australia).
'aayiz/'ayza attaṣal bi (ustrālya) (m/f) — عايز أتّصل ب (أستراليا).

The number is ...	il nimra ...	النّمرة ...
It's engaged.	mashghool	مشغول.
I've been cut off.	il khaṭ it^{c}aṭa'	الخط إتقطع.
operator	'aamil/'aamlit tilifōnaat (m/f)	عامل تليفونات
phone book	daleel tilifōnaat	دليل تليفونات
phone box	kabeenit tilifōn	كابينة تليفون
phonecard	kart tilifōn	كارت تليفون
telephone	tilifōn	تليفون
telephone office	sintrāl	سنترال
urgent	ḍaroori	ضروري

Making a Call الإتصال بالتليفون

Hello, is ... there?
alō, ... mawgood/a? (m/f) ألو،... موجود؟

Hello. (answering a call) alō ألو.

May I speak to ...? mumkin akallim ...? ممكن أكلّم ...؟

Who's calling? meen biyitkallim? مين بيتكلّم؟

It's .... ana ... أنا ...

Yes, (he/she) is here.
aywa, (huwa/hiyya) mawgood/a (m/f) أيوه، (هو) موجود.

One moment, (please).
sanya waHida (min fadlak/ik) (m/f) ثانية واحدة، من فضلك.

I'm sorry, he's not here.
lil ʿasif, mish mawgood للأسف مش موجود.

What time will she be back?
Hatirga' imta? حترجع إمتى؟

Can I leave a message?
mumkin aseeb risaala? ممكن أسيب رسالة؟

Please tell him I called.
min faḍlak 'ulu inni itaṣalt من فضلك قول له إنّي إتّصلت.

Please tell her I called.
min faḍlik, 'uleelha inni itaṣalt من فضلك قوليلهاإنّي إتّصلت.

My number is ...
nimriti ... نمرتي ...

I don't have a contact number.
ma'andeesh nimrat it tilifōn معنديش نمرة التّليفون.

I'll call back later.
Hattaṣal beeh/beeha ba'deyn (m/f) حاتّصل بيه/بيها بعدين.

What time should I call?
attaṣal imta? إتّصل إمتى؟

THE INTERNET
الإنترنت

Is there a local Internet cafe?
fee kafay internet hina? — فيه كافّيه إنترنت هنا؟

I need to get Internet access.
'aayiz/'ayza astakhdam il internet (m/f) — عايز أستخدم الإنترنت.

I'd like to check my email.
'aayiz/'ayza ashoof il e-mayl bitaa'i (m/f) — عايز أشوف الإيميل بتاعي.

I'd like to send an email.
'aayiz/'ayza aba'at e-mayl (m/f) — عايز أبعت إيميل.

SIGHTSEEING
السّياحة

Where's the tourist information office?
maktab is siyaaHa fayn? — مكتب السّياحة فين؟

Do you have a local map?
'andak/ik kharita maHalliyya? (m/f) — عندك خريطة محلّيّة؟

Do you have a guidebook in English?
fee kitaab irshaadi bil ingileezi? — فيه كتاب إرشادي بالإنجليزي؟

What are the main attractions?
ay ahham il muzarāt hina? — أيه أهم المزارات هنا؟

We only have one day/two days.
'andina yōm/yōmeyn bas — عندنا يوم/يومين بس.

I'd like to see ...
'aayiz/'ayza ashoof ... (m/f) — عايز أشوف ...

May we take photographs?
mumkin nakhud soora? — ممكن ناخد صورة؟

I'll send you the photograph.
Hab'atlak/lik is soora (m/f) — حا بعتلك الصّورة.

Could you take a photograph of me?
mumkin tisawwarni? — ممكن تصوّرني؟

Getting In — الدّخول

What time does it open?
biyiftaH imta? — بيفتح إمتى؟

What time does it close?
biyi'fil imta? — بيقفل إمتى؟

Is there an admission charge?
fee rasm id dukhool? — فيه رسم الدّخول؟

Is there a discount for ...?	fee takhfeeḍ ...?	فيه تخفيض...؟
children	lil aṭfāl	للأطفال
students	liṭ ṭalba	للطّلبة

The Sights — معالم

What's that building?
ey il mabna da? — إيه المبنى ده؟

What's this monument?
ey il asar da? — إيه الأثر ده؟

What's that?	ey da?	إيه ده؟
How old is it?	baᶜaalu addi ey da?	بقاله قد إيه ده؟

ON THE RIGHT TERMS

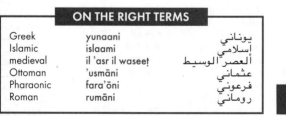

Greek	yunaani	يوناني
Islamic	islaami	إسلامي
medieval	il 'asr il waseeṭ	العصر الوسيط
Ottoman	'usmāni	عثماني
Pharaonic	fara'ōni	فرعوني
Roman	rumāni	روماني

ancient	ᶜadeem	قديم
antiquities	asār	آثار
castle	al'a	قلعة
church	kaneesa	كنيسة
cathedral	kateedrāᶜiyya	كتدرائية
cinema	sinima	سينما
column	'amood	عمود
concert	Hafla museeqiyya	حفلة موسيقيّه
Coptic	ibṭi	قبطي
court(yard)	Hōsh	حوش
crowded	zaHma	زحمة
dynasty	usra	أسرة
exhibition	ma'raḍ	معرض
god	ilaa	الاه
Islamic	islaami	إسلامي
medieval	min il 'uṣoor il wusṭa	من العصور الوسطى
monastery/convent	dayr	دير
mosque	gaami'	جامع
mummy	mumya	موميا
museum	matHaf	متحف
palace	qaṣr	قصر
papyrus	babeerus; wara' il bardi	بابيروس/ ورق البردي
pharaonic	fara'ōni	فرعوني
pyramid	haram	هرم
The Pyramids (Giza)	il ahraam	الأهرام
reliefs	buruzaat	بروزات
statue	timsaal	تمثال
the Sphinx	abul hōl	أبو الهول
temple	ma'bad	معبد
tomb	maqbara	مقبرة
university	gaama'a	جامعة
Valley of the Kings	waadi il mulook	وادي الملوك
Valley of the Queens	waadi il malikāt	وادي الملكات

ISLAMIC ARCHITECTURAL TERMS
مصطلحات معمارية إسلاميّة

khaan — خان
hostel for traders

khanqa — خانقة
hostel for sufi mystics

kuttaab — كتّاب
charitable primary school, usually attached to a mosque and public fountain

madrasa — مدرسة
theological school

mashrabiyya — مشرّبيّة
lattice-like woodwork screen usually used in windows

miHrāb — محراب
niche, usually in a mosque, indicating the direction of Mecca

minbar — منبر
pulpit in a mosque

sabeel — سبيل
public fountain

wikaala — وكالة
hostel for traders

SIGNS

دخول	ENTRANCE
خروج	EXIT
سخن	HOT
بارد	COLD
ممنوع الدّخول	NO ENTRY
ممنوع التّدخين	NO SMOKING
مفتوح/مغلق	OPEN/CLOSED
ممنوع	PROHIBITED
دورة المياه	TOILETS
سيّدات	WOMEN
رجال	MEN

TOURS جولات

Are there regular tours we can join?
fee gawalaat muntazima mumkin nindam liha? فيه جولات منتظمة ممكن ننضمّ لها؟

Can we hire a guide?
'ayzeen murshid khāṣ عايزين مرشد خاص.

How much is a guide?
il murshid/a bikam? (m/f) المرشد بكم؟

How long is the tour?
il gawla kam saa'a? الجولة كم ساعة؟

Will we have free time?
fee gawla Hurra? فيه جولة حرّة؟

How long are we here for?
Han°ad hina addi ey? حنقعد هنا قدّ إيه؟

What time should we be back?
il mafrooḍ nirga' imta? المفروض نرجع إمتى؟

The guide has paid/will pay.
il murshid dafa'/hayidfa' المرشد حيدفع.

I'm with them.
ana ma'a hum أنا معهم.

Have you seen a group of (Australians)?
inta/inti shuft/ee magmoo'at (ustrāliyyeen)? (m/f) شفت مجموعة (أستراليين)؟

I've lost my group.
ḍā'it il magmoo'a bita'ti ضاعت المجموعة بتاعتي.

BAKHSHEESH

Bakhsheesh, 'tipping', is an essential part of the Egyptian experience. For those receiving the tips, the extra income supplements a wage that is often shocking by Western standards. **Bakhsheesh** is made when small services are rendered such as carrying bags and opening doors and to waiters and to anyone being extra helpful. **Bakhsheesh** isn't reserved for tourists only. Egyptians tip at every opportunity and for the most basic of daily needs.

سوبر ماركت
محل
تذكارات

PAPERWORK

إجراءات رسميّة

address	'unwaan	عنوان
age	sinn	سن
customs	gamaarik	جمارك
date of birth	tarikh il milaad	تاريخ الميلاد
drivers licence	rukhsit siwaaʿa	رخصة سواقة
identification	baṭaʿa	بطاقة
immigration	gawazaat	جوازات
marital status	il Halit il igtimaa'iyya	الحالة الإجتماعيّة
divorced	muṭallaq/a (m/f)	مطلّق
married	mutazawwig/a (m/f)	متزوّج
single	a'azib/a (m/f)	أعزب
widowed	armal/a (m/f)	أرمل
name	ism	إسم
nationality	ginsiyya	جنسيّة
passport number	raqm ib basboor	رقم الباسبور
place of birth	maHal il milaad	محل الميلاد
profession/work	mihna	مهنة
purpose of visit	sabab iz ziyāra	سبب الزّيارة
reason for travel	sabab si safar	سبب السّفر
business	shughl	شغل
holiday	ʿagaaza	أجازة
visiting relatives	ziyarat il aqārib	زيارة الأقارب
religion	diyaana	ديانة
sex	gins	جنس
visa	feeza	فيزا

الخروج بالليل GOING OUT

In a country where the vast majority of the population are teetotallers, nightlife isn't always as rollicking as it might be in the West. Cairo is, of course, a cosmopolitan metropolis with bars, cafes, cinemas and galleries. There the evening tends to start late. Locals, whether Egyptian or foreign, rarely eat dinner before 10 pm, and it's not unusual for restaurants in the well-heeled areas of Mohandiseen and Zamalek or in the major hotels to be buzzing until 1 or 2 am. Nightclubs are few and far between but there are always a few popular places, mostly attached to large hotels.

For most of Egypt's male inhabitants, though, socialising outside the home is done in cafes, where you can smoke a sheesha, drink tea, watch a football match or play backgammon – just like in English pubs, only without the alcohol or the women.

WHERE TO GO السّهرات

What's there to do in the evenings?
mumkin na'amil ey hina bil layl? — ممكن نعمل إيه هنا بالليل؟

What's on tonight?
fee ey yit'amal il layla? — فيه إيه يتعمل الليلة؟

Where are concerts listed?
fayn daleel il Hafalaat hina? — فين دليل الحفلات هنا؟

In the entertainment guide.
fee daleel il tarfeeh — في دليل الترفيه.

I feel like going to a/the ...	'aayiz/'ayza arooH ... (m/f)	عايز أروح ...
bar	bār	بار
cafe	ahwa	قهوة
cinema	is sinima	السّينما
concert	Hafla musiqiyya	حفلة موسيقيّة
nightclub	disku	ديسكو
opera	il ubira	الأوبرا
a restaurant	maṭ'am	مطعم
the theatre	masraH	مسرح
I feel like ...	'aayiz/'ayza (m/f)	عايز ...
a stroll	atmasha	أتمشّى
dancing	ar'uṣ	أرقص
going for a coffee/drink	akhad mashroob	أخد مشروب

TIP

Remember the capital H is pronounced as a strongly whispered 'h', rather like a loud sigh of exasperation, all the way from the back of the throat.

INVITATIONS عزومات

What are you doing this evening/this weekend?
Hat'amil/ee ey bil layl/ fil nihayet il usboo'? (m/f) — حاتعمل أيه بالليل/ في نهاية الأسبوع؟

Would you like to go out somewhere?
tiHibb/ee tukhrug/ee ma'aaya? (m/f) — تحب تخرج معايا؟

Would you like to do something ...?	tiHibb/ee ti'amal/ee Haaga ...? (m/f)	تحب تعمل حاجه...؟
tonight	il layla di	الليلة دي
tomorrow	bukra	بكره
at the weekend	fee nihayit il usboo'	في نهاية الأسبوع

Where would you like to go?
tiHibb/ee tirooH/ee fayn? (m/f) تحب تروح فين؟

Do you know a good restaurant (that is cheap)?
ta'rif/ee maṭ'am kwayyis (wi rakheeṣ)? (m/f) تعرف مطعم كويّس (و رخيص)؟

Would you like to go for a drink or a meal?
tiHibb/ee tishrab/ee aw taakul/ee Haaga? (m/f) تحب تشرب او تاكل حاجه؟

My shout. (I'll buy.)
ana Hadfa' أنا حادفع.

Do you want to come to the ... concert with me?
tiHibb/ee tirooH/ee Haflat ... ma'aaya? (m/f) تحب تروح حفلة ... معايا؟

We're having a party.
Hana'mil Hafla حنعمل حفلة.

Come along. ta'āla/ta'ālee (m/f) تعال.

Responding to Invitations الرّد على العزومة

Women should be careful how they use rejections. If trying to get rid of someone who's approached you on the street, the best strategy is to ignore them. If you use anything stronger than these expressions, you're likely to encourage, rather than discourage, attention.

Sure! akeed! أكيد!
Yes, I'd love to. yarayt ياريت.

Yes, let's. Where shall we go?
maashi. HanrooH fayn? ماشي. حنروح فين؟

What about tomorrow?
mumkin bukra? ممكن بكرة؟

No, thank you.
la' shukran لأ شكرا.

I'm here with my girlfriend/boyfriend.
ana hina ma' ṣadeeqti/ṣadeeqi أنا هنا مع صديقتي/صديقي.

I'm afraid I'm busy.
ana aasif/a, ana mashghool/a (m/f) — أنا آسف، أنا مشغول.

No, I'm afraid I can't.
aasif/a, maᶜadarsh (m/f) — آسف مقدرش.

Thanks, but I'd rather not.
shukran laakin mish Hayinfa' — شكرًا لكن مش حينفع.

I'm sorry, I've got better things to do.
aasif/a, ana 'andi Hagaat tanya a'milha (m/f) — آسف عندي حاجات تانية أعملها.

Leave me alone!
seebni li waHidi! — سيبني لوحدي!

Excuse me, I have to go now.
min faḍlak/min faḍlik laazim amshi — من فضلك لازم أمشي.

I'm not interested!
ana mish 'aayiz/'ayza! (m/f) — أنا مش عايز!

Get lost! — imshi! — إمشي!

NIGHTCLUBS & BARS — النّوادي الليليّة و البارات

Are there any good nightclubs?
fee hina nawaadi layliyya kuwayyisa? — فيه هنا نوادي ليليّة كويسة؟

Shall we dance?
neegi nurᶜuṣ? — نيجي نرقص؟

I'm sorry, I'm a terrible dancer.
ana aasif/a, mish bar'us kuwayyis (m/f) — أنا آسف، مش برقص كويّس.

Do you have to pay to enter?
laazim adfa' 'ashaan adkhul? — لازم أدفع علشان أدخل؟

No, it's free.
laᶜ, id dukhool bibalaash — لأ، الدّخول ببلاش.

Yes, it's 30 pounds.
aywa, id dukhool bi talateen ginay — أيوه، الدّخول ب ٣٠ جنيه.

This place is great!
da makaan rāi^{c}'!
ده مكان رائع!

I don't like the music here.
mish 'agbaani il museeqa hina
مش عاجباني الموسيقى هنا.

Shall we go somewhere else?
mumkin nirooH makan taani?
ممكن نروح مكان تاني؟

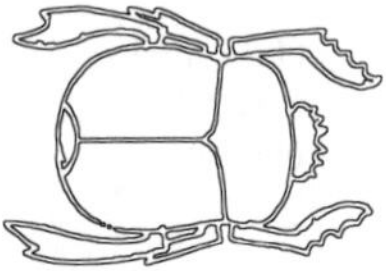

ARRANGING TO MEET الإتّفاق على اللقاء

What time shall we meet?
Hanit^{c}aabil imta?
حنتقابل إمتى؟

Where shall we meet?
Hanit^{c}aabil fayn?
حنتقابل فين؟

Let's meet at (eight) o'clock at the ....
mumkin nit^{c}aabil is saa'a (tamanya) fil ...
ممكن نتقابل السّاعه (ثمانية) في ...

OK. I'll see you then.
maashi, Hashoo/fak Hashoofik hinaak (m/f)
ماشي، حا شوفك هناك.

I'll come over at (six).
Hageelak/Hageelik is saa'a (sitta) (m/f)
حاجيلك السّاعة (ستّة).

I'll pick you up at (nine).
Haagi akhadak/akhadik is saa'a (tisa'a) (m/f)
حاجي اَخدك السّاعة (تسعة).

If I'm not there by (nine), don't wait for me.
low mali^{c}eytneesh hinaak is saa'a (tisa'a), matistanaash/matistaneesh (m/f)
لو ملقيتنيش هناك السّاعة (تسعة)، متستنّاش.

I'll be along later; where will you be?
Haagi ba'd kida; inta/
inti Hatkoon/ee fayn? (m/f) — حاجي بعد كده؛ أنت حتكون فين؟

See you later/tomorrow.
Hashoofak/Hashoofik
ba'd kida/bukra (m/f) — حاشوفك بعد كده/بكرة.

Sorry I'm late.
aasif/a inni ta^{c}akhart (m/f) — آسف أنّي تأخّرت.

I'll try to make it.	HaHaawil	حاحاول.
OK!	maashi!	ماشي!
Never mind.	ma'lish	معلش.

إهتمامات INTERESTS

COMMON INTERESTS إهتمامات عاديّة

What do you do in your spare time?
bit'amal/i ey fee ᶜawaat farāghak/farāghik? (m/f) — بتعمل أيه في أوقات فراغك؟

Do you like ...?	bitHibb/i ... (m/f)	بتحب ...؟
I like ...	ana baHibb ...	أنا بحب ...
I don't like ...	ana mabaHibbish ...	أنا مبحبّش ...
basketball	kōrit is silla	كورة السلّة
dancing	ir raᶜs	الرّقص
films	il aflaam	الأفلام
food	akl	أكل
football	ik kōra	الكورة
hiking	it tasalluq	التسلّق
music	il museeqa	الموسيقى
photography	it taṣweer	التصوير
reading	il qirāᶜa	القراءة
shopping	it tisawwuq	التسوق
skiing	is skeeying	السكيينج
swimming	is sibaaHa	السّباحة
talking	ik kalaam	الكلام
travelling	is safar	السّفر

STAYING IN TOUCH البقاء على اتصال

Tomorrow is my last day here.
bukra aakhir yōm liyya hina — بكرة آخر يوم ليا هنا.

Let's swap addresses.
yella nitbaadil il 'anaween — يالاّ نتبادل العناوين.

Do you have a pen and paper?
'andak/'andik wara' wa ᶜalam? (m/f) — عندك ورق و قلم؟

What's your address?
'inwānakik ey? — عنوانك أيه؟

Here's my address.
da 'unwāni — ده عنواني.

If you ever visit (Scotland), you must come and visit us.
low zurt/i (iskutlanda) laazim tigi tizurna/tizureena (m/f) — لو زرت (إسكتلندا) لازم تزورنا.

If you come to (London), you've got a place to stay.
low gayt/i (london) mumkin tu'"d 'andi (m/f) — لو جيت (لندن) ممكن تقعد عندي.

Do you have an email address?
'andak/'andik e-mayl? (m/f) — عندك إيميل؟

Do you have access to a fax machine?
'andak faaks? — عندك فاكس؟

I'll send you copies of the photos.
Haba'atlakik is suwwar (m/f) — حابعتلك الصور.

Don't forget to write!
matinsaash/tinseesh tiktib/i! (m/f) — متنساش تكتب!

It's been great meeting you.
ana mabsooṭ/a awi inni 'abiltak/'abiltik (m/f) — أنا مبسوط قوي إني قابلتك.

I'll miss you.
HatiwHashni (to a man) — حتوحشني.
HatiwHasheeni (to a woman) — حتوحشيني.

Keep in touch!
khaleena 'ala ittiṣāl! — خلّينا على إتّصال!

ART — الفن

Seeing Art — مشاهدة الفن

When is the gallery open?
ṣalit 'arḍ il funoon bitiftaH imta? — صالة عرض الفنون بتفتح إمتى؟

What kind of art are you interested in?
inta/inti muhtamm/a bi anhi fann? (m/f) — أنت مهتم بأنهى فن؟

I'm interested in ...	ana muhtamm/a bi ... (m/f)	أنا مهتم ب ...
calligraphy	zakhrafa	زخرفة
carpets	sagageed	سجاجيد
ceramics	khazaf	خزف
graphic art	fann il girāfeek	فن الجرافيك
icons	iqunāt	ايقونات
Islamic art	il fann il islāmi	ألفن الإسلامي
jewellery	migaw harāt	مجوهرات
painting	fann ir rasm	فن الرّسم
pottery	il fukhār	الفخّار
sculpture	naHt	نحت
weaving	naseeg	نسيج

What's in the collection?
il magmu'a feeha ey? المجموعة فيها أيه؟

There's a good collection of ...
fee magmu'a ... kuwayyisa. فيه مجموعة ... كويّسة.

building	mabna	مبنى
cartouche	kharṭoosh	خرطوش
church	kaneesa	كنيسة
epoch	'aṣr	عصر
mummy	moomya	موميا
paintings	lōHāt	لوحات
papyrus	wara' il bardi	ورق البردي
photographer	muṣawwir/a	مصور
relief	burooz	بروز
sarcophagus	taboot	تابوت
sculptor	naHāt	نحّات
slide	slayd	سلايد
souvenir shop	maHall tizkarāt	محل تذكارات
statue	timsaal	تمثال

Opinions آراء

I like the works of ...
ana baHibb shughl ... أنا بحب شغل ...

What do you think of ...?
ey rayyik fee ...? أيه رايك في ...؟

It's ...	huwa/hiyya ... (m/f)	هو/هي ...
awful	wiHish/wittsha (m/f)	وحش
beautiful	gameel/a (m/f)	جميل
dramatic	drāmi	درامي
incomprehensible	mish mafhoom	مش مفهوم
interesting	mumti'	ممتع
marvellous	rāi''	رائع
unusual	mish 'ādi	مش عادي

It's not as good as ...
mish kuwāyis/a zay ... (m/f) مش كويّس زيّ ...

It's reminiscent of ...
bifakkarni bi ... بيفكّرني ب ...

Doing Art ممارسة الفن

artwork	'amal fanni	عمل فنّي
bookshop	maktaba	مكتبة
canvas	kanaava	كانافا
exhibit/exhibition	ma'rad	معرض
opening	iftitaaH	إفتتاح
painter	rassaam/a (m/f)	رسّام
studio	stoodyu	ستوديو
style	usloob	أسلوب
technique	tekneek	تكنيك

TIP

Don't let the emphatic consonants ṣ, ḍ, ṭ and ẓ put you off. Even if you pronounce them in exactly the same way you would normally pronounce these letters, your Arabic will still be clearly understood.

MUSIC الموسيقى

Twentieth century Egyptian music can be broadly divided into classical, pop and traditional. Classical music had its peak in the 1940s and 50s, and its star was the legendary Umm Kalsoum, whose powerful voice is still revered by Egyptians and other Arabs. Her backup orchestra, like others of the time, combined Western and traditional Arabic instruments to create their own distinctive Arab sound. In the 1970s, a new kind of pop music called il geel, 'the generation', was born. With its streetwise and often political lyrics, and synthesised melodies, it was a hit with the young and later spawned sha'bi, 'popular', music, which is considered the music of the working class. Away from Cairo's dominant musical culture are the diverse traditional rhythms of the Sa'eed (Upper Egypt) and Nubia.

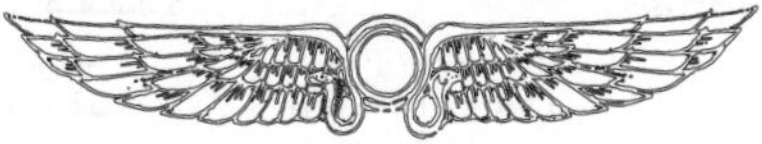

Do you like ...?	bitHibb/i ...? (m/f)	بتحب ...؟
to dance	turᶜuṣ/i (m/f)	ترقص
listening to music	tisma'/i museeqa? (m/f)	تسمع موسيقى

Do you play an instrument?
bita'zif Hāga? بتعزف حاجة؟

Do you sing?
bitghanni? بتغنّي؟

What music do you like?
bitHibb anhi museeqa? بتحب أنهي موسيقى؟

Which bands do you like?
bitHibb ayy fareeᶜ museeqi? بتحب أي فريق موسيقي؟

I like (the) ...
ana baHibb ... أنا بحب ...

Have you heard the latest record by ...?
sama't/i aakhir shireeṭ li ...? (m/f) سمعت آخر شريط ل ...؟

Where can you hear traditional music around here?
mumkin nisma' museeqa sha'biyya fayn hina? — ممكن نسمع موسيقة شعبيّة فين هنا؟

Shall we go closer to the stage?
mumkin niᶜrab min il masraH? — ممكن نقرّب من المسرح؟

What a fantastic concert!
dee Hafla Hilwa awi! — دي حفلة حلوة قوى!

It's terrible!
hiyya wiHsha! — هي وحشة!

This singer is brilliant.
il mughanni/yya da/dee 'aẓeem/a (m/f) — المغنّي ده عظيم.

See also On Tour, page 193.

Useful Words — كلمات مفيدة

band	firᶜa musiqiyya	فرقة موسيقيّة
concert	Hafla musiqiyya	حفلة موسيقيّة
concert hall	ṣālit Hafalat musiqiyya	صالة حفلة موسيقيّة
drums	ṭabla	طبلة
famous	mashhoor	مشهور
guitar	gitār	جيتار
musician	'aazif/a (m/f)	عازف
opera	ubera	أوبّرا
opera house	dār il ubera	دار الأوبّرا
orchestra	urkistra	أوركسترا
performance	'arḍ	عرض
song	ughniyya	أغنية
show	Hafla	حفلة
singer	mughanni/yya (m/f)	مغنّي
stage	khashabit il masraH	خشبة المسرح
tickets	tazaakir	تذاكر
ticket office	shibaak it tazaakir	شباك التّذاكر
tune	naghama	نغمة
venue	sāHa	ساحة
voice	ṣōt	صوت

ARABIC INSTRUMENTS

muzmār — مزمار
wind instrument used in traditional music and consisting of two reed pipes; makes a sound similar to an oboe

nay — ناي
reed pipe that sounds like a breathy flute

'ood — عود
similar to a lute

qanoon — قانون
zither

rabāba — ربابة
single-stringed instrument played with a bow; features in Sa'eedi music

ṭabla — طبلة
drum, similar to a bongo with an elongated wooden or clay base

CINEMA & THEATRE سينما ومسرح

I feel like going to a ...	'aayiz/'ayza ashoof ... (m/f)	عايز أشوف ...
ballet	balay	باليه
comedy	kumeedya	كوميديا
film	film	فيلم
play	masraHiyya	مسرحيّة

What's on at the cinema tonight?
fee ey fis sinima il layla di? — في أيه في السّينما الليلة دي؟

Where can I find a cinema guide?
alaʿi daleel sinima fayn? — ألاقي دليل سينما فين؟

Are there any tickets for ...?
fee tazaakir li ...? — فيه تذاكر ل...؟

Is it in English?
huwa bil ingileezi? — هو بالإنجليزي؟

Does it have English subtitles? fee targama ingileezi?		فيه ترجمة إنجليزيّة؟
Are there ads before the film? fee i'lanaat ᶜabl il film?		فيه إعلانات قبل الفيلم؟
Are those seats taken? il karaasi dee faḍya?		الكراسي دي فاضية؟
Have you seen ...? shuft/i ...? (m/f)		شفت ...؟
Have you seen the latest film by (Yousef Chahine)? shuft aakhir film li (Yousef Chahine)?		شفت آخر فيلم ل (يوسف شاهين)؟
Who's in it? meen il mumassileen?		مين الممثّلين؟
It's been very well reviewed. katabu 'anha kuwayyis		كتبوا عنها كويّس.
It stars ...	biṭoolit ...	بطولة ...
It's directed by ...	ikhrāg ...	إخراج ...
I like/don't like ...	ana baHibb/ mabaHibbish ...	أنا بحبّ/ أنا مبحبّش ...
action movies	aflaam akshun	أفلام أكشن
animated films	aflaam kartoon	أفلام كارتون
black comedy	kumeedya sawdā'	كوميديا سوداء
classical theatre	masraH klaseeki	مسرح كلاسيكى
comedy	kumeedya	كوميدية
documentaries	aflaam tasgeeliyya	أفلام تسجيليّة
drama	drāma	دراما
horror movies	aflaam ra'b	أفلام رعب
period dramas	aflaam tarikhiyya	أفلام تاريخيّة
realism	wāq'iyya	واقعيّة
sci-fi movies	aflaam il khayaal il 'ilmi	أفلام الخيال العلمي
short films	aflaam uṣayyara	أفلام قصيرة
thrillers	aflaam ithāra	أفلام إثارة
war films	aflaam Huroob	أفلام حروب

Opinions آراء

Did you like the ...?	a'gibak/a'gibik il ... ? (m/f)	عاجبك ال ...؟
film	film	فيلم
performance	'ard	عرض
play	masraHiyya	مسرحيّة

I liked it very much.
'aagibni awi — عاجبني قوي.

I didn't like it very much.
ma'gibneesh awi — معجبنيش قوي.

I thought it was ...
kunt faakir/fakra innu ... (m/f) — كنت فاكر إنّه ...

I had a few problems with the language.
kaan 'andi mushkila baseeṭ a ma' il lugha — كان عندي مشاكل بسيطة مع اللغة.

Excellent.	mumtaaz	ممتاز.
It's OK.	mish baṭāl	مش بطّال.

THEY MAY SAY ...

aasif/a, it tazaakir khilsit (m/f)
Sorry, we're sold out.

LITERATURE أدب

Who's your favourite author?
meen kaatibak/kaatibik il mufaḍḍal ? (m/f) — مين كاتبك المفضّل؟

I read (Naguib Mahfouz).
baʿra (nagib maHfooẓ) — باقرا(نجيب محفوظ).

I've read everything by (Nawal al-Saadawi).
ʿarayt kulli Hagaat (nawal al-saadawi) — قريت كل حاجات (نوال السعداوي).

I prefer the works of (Taha Hussein).
bafaḍḍal 'amaal (taha Hussein) — أنا بفضّل أعمال (طّه حسين).

What kind of books do you read?
ey nu' il kutub illi inta/inti biti^{c}raha/biti^{c}riha ? (m/f) — أيه نوع الكتب اللي انت بتقراها؟

I like/don't like ... — ana baHibb/mabaHibbish ... (m/f) — أنا بحب/مبحبش ...

anthologies	mukhtārāt	مختارات
biography	seera	سيرة
the classics	il klaseekiyaat	الكلاسيكيّات
comics	magalaat hazliyya	مجلاّت هزليّة
contemporary literature	il adab il mu'āṣir	الأدب المعاصر
crime/detective novels	ruwayaat buleesiyya	روايات بوليسيّة
fantasy	adab il fantazya	أدب الفانتازيا
fiction	khayaali	خيالي
non-fiction	ghayr khayaali	غير خيالي
novels	ruwayaat	روايات
poetry	shi'r	شعر
romance	qiṣaṣ gharāmiyya	قصص غراميّة
science-fiction	khayaal 'ilmi	خيال علمي
short stories	qiṣaṣ ^{c}uṣayyara	قصص قصيرة
travel writing	adab il riHlaat	أدب الرّحلات

Have you read (Mahfouz)?
arayt/i (maHfooẓ)? (m/f) — قريت (محفوظ)؟

What did you think of ...?
ey rayyak/rayyik fee ...? (m/f) — أيه رايك في ...؟

Can you recommend a book for me?
mumkin tirashaHli kitaab a^{c}rāhu? — ممكن ترشّح لي كتاب أقراه؟

Opinions آراء

I thought it was ...	ana kunt faakir/a innu ... (m/f)	أنا كنت فاكر أنّه ...
entertaining	musalli/yya (m/f)	مسلّي
well-written	maktoob kuwayyis	مكتوب كويّس
better/worse than the previous book	aHsan/awHash min il kitaab illi faat	أحسن/أوحش من الكتاب اللي فات
boring	mumil/a (m/f)	مملّ
badly written	maktoob wiHish	مكتوب وحش

HOBBIES هوايات

Do you have any hobbies?
’andak/’andik ayyi huwāyāt? (m/f) عندك أي هوايات؟

I like (to) ...	baHibb ...	بحبّ ...
cook	aṭbukh	أطبخ
draw	arsim	أرسم
paint	arsim	أرسم
sew	akhayyat	أخيّط
take photographs	aṣawwar	أصوّر
travel	is safar	السّفر

I make ...	ana ba’mal ...	أنا بعمل ...
jewellery	mugaw harāt	مجوهرات
pottery	fukhār	فخّار

I collect ...	bagamma’ ...	بجمّع ...
books	kutub	كتب
coins	’umla	عملة
comics	magalaat hazliyya	مجلاّت هزليّة
dolls	’araayis	عرايس
stamps	ṭawābi’	طوابع

ANCIENT EGYPTIAN

Ancient Egyptian belongs to the Hamito-Semitic group of languages and is distantly related to Arabic. Some Arabic words that are also found in ancient Egyptian share a common root, while others are ancient Egyptian words that have survived via Coptic (the latest stage of ancient Egyptian, which still survives as a liturgical language in the Coptic church).

Unlike the alphabetic Arabic script, ancient Egyptian was written in hieroglyphs, a script that combined different types of signs: uniliterals, biliterals and triliterals (alphabetic signs), logograms (signs that could stand for a whole word) and determinatives (signs that come at the end of a word and indicate to what class of word it belongs). Apart from the determinatives, all the signs had phonetic values.

The following uniliteral signs comprise the ancient Egyptian alphabet:

𓄿	Egyptian vulture, ꜣ, as the 'a' in 'hard' (Semitic *Aleph*)	𓃀	foot, *b*
𓇋	flowering reed, *ỉ*, as the 'i' in 'in' (Semitic *Jod*)	𓊪	stool, *p*
𓇌, 𓏭	two flowering reeds; oblique strokes, *y*, as the 'y' in 'baby'	𓆑	horned viper, *f*
𓂝	forearm, ', glottal stop (Semitic *Ajin*)	𓅓	owl, *m*
𓅱	quail chick, *w*, as the 'w' in 'way'	𓈖	water, *n*
		𓂋, 𓃭	mouth, lion, *r*

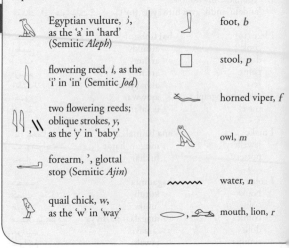

 reed shelter in fields, *h*

 wick of twisted flax, *ḥ*, emphatic, as the 'h' in 'Hugh'

 placenta (?), *ḫ*, as the 'ch' in Scottish 'loch'

 animal's belly with teats, *ẖ*, as the 'ch' in German 'ich'

 bolt, *z*, as the 's' in 'nose'

 folded cloth, *s*

 *š*, as the 'sh' in 'shape'

 hill slope, *ḳ*, *q*, (Semitic *Kaf*)

 basket with handle, *k*

 stand for jar, *g*

 loaf, *t*

 tethering rope, *ṯ*, as the 'tch' in 'itch'

 hand, *d*

 snake, *ḏ*, as the 'j' in 'jungle'

 In Greek names stands for the vowel 'o'

Examples of biliterals are  *ms*,  *wn*,  *wr*; a well-known triliteral is  *ʿnḫ* (ankh); a logogram is , a soldier, standing for 'army'. Some determinatives are  for words designating eating, drinking, thinking;  designating verbs of motion;  the papyrus roll designating abstract concepts.

TALKING ABOUT TRAVELLING — الكلام عن السفر

Have you travelled much?
safirt/i kiteer? (m/f) — سافرت كثير ؟

How long have you been travelling?
ba^caalak/ba^caalik ^caddi ey masaafir/a? (m/f) — بقيلك قد أيه مسافر ؟

I've been travelling for (two months).
ana masaafir/a li muddit (shahrayn) (m/f) — أنا مسافر لمدّة (شهرين).

Where have you been?
kunt/i fayn ^cabl ma tigi hina? (m/f) — كنت فين قبل متيجي هنا؟

I've been to ...
ana kunt fee ... — أنا كنت في ...

What did you think of (Athens)?
ey rayyik fee (ateena)? — أيه رايك في (أتينا)؟

I thought it was ...	kunt faakir/a innu ...	كنت فاكر إنّه ...
boring	mumil	مملّ
great	'azeem	عظيم
OK	mish baṭāl	مش بطّال
too expensive	ghaali	غالي
horrible	wiHish	وحش

There are too many tourists there.
fee suyāH kiteer hinaak — فيه سيّاح كتير هناك.

Not many people speak (English).
mafeesh naas kiteer biyitkallimu (ingileezi) — مفيش ناس كتير بيتكلّموا (إنجليزي).

I was ripped off in (Cairo).
itnaṣab 'alaya fee (al qāhira) — إتنصب عليّ في (القاهرة).

People are really friendly there.
in naas waduda awi hinaak — النّاس ودودة قوي هناك.

INTERESTS

What is there to do in (Brussels)?
fee ey yit'amal fee (brussels)? فيه إيه يتعمل في (بروكسل)؟

There's a really good restaurant there.
fee maṭ'am kwayyis awi hināk فيه مطعم كويّس قوي هناك.

I'll write down the details for you.
Haktiblak/Haktiblik il tafaṣeel (m/f) حاكتبلك التفاصيل.

The best time to go is in (December).
aHsan fatra tirooH feeha hiyya (disimber) أحسن فترة تروح فيها هي (ديسمبر).

Is it expensive?
huwa ghaali/hiyya ghalya? (m/f) هو غالي؟

Did you go alone?
ruHt/i li waHidak? (m/f) رحت لوحدك؟

Is it safe for women to travel alone?
huwa/hiyya amaan/a lil sittaat illi bisaafiroo li waHduhum? (m/f) هو أمان للستّات اللي بيسافروا لوحدهم؟

PLACE NAMES

Not all Egyptian towns have the same name in Arabic that we use in English. Below are a few placenames that have different pronunciations in the two languages. Note that Cairo is often referred to by the same word as Egypt (which says something about the importance of the metropolis to the rest of the country).

Alexandria	il iskandariyya	الإسكندريّة
Cairo	il qāhira; maṣr	ألقاهرة/مصر
Egypt	maṣr	مصر
Hurghada	il ghardaqa	الغردقة
Luxor	il luᶜṣur	الأقصر
Port Said	boor sa'eed	بور سعيد
Sinai	seena	سيناء

ASTRONOMY علم الفلك

Are you interested in astronomy?
inta/inti muhtamm/a bil tangeem? (m/f) أنت مهتم بالتّنجيم؟

I'm interested in astronomy.
ana muhtamm/a bil tangeem (m/f) أنا مهتم بالتّنجيم.

Do you have a telescope?
'andak/'andik teliskōp? (m/f) عندك تليسكوب؟

Will it be cloudy tonight?
Haykoon mighayyim bil layl? حيكون مغيّم با لليل؟

When can I see ...? mumkin ashoof ... imta? ممكن أشوف ... إمتى؟

Mars	il mareekh	المرّيخ
Mercury	'aṭārid	عطارد
Pluto	plutō	بلوتو
Uranus	urānus	أورانوس

What time does it rise?
biyiṭla' imta? بيطلع إمتى؟

What time will it set?
Hayinzil imta? حينزل إمتى؟

Can I see it at this time of year?
mumkin a shufu fil waᶜt da min is sana? ممكن أشوفه في الوقت ده من السنة؟

Which way is north?
ish shimāl fayn? الشّمال فين؟

Is that Orion?
da it talata 'aṣi? ده التّلاتة عصي؟

astronaut	ragul il faḍāᶜ	رجل الفضاء
astronomer	'aalim felaki	عالم فلكي
atmosphere	il ghulāf il gawi	الغلاف الجوّي
comet	shahab	شهب
Earth	il arḍ	الأرض
full moon	il badr	البدر
galaxy	maggara	مجرة
The Little Bear	id dib il aṣghar	الدّب الأصغر
meteor	shuhub	شهب
Milky Way	darb it tabbaana	درب التبّانة
moon	ᶜamar	قمر
planet	kawkab	كوكب
shuttle	makuk il faḍāᶜ	مكّوك الفضاء
sky	samaaᶜ	سماء
space	il faḍāᶜ	الفضاء
stars	nugoom	نجوم
sun	shams	شمس
telescope	teliskōp	تليسكوب
universe	il kun	الكون
Ursa Major/The Great Bear/The Big Dipper	id dib il akbar	الدّب الأكبر

SWEET STICKY MORNINGS

Egyptians are experts at turning everyday phrases into mock-flowery wordplay. So, for example, a simple good morning can turn into the following:

ṣabaH il 'ishṭa	(lit: morning of cream)	صباح القشدة
ṣabaH il full	(lit: morning of jasmin)	صباح الفلّ
ṣabaH il ward	(lit: morning of roses)	صباح الورد
ṣabaH il 'asal	(lit: morning of honey)	صباح العسل

THE UNEXPLAINED الغير معلوم

Do you believe in ...?	bitsadda' fee ...?	بتصدّق في ...؟
black magic	is siHr il iswid	السّحر الأسود
extraterrestrials	makhluqāt faḍāᶜiyya	مخلوقات فضائيّة
ghosts	ashbaaH	أشباح
life after death	il Hayat ba'd il mawt	الحياة بعد الموت
mediums	wasiṭ ruhi	وسط روحي
miracles	mu'gizaat	معجزات
UFOs	aṭ bāq ṭāira	أطباق طائرة

Are there haunted places in Egypt?
fee amaakin maskoona fee maṣr?
فيه أماكن مسكونة في مصر؟

People here/in my country tend (not) to be ...	in naas hina/fee baladna aghlabhum (mish)...	النّاس هنا/في بلدنا أغلبهم (مش) ...
imaginative	khayaali	خيالي
realistic	wāq'i	واقعي
scientific	'ilmi	علمي
superstitious	khurāfāt	خرافات

مسائل إجتماعيّة SOCIAL ISSUES

POLITICS السّياسة

Issues at the forefront of Egyptian politics include political freedom, human rights, the status of women, and economic development. Egyptians may be cynical about politics and often use it as the subject of jokes. However, with a foreigner, particularly if he or she is a stranger, people are likely to be more circumspect and refrain from direct criticism of their political system.

Did you hear about ...?
sama't/i 'an ...? (m/f) — سمعت عن ...؟

I read in (Al-Ahram) today that ...
arayt fee (il ahrām) innaharda in ... — قريت في (الأهرام) االنهارده ان ...

What type of government do you have in your country?
ey no' Hukooma i'ndukom fee baladak? — أي نوْع حكومة عندكم في بلدك ؟

I (don't) agree with the policy on ...	ana (mish) muwāfi^c/a 'ala siyaasit ... (m/f)	أنا (مش) موافق على سّياسة ...
drugs	il mukhadarāt	المخدّرات
the economy	il iqtiṣād	الإقتصاد
education	it-ta'leem	التّعليم
the environment	il bee'a	البيئة
human rights	Hu^coo^c il insaan	حقوق الإنسان
the military	il quwāt il musallaHa	القوّات المسلّحة
privatisation	il khaṣkhaṣa (m/f)	الخصخصة
social welfare	ar-rafaaha il igtimaa'iyya	الرّفاهة الإجتماعيّة
unemployment	biṭāla	البطالة

I'm ...	ana ...	أنا ...
communist	shiyoo'i/yya (m/f)	شيوعي
conservative	mutaHāfiz/a (m/f)	محافظ
green	akhḍar/khaḍra (m/f)	أخضر
socialist	ishtirāki/yya (m/f)	إشتراكي
I'm an anarchist.	ana fawḍawi/yya (m/f)	أنا فوضوي.

In my country we have a (socialist) government.
'andina Hukuma (ishtirākiyya) fee baladna
عندنا حكومة (إشتراكيّه) في بلدنا.

Politicians are all the same.
is siyaasiyyeen kulluhum zay ba'ḍ
السّيا سيّين كلّهم زي بعض.

EGYPTIAN POLITICAL PARTIES

Arab Democratic Nasserist Party
il Hizb il 'arabi il dimuqrāṭi il nāṣiri
الحزب العربي الديمقراطي النّاصري

Labour Party
Hizb il 'amal
حزب العمل

Liberal Party Hizb
il ahrār
حزب الأحرار

Muslim Brotherhood (banned)
il ikhwaan il muslimeen
الإخوان المسلمين

National Democratic Party Hizb
il waṭani il dimuqrāṭi
الحزب الو طني الديمقراطي

Nationalist Unionist Progressive Party
it tagammu'
التّجمّع

Wafd (Delegation)
Hizb il wafd
حزب الوفد

candidate's speech	khuṭbat il murashaH	خطبة المرشّح
censorship	riqāba	رقابة
corrupt	faasid	فاسد
corruption	fasaad	فساد
democracy	dimuqrāṭiya	ديمقراطيّة
demonstration	muẓahra	مظاهرة
elections	intikhabaat	إنتخابات
electorate	nakhibeen	ناخبين
exploitation	istaghaal	إستغلال
extremist	mutaṭarrif	متطرّف
freedom	Hurriya	حرّية
fundamentalist	uṣooli	أصولي
islamist	islāmi	إسلامي

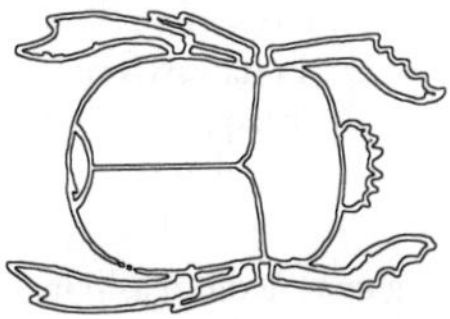

legislation	tashree'	تشريع
parliament	barlamān/ maglis ish sha'b	برلمان/مجلس الشّعب
policy	siyaasa	سياسة
president	ra'ees	رئيس
prime minister	ra'ees il wuzara	رئيس الوزراء
racism	tafri'a 'unṣuriyya	تفرقة عنصريّة
rally	muẓahra	مظاهرة
sexism	tafri'a ginsiyya	تفرقة جنسيّة
strike	iḍrāb	إضراب
term of office	muddit il manṣib	مدّة المنصب
trade union	niqāba	نقابة
unemployment	biṭāla	بطالة
vote	ṣōt	صوت
violence	'unf	عنف

ENVIRONMENT البيئة

Does (Egypt) have a pollution problem?
fee (maṣr) mushkilat it talawus?
فيه (مصر) مشكلة تلوّث؟

Does (Cairo) have a recycling program?
fee i'aadit tashgheel iz zibaala fil (qāhira)?
فيه إعادة تشغيل الزّبالة في (القاهرة)؟

Are there any protected species here?
fee hina kaʿinaat maHmiyya?
فيه هنا كائنات محميّة؟

Is this a protected area?
dee maHmiya?
دي محميّة؟

What's your opinion about ...?	ey rayyak/ rayyik fee ... ? (m/f)	أيه رايك في...؟
pollution	it talawwus	التلوّث
nuclear ...	... in nawawiyya	... النوويّة
energy	ittāqa	الطّاقة
weapons testing	iHtabarāt il asliHa	إحتبارات الأسلحة

anti-nuclear group	gamaa 'a ḍid il asliHa in nawawiyya	جماعة ضدّ الأسلحة النّوويّة
conservation	Himaaya	حماية
disposable	tustakhdam wi titrimi	تستخدم و تترمي
drought	gafaaf	جفاف
ecosystem	nizām il beeʿa	نظام البيئة
endangered species	kā'ināt mu'arraḍa lil inqirāḍ	كائنات معرّضة للإنقراض
hunting	ṣayd	صيد
hydroelectricity	kahru māʿiya	كهرو مائيّة
industrial pollution	it talawwus iṣ ṣanā'i	التلوث الصّناعي
irrigation	rayy	ري
ozone layer	ṭabaqat il ōzōn	طبقة الأوزون
pesticides	mubidaat	مبيدات
toxic waste	il nifayaat is saama	النفايات السّامّة
water supply	mawrid il miyaa	مورد المياه

SOCIAL ISSUES مواضيع إجتماعية

How do people feel about ...?
ey ray in naas fee ...? أيه راي الناس في ...؟
What do you think about ...?
ey rayyak/rayyik fee ...? (m/f) أيه رأيك في ...؟

I'm in favour of ...	ana uᶜayyid ...	أنا أؤيّد ...
I'm against ...	ana ḍid ...	أنا ضد ...
civil society	il mugtama' il madani	المجتمع المدني
equal opportunity	takaafuᶜ il furu	تكافؤ الفرص
press freedom	Hurriyit iṣ ṣaHāfa	حرّية الصّحافة
human rights	Huᶜooᶜ il insān	حقوق الإنسان
racism	at-tafriᶜa 'unṣuriyya	التفرقة عنصرية
taxes	ḍarayib	الضّرايب
unions	an-niqābaat	النّقابات
women's rights	Huᶜooᶜ il marᶜa	حقوق المرأة

Is there an (unemployment) problem here?
fee mushkilat (biṭāla) hina? فيه مشكلة (بطالة) هنا؟
Is there an adequate social welfare program?
fee burnaamig lil rifaaha il igtimaa'iya hina? فيه برنامج للرفاهه الإجتماعيّة هنا؟

What assistance is there for ...?	fee musaa'da Hukumiyya li ...?	فيه مساعدة حكومية ل ...؟
the aged	kibār is sinn	كبار السّن
the homeless	musharideen	المشرّدين
street kids	aṭfāl ish shawaari	أطفال الشّوارع

activist	nashiṭ/a (m/f)	نشط
citizenship	al-muwāṭina	المواطنة
class system	in niẓam iṭ ṭabaqi	النّظام الطّبقي
demonstration	al-muẓāhra	المظاهرة
equality	il musawaah	المساواه
human rights	Hu^{c}oo^c il insaan	حقوق الانسان
inequality	it tafāwit	التفاوت
petition	il timaas	التماس
poverty	il faqr	الفقر
protest	il iHtigaag	الإحتجاج
social security	it ta^{c}meen il igtimaa'i	التأمين الإجتماعي
strike	il iḍrāb	الإضراب
unemployment	il biṭāla	البطالة
welfare	ir rifaaha	الرفاهه
political speech	khuṭba siyasiyya	خطبة سياسيّة

DRUGS

Although there are drugs in Egypt, trafficking carries the death sentence and possession can lead to heavy penalties.

I don't take drugs.
ma bakhudsh mukhaddarāt — مباخدش مخدّرات.

I'm not interested in drugs.
ana mabaHibbish il mukhaddarāt — أنا مبحبّش المخدّرات.

I smoke (hashish) regularly.
ana bashrab (Hashish) — أنا بشرب حشيش.

نشاطات ACTIVITIES

Egypt is fast becoming a destination for outdoor sports enthusiasts. The coral reefs off the Red Sea and and Sinai coasts are world-renowned for their beauty, and attract thousands of scuba divers and snorkellers each year. On dry land, camel and four-wheel drives are taking off in Egypt's deserts. In Sinai's rock mountains, which cars can't access, Bedouins guide growing numbers of trekkers.

TYPES OF SPORT أنواع الرياضة

What sport do you play?
bitila'b/i anhi riyāḍa? بتلعب أنهى رياضة؟

I play/practise ...	bala'b ...	بلعب ...
aerobics	irōbiks	أيروبيكس
American football	kōrat il qadam il amrikiyya	كورة القدم الأمريكيّة
baseball	baysbaal	بيسبول
basketball	kōrat is salla	كورة السلّة
boxing	mulakma	ملاكمة
cricket	kirikit	كريكت
cycling	rukoob 'agal	ركوب العجل
diving	ghaṭs	غطس
football (soccer)	kōra	كورة
handball	kōrat il yad	كورة اليد
hockey (field)	huki	هوكي
martial arts	al'aab quwwa	ألعاب قوّة
roller blading	batinaazh	باتيناج
rowing	tagdeef	تجديف
surfing	tabHeer	تبحير
swimming	sibaaHa	سباحة
tennis	tinis	تنس
gymnastics	zhimnastik	جيمنا ستيك
volleyball	kōrat ṭayra	كورة طائرة
weightlifting	rafa' il asqāl	رفع الأثقال
yoga	yooga	يوجا

TALKING ABOUT SPORT الكلام عن الرياضة

Do you like sport?
bitHibb/i ir riyāḍa? (m/f) — بتحب الرّيا ضة ؟

Yes, very much.
aywa, awi — أيوه، قوي.

No, not at all.
la', mabaHibhaash — لأ، مبحبّهاش.

I like watching it.
baHibb atfarrag 'alayha — بحب اتفرّج عليها.

What sports do you follow?
ey noo' ir riyāḍa illi inta/i bititfarrag/i 'alayha? (m/f) — ايه نوع الريا ضة اللي انت بتتفرّج عليها؟

I follow (like) ...
ana baHibb ... — أنا بحب ...

Who's your favourite player?
meen il mufaḍḍal laa'ib/a 'andak/ik? (m/f) — مين المفضّل لاعب عندك ؟

What's your favourite team?
ey fari' ak il mufaḍḍal? — أيه فريقك المفضّل؟

I support ...
ana bashagga' ... — أنا بشجّع ...

How do you play (basketball)?
bitil'ab (kōrat salla) iz zay? — بتلعب (كورة سلّة) إزّاي؟

Can you play (football)?
ta'arif/i tila'b/i (kōra)? (m/f) — تعرف تلعب (كورة)؟

Yes, I know how to play.
aywa, ba'araf — أيوه، بعرف.

No, I don't know how to play.
la', mish 'aarif/'arfa (m/f) — لأ، مش عارف.

Do you feel like (going for a run)?
tiHibb/i (tigri)? (m/f) — تحب (تجري)؟

Do you want to go (diving) this weekend?
tiHibb/i tirooH/i (tighṭas) fee nihāyit il usboo'? تحب تروح (تغطس) في نهاية الأسبوع؟
Come and watch us play.
ta'aala/i itfarrag/i 'alayna wa iHna binila'b (m/f) تعالى إتفرج علينا و احنا بنلعب.
Can I join in?
mumkin ala'b ma'akum? ممكن ألعب معكم؟

SOCCER كورة القدم

Soccer is by far Egypt's most popular team sport, and attending a match is one way to interact with ordinary Egyptians away from the hassle of touristic sites. Soccer fans are passionate about their sport and when an important game is on television, Cairo's streets are emptied of their usual chaotic traffic as the city gathers around the nearest set to watch.

Do you follow soccer?
bitHibb/i ik kōra? بتحب الكورة؟
Who do you support?
bitshagga'/i meen? بتشجّع مين؟
I support (Zamalek).
bashagga' (zamaalik) بشجّع (ليفربول).
What a terrible team!
fari^c ta'baan! فريق تعبان!
Who's the best team?
meen ahsan fareeq? مين أحسن فريق؟

A TO Z OF SOCCER TEAMS

Egypt's dawri mumtāz, 'top league', consists of 14 teams which compete for the dir' id dowri, 'league shield'. The top seven teams in the league go on to compete for the kās maṣr, 'Egypt Cup'. Usually, the contest ends up being between two Cairo-based teams, Ahli and Zamalek.

Who's at the top of the league? meen il awwal fil dawra?	مين الأوّل في الدورة؟
Who plays for (Ahli)? meen biylā'b (ahli)?	مين بيلاعب (أهلي)؟
My favourite player is ... afḍal laa'ib 'andi ...	أفضل لاعب عندي ...
He's a great player. huwa la'eeb	هو لعّيب.
He played brilliantly in the match against (Italy). li'ib kuwayyis giddan fee matsh ma'a (iṭālya)	لعب كويّس جدا في ماتش مع (إيطاليا).
Would you like to go to a match? tiHibb/i tirooH/i il matsh? (m/f)	تحب تروح الماتش؟
Where's it being held? Hayibᶜa fayn?	حيبقى فين؟
How much are the tickets? it tazaakir bikam?	التذاكر بكم؟
What time does it start? Hayibtidi imta?	حيبتدي إمتى؟
Who's playing? meen biyil'ab?	مين بيلعب؟

At the Match

في الماتش

Who do you think will win? meen hayfooz?	مين حيفوز؟
Who are you supporting? bitshagga' meen?	بتشجّع مين؟
I'm supporting ... bashagga' ...	بشجّع ...
Who's winning? meen faayiz?	مين فايز؟
Which team is winning/losing? meen faayiz/khasrān?	مين فايز/خسران؟
What's the score? kam kam?	كم كم؟

He's/She's good.
  huwa/hiyya la'eeb/a — هولعّيب.

The referee has disallowed it.
  il Hakam laghaah — الحكم لغاه.

How much time is left?
  nā^{c}iṣ kam 'alal matsh? — ناقص كم على الماتش؟

That was a really good game!
  kaan matsh gameel! — كان ماتش جميل!

What a boring game.
  matsh mumil — ماتش ممل.

What was the final score?
  khiliṣ kam kam? — خلص كم كم؟

It was a draw.
  kaan t'aadul — كان تعادل.

What a ...!	ya salaam 'ala ...!	يا سلام على ...!
goal	gōl	جول
kick	shooṭa	شوطة

coach	kōtsh	كوتش
corner	ḍarabit rukniyya	ضربة ركنيّة
cup	kaas	كاس
fans	gumhoor	جمهور
first half	ish shooṭ il awwil	الشّوط الأوّل
free kick	ḍarabit Hurra	ضربة حرّة
direct	mubashara	مباشرة
indirect	ghayr mubashara	غير مباشرة
foul	fawl	فاول
the goal	il marma	المرمى
goalkeeper	Haaris marma	حارس مرمى
international championships	biṭoola dawliyya	بطولة دوليّة
kick off	bada'shoot il awwil	بدأ شوط الأوّل
league	dawra	دورة
manager	mudeer il fari'	مدير الفريق
medal	meedalya	ميداليّة
national championships	biṭoola maHalliyya	بطولة محليّة
offside	it tasallul	التسلّل
Olympic Games	il al'aab il ulimbiyya	الألعاب الأوليمبيّة
penalty	gazā'	جزاء
penalty kick	ḍarbit gazā'	ضربة جزاء
player	laa'ib/a (m/f)	لاعب
referee	Hakam	حكم
seat	kursi	كرسي
to shoot	shooṭ	شوط
soccer	kōra	كورة
supporters	gumhoor	جمهور
ticket	tazkara	تذكرة
ticket office	shibaak tazaakir	شبّاك تذاكر

FOOTBALL & RUGBY كورة قدم ورجبي

I play ...	ana bal'ab ...	أنا بلعب ...
Have you ever seen ...?	'umrak shuft ...?	عمرك شوفت ...؟
Are you familiar with ...?	ti'rif ...?	تعرف ...؟
American football	kōrit il qadam il amrikiyya	كورة القدم الأمريكيّة
Aussie Rules	kōra ustraliyya	كورة أسترالية
rugby	rugby	رجبى

Do you want me to teach you to play?
'aayizni/'ayzani a'llimak tila'b? (m/f)
عايزني أعلمك تلعب؟

TRYING TO SCORE

draw/even	ta'aadul	تعادل
goal	gōl	جول
match-point	nu^{c}ṭit tamās	نقطة تماس
nil (zero)	ṣifr	صفر
to score	yigib gōl	يجيب جول

KEEPING FIT المحافظة على المرونة البدنيّة

Where's the nearest ...?	fayn a^{c}rab ...?	فين أقرب ...؟
gym	zhim	جيم
swimming pool	Hamaam is sibaaHa	حمّام السّباحة
tennis court	mala'b tinis	ملعب تنس
What's the charge per ...?	bikam il ...?	بكم ال...؟
day	yōm	يوم
game	la'ba	لعبة
hour	saa'a	ساعة

Where are the changing rooms?
fayn taghayyir il malaabis?
فين تغيّر الملابس؟

Where's the best place to jog/ run around here?
fayn aHsan makaan lil gari? — فين أحسن مكان للجري؟

jogging	il gari	الجّري
massage	masāzh	مسّاج
rowing machine	makanat tagdeef thabta	مكنة تجديف ثابتة
sauna	sawna	ساونة
shower	dush	دش
towel	foota	فوطة

AQUATIC SPORTS — رياضة مائيّة

dinghy	lunsh	لنش
motor	mutoor	موتور
motorboat	lunsh	لنش
oars	magādeef	مجاديف
sail	shurā'	شراع
sailing (the sport)	tabHeer	تبحير
swimming	sibaaHa	سباحة
waterskiing	tazaHluq 'alal mayya	تزحلق على الميّة
wave	moog	موج
windsurfing	tabHeer il hawaa'i	تبحير الهوائي

Diving & Snorkelling — الغطس

Are there good diving sites here?
fee amaakin ghaṭs kuwayyis hina? — فيه أماكن غطس كويس هنا؟

I'm interested in exploring wrecks.
ana muhtamm bi iktishāf aṭlāl is sufun — أنا مهتم بإكتشاف أطلال السفن.

Can we hire a diving boat/guide?
mumkin n'aggar markib/murshid? — ممكن نأجّر مركب/مرشد؟

We'd like to hire diving equipment.
'ayzeen nᶜaggar 'iddit il ghaṭs — عايزين نأجّر عدة الغطس.

ACTIVITIES

to dive	ghitis, yightas	غطس
a dive	ghatsa	غطسة
diving	ghats	غطس
diving equipment	aghizit il ghats	أجهزة الغطس
fin	za'nif	زعنف
fins	za'aanif	زعانف
goggles/mask	naddārit ghats	نضّارة غطس
recompression chamber	ghurfit daght	غرفة ضغط
regulator	munazzam	منظّم غطس
scuba diving	il ghats	الغطس
snorkel	sinorkil	سنوركل
snorkelling	ghōs	غوص
tank	ambooba	أمبوبة
wetsuit	badlit ghats	بدلة غطس

HORSE & CAMEL RIDING ركوب الخيل والجمل

Is there a horse-riding school around here?
fee istabl urayyib min hina? فيه إسطبل قريب من هنا؟

Are there rides available?
fee khayl fādi? فيه خيل فاضي؟

How long is the ride?
kam muddit ir rukoob? كم مدّة الركوب؟

How much does it cost?
bikam? بكم؟

Do you offer rides for beginners?
fee rukoob lil mubtadiᶜeen? فيه ركوب للمبتدئين؟

I'm an experienced rider.
'andi khibra fil rukoob عندي خبرة في الركوب.

Can I rent a hat and boots?
mumkin aᶜaggar khōza wa boot? ممكن أأجّر خوذة و بوت؟

I want to gallop.
'aayiz/'ayza agri (m/f) عايز أجري.

ACTIVITIES

bit	ligaam	لجام
camel	gamal	جمل
gallop	yigri	يجري
horse	faras	فرس
horse riding	rukoob khayl	ركوب خيل
mare	farasa	فرسة
reins	sur'a	سرع
saddle	sarg	سرج
stables	iṣtabl	إصطبل
stallion	Huṣān	حصان
stirrup	rikaab	ركاب

CARDS الكتشينة

Do you want to play ...?	tiHibb/i tila'b/i ...?	تحب تلعب ...
bridge	bridzh	بريدج
cards	kutsheena	كتشينة
poker	bōkir	بوكر

POKER LINGO

four of a kind	karay	كارى
full hand	fool	فول
pair	gōz	جوز
poker	bōkir	بوكر
royal flush	ruyal flush	رويال فلش
three of a kind	trees	تريس
two pairs	gōzayn	جوزين

I don't know how to play.
mish 'aarif/'arfa ala'b (m/f) مش عارف ألعب.

I'll teach you.
Ha'allimak حاعلّمك.

I'll bet (200) Egyptian pounds.
arahhin bi (mitayn) ginay أرهّن ب (متين) جني.

I'll raise you (100) Egyptian pounds.
azawwid (meet) ginay. أزوّد(مية) جني.

It's your turn to pick up a card.
dōrak 'ashaan takhud kart — دورك علشان تاخد كرت.

I can't go.	pās	باس.
I'll see you.	ana kamaan	أنا كمان.
I'm winning.	ana fāyiz/fayza (m/f)	أنا فايز.
I'm losing.	ana khasrān/a (m/f)	أنا خسران.
Stop cheating!	kifāya ghish!	كفاية غش!

ace	ays	أيس
king	shayib	شايب
queen	bint	بنت
jack	walad	ولد
joker	zhōkir	جوكر
spades	sibaads	سباتس
clubs	warda	وردة
diamonds	sambuksa	سمبكسة
hearts	ᶜalb	قلب
to deal	faraᶜ	فرق
to shuffle	funnaṭ	فنّط

CHESS — الشطرنج

Do you like chess?
bitHibb/i il shaṭarang? (m/f) — بتحب الشّطرنج؟

Shall we play chess?
tiHibb/i tila'b/i shaṭarang? (m/f) — تحب تلعب شطرنج؟

KISH MAAT!

White starts.	il abyaḍ yibtidi	الأبيض يبتدي.
It's my move.	doori	دوري.
Hurry up and make a move!	khalaṣ wa ila'b!	خلص و العب!
Check!	kish!	كش!
Check to the king!	kish malik!	كش ملك!
Checkmate!	kish maat!	كش مات!
Cheat!	ghashaash!	غشّاش!

bishop	feel	فيل
black pieces	qiṭa'sōda	قطع سودة
castle; rook	ṭābya	طابية
chess board	ā'dit shaṭarang	قاعدة شطرنج
chess tournament	dawrit shaṭarang	دورة شطرنج
king	malik	ملك
knight	Huṣān	حصان
pawn(s)	'askari ('asākir)	عسكري
pieces	qiṭ'a	قطعة
queen	wazeer	وزير
stalemate	t'aadul	تعادل
white pieces	qiṭa' bayḍa	قطع بيضة

TV التليفزيون

Do you mind if I put the TV on?
mumkin aftaH it tilivizyōn? ممكن أفتح التليفزيون؟

Can I change the channel?
mumkin aghayyar il qanā? ممكن أغيّر القناة؟

The TV isn't working.
it tilivizyōn 'aṭlān التليفزيون عطلان.

التسوّق SHOPPING

From the medieval alleyways of Cairo's labyrinthine Khan al-Khalili bazaar to the stalls in a country market, Egypt is a shopper's paradise. Whether you're looking for a kitsch Pharaonic souvenir, some famed Egyptian cotton or a scarf embroidered by a Bedouin woman, you'll be in luck.

In Cairo, there are a number of produce markets in the old city and in areas like Bab il-Louq or Ataba. Most shops close on Sunday, a hangover from colonial times. Many small grocery stores and supermarkets, however, stay open until late at night.

LOOKING FOR ... البحث عن ...

Where can I buy ...?	ashtiri ... minayn?	أشتري ... منين ؟
Where's the nearest ...?	fayn il a'rab ...?	فين الأقرب ...؟
bank	bank	بنك
barber	Hallaa^c	حلاّق
bookshop	maktaba	مكتبة
camera shop	maHall kamiraat	محل كاميرات
chemist	ṣaydaliyya	صيدليّة
clothing store	maHall malaabis	محل ملابس
department store	maHall	محل
grocer	ba^caal	بقّال
laundry	maghsala	مغسلة
market	soo^c	سوق
newsagency	maktaba	مكتبة
optician	maHall naḍārāt	محل نظّارات
music shop	maHall isṭiwānaat	محل إسطوانات
shoe shop	maHall gizam	محل جزم
souvenir shop	maHall it tizkaraat	محل تذكارات
stationers	maktaba	مكتبة
supermarket	subirmarkit	سوبرماركت
tailor	tarzi	ترزي
travel agency	maktab is siyaaHa	مكتب السّياحة

MAKING A PURCHASE شراء

I'm just looking.	batfarrag bas	بتفرّج بس.
How much is this?	bikam da?	بكم ده؟
Do you have others?	fee taani?	فيه تاني؟
Can I look at it?	mumkin ashoofu?	ممكن أشوفه؟
I don't like it.	mish 'agibni	مش عاجبني.

Can you write down the price?
mumkin tiktib/i it taman? (m/f) — ممكن تكتب الثّمن؟

I'd like to buy ...
'aayiz/'ayza ashtiri ... (m/f) — عايز أشتري ...

Do you accept credit cards?
bitakhud/i kredit kard? (m/f) — بتاخد كريدت كارد؟

Could I have a receipt, please?
'aayiz/'ayza waṣl, low samaHt — عايز وصل، لو سمحت.

Does it have a guarantee?
fee ḍamān? — فيه ضمان؟

Can I have it sent overseas/abroad?
mumkin aba'at ha barra? — ممكن أبعتها برّة؟

Please wrap it.
liffuh/liffeeh low samaHt (m/f) — لفّه، لو سمحت.

I'd like to return this, please.
'aayiz/'ayza aragga'uh, low samaHt (m/f) — عايز أرجّعه لو سمحت.

I'd like my money back.
'aayiz il filoos bitaa'ti — عايز الفلوس بتاعتي.

It's faulty.	mish shaghghaal	مش شغّال.
It's broken.	huwa/hiyya 'aṭlān (m/f)	هو عطلان.

BARGAINING المفاصلة

While bargaining is standard practice in markets and most souvenir shops, it isn't done in supermarkets, Western-style boutiques or in shops with clearly marked prices.

I think it's too expensive.
da ghaali awi — ده غالي قوي.

Can you lower the price?
mumkin tinazzil it taman? ممكن تنزّل التّمن؟

Do you have something cheaper?
'andak/'andik Haaga arkhaṣ? (m/f) عندك حاجة أرخص؟

Really?	Ha^{c}ee^{c}i?	حقيقي؟
I'll give you ...	Hadfa' ...	حادفع ...
Let's say ...	khalleena ni^{c}ool ...	خلّينا نقول ...
No more than ...	mish aktar min ...	مش أكتر من ...

ESSENTIAL GROCERIES البقالة الضروريّة

Where can I find ...?	alaa^{c}ee ... fayn?	ألاقي... فين؟
I'd like (a/some) ...	'aayiz/'ayza ... (m/f)	عايز ...
batteries	baṭariyāt	بطّاريّات
bread	'aysh	عيش
butter	zibda	زبدة
candles	shama'	شمع
cheese	gibna	جبنة
chocolate	shikōlāta	شيكولاتة
eggs	bayḍ	بيض
flour	di^{c}ee^c	دقيق
gas cyclinder	ambubit butagaaz	أمبوبة بوتجاز
honey	'asal	عسل
matches	kibreet	كبريت
milk	laban	لبن
mosquito coils	ṭārid in namoos	طارد النّاموس
pepper	filfil	فلفل
salt	malH	ملح
shampoo	shamboo	شامبو
soap	ṣāboon	صابون
sugar	sukkar	سكّر
toilet paper	wara^c tuwalit	ورق تواليت
toothpaste	ma'goon asnaan	معجون أسنان
washing powder	ṣāboon ghaseel	صابون غسيل
yogurt	zabaadi	زبادي

SOUVENIRS — هدايا تذكاريّة

alabaster	marmar	مرمر
applique	khayyamiyya	خيّاميّة
basket/s	sabat/isbita (sg/pl)	سبت
brassware	naHaas	نحاس
carpets	sagageed	سجاجيد
cartouche	kharṭoosha	خرطوشة
handicraft	shughl yadawi	شغل يدوي
papyrus	wara^{c} il bardi	ورق البردي
jewellery	mugaw harāt	مجوهرات

CLOTHING — ملابس

boots	boot	بوت
clothing	hudoom	هدوم
coat	balṭu	بالطو
dress	fustaan	فستان
jacket	zhakit	جاكت
jeans	zhinz	جينز
jumper (sweater)	biloovar	بلوفر
pants (trousers)	banṭalōn	بنطلون
raincoat	baltō maṭar	بالطو مطر
shirt	^{c}āmiṣ	قميص
shoes	gazma	جزمة
socks	sharāb	شراب
swimsuit	maayu	مايو
T-shirt	tishirt	تي شيرت
underwear	malaabis dakhiliyya	ملابس داخليّة

Can I try it on?
  mumkin a^{c}ees? ممكن أقيس؟

My size is ...
  ma^{c}aasi ... مقاسي ...

It doesn't fit.
  huwa/hiyya mish maẓbooṭ/a (m/f) هو مش مظبوط.

It's too ...	huwa/hiyya ... (m/f)	هو ...
big	waasi'/a (m/f)	واسع
small	ṣughayyar/a (m/f)	صغير
short	^{c}usayyar/a (m/f)	قصير
long	ṭaweel/a (m/f)	طويل
tight	dayyi^{c}/a (m/f)	ديّق
loose	waasi'/a (m/f)	واسع

MATERIALS مواد

brass	naHaas aṣfar	نحاس أصفر
ceramic	khazaf	خزف
cotton	^{c}uṭn	قطن
copper	naHaas aHmar	نحاس أحمر
glass	^{c}izaaz	قزاز
gold	dahab	دهب
handmade	shughl yadawi	شغل يدوي
leather	gild	جلد
metal	ma'dan	معدن
plastic	bilastik	بلاستيك
silk	Hareer	حرير
silver	faḍḍa	فضّه
stainless steel	istaynlis steel	استينلس ستيل
synthetic	alyaaf ṣanā'iyya	ألياف صناعيّة
wood	khashab	خشب
wool	ṣoof	صوف

COLOURS — ألوان

dark ...	... ghaami^c	... غامق
light ...	... faatiH	... فاتح
black	iswid/sōda (m/f)	إسود
blue	azra^c/zar^{c}a (m/f)	أزرق
brown	bunni/bunya (m/f)	بنّي
burgundy	nibiti	نبيتي
green	^{c}akhḍar/khaḍra (m/f)	أخضر
grey	ruṣāsi	رصاصي
orange	burtu'āni	برتقالي
pink	bambi	بمبي
purple	binafsigi	بنفسجي
red	aHmar/Hamra (m/f)	أحمر
white	abyaḍ/bayḍa (m/f)	أبيض
yellow	aṣfar/ṣafra (m/f)	أصفر

TOILETRIES — أدوات الزينة

aftershave	kulunya ba'd il Helaa^{c}a	كولونيا بعد الحلاقة
bath/shower gel	shower gel	شاور جيل
comb	mishṭ	مشط
condoms	kaboot (**slang**); 'aazil zakary	كابوت/ عازل ذكري
dental floss	khayṭ lil asnaan	خيط أسنان
deodorant	muzeel li reeHt il 'ara^c	مزيل لريحة العرق
hairbrush	fursha	فرشة
moisturiser	kraym	كريم
pregnancy test kit	taHleel Haml	تحليل حمل
razor	moos	موس
razor blades	amwās Halāqa	أمواس حلاقة
shaving cream	kraym Halaa^{c}a	كريم حلاقة
sunblock	kraym ḍid ish shams	كريم ضدّ الشّمس
tampons	tampax	تامبكس
tissues	manadeel	مناديل
toothbrush	furshit asnaan	فرشة أسنان

FOR THE BABY للطّفل

baby powder	budrat talk lil baybi	بودرة تلك للبيبي
bib	bavetta	بافتّة
disposable nappies	bambers	بامبرس
dummy (pacifier)	titeena	تتّينة
feeding bottle	biberōna	ببرونة
nappy (diaper)	kafoola	كفولة
nappy rash cream	kraym lil tasalukhāt	كريم للتّسلّخات
powdered milk (formula)	laban mugafaf lil baybi	لبن مجفّف للبيبى
teat	bazāza	بزازة
tinned baby food	akl lil baybi fil 'ilab	أكل للبيبى في العلب

STATIONERY & PUBLICATIONS ومكتبات قرطاسيّة

Is there an English-language bookshop nearby?
fee maktaba bitbee' Hagaat ingliziyya 'urayyiba min hina?
فيه مكتبة بتبيع حاجات إنجليزيّة قريّبة من هنا؟

Is there an English-language section?
fee qism ingileezi?
فيه قسم إنجليزي؟

Is there a local entertainment guide in English?
fee daleel lil tarfeeyya bil ingileezi?
فيه دليل للترفية بالإنجليزي؟

Do you have any books in English by (Neguib Mahfouz)?
'andak kutub bil ingileezi min (negeeb maHfooẓ)?
عندك كتب بالإنجليزي من (نجيب محفوظ)؟

Do you sell ...?	bitbee'...?	بتبيع ...؟
dictionaries	qamoos	قاموس
envelopes	zarf	ظرف
magazines	magallaat	مجلّات
newspapers	garāyid	جرايد
newspapers in English	gurnāl bil ingileezi	جرنال بالإنجليزي
paper	wara'	ورق
pens (ballpoint)	alam	قلم
postcards	kuroot bustāl	كروت بوستال
stamps	ṭābi'	طابع
... maps	khareeṭa ...	خريطة ...
city	il medina	المدينة
regional (provincial)	il muHafẓa	المحافظة
road	ṭaree'	طريق

MUSIC موسيقى

I'm looking for a ... CD.
badawwar 'ala CD ... بدوّر على سي دي ...

Do you have any ...?
'andak ...? عندك ...؟

What's his/her best tape/CD?
ey aHsan shireet/ CD luh/laha? أيه أحسن شريط/ سي دي له/لها؟

I heard a singer called ...
ana sama't mughanni/ yya ismuh/ismaha ... (m/f) أنا سمعت مغنّي إسمه ...

Can I listen to this CD here?
mumkin agarrab il CD da hina? ممكن أسمع السّي دي ده هنا؟

I need a blank tape.
ana 'aayiz/'ayza shireet tasgeel (m/f) أنا عايز شريط تسجيل.

PHOTOGRAPHY تصوير

How much is it to process this film?
taHmeed il film da bikam? تحميض الفيلم ده بكم؟

When will it be ready?
Haykoon gāhiz imta? حيكون جاهز إمتى؟

I'd like a film for this camera.
'aayiz/'ayza film lil kamira da (m/f) عايز فيلم للكاميرا ده.

battery	baṭariyya	بطّارية
camera	kamira	كاميرا
flash (bulb)	flash	فلاش
lens	'adasa	عدسة
slides	slaydz	سلايدز
videotape	shireeṭ veedyu	شريط فيديو
... film	film ...	فيلم ...
B&W	abyaḍ wa iswid	أبيض و إسود
colour	milawwin	ملون

SMOKING التدخين

A packet of cigarettes, please.
'ilbit sigaayar, low samaHt/i (m/f) علبة سجاير، لو سمحت.

Are these cigarettes strong or mild?
is sigaayar di tiʿeela walla khafifa? السّجاير دي تقيلة ولاّ خفيفة؟

Do you have a light?
'andak/'andik wallaa'a? (m/f) عندك ولاّعة؟

Please don't smoke.
matdakhansh, low samaHt ما تدخّنش، لو سمحت.

Do you mind if I smoke?
mumkin ashrab sigāra? ممكن أشرب سيجارة؟

I'm trying to give up.
ana baHawwil abaṭṭal il tadkheen أنا بحاول أبطّل التّدخين.

cigarettes	sigaayar	سجاير
cigarette papers	wara^{c} bafra	ورق بفرة
filtered	bil filtr	بالفلتر
lighter	wallaa'a	ولّاعة
matches	kibreet	كبريت
pipe	bayb	بايب
tobacco	dukhaan	دخان

(See page 160 for Smoking the Sheesha.)

SIZES & COMPARISONS الحجم والمقارنة

also	kamaan	كمان
big	kibeer/a (m/f)	كبير
enough	kifaaya	كفاية
heavy	ti^{c}eel/a (m/f)	ثقيل
light	khafeef/a (m/f)	خفيف
little (amount)	ulayyil/a (m/f)	قليل
a little bit	shiwayya	شوية
many	kiteer	كثير
more	aktar	أكثر
small	ṣughayyar/a (m/f)	صغير
too much/many	aktār min il laazim	أكثر من اللازم

Breakfast in Egypt tends to be savoury rather than sweet, although milk-based sweet dishes are sometimes on offer. Lunch was traditionally a heavy meal that was eaten between 2 and 4 pm and followed by a siesta. However, as business hours change and urban life becomes increasingly chaotic, the siesta is being lost and lunch is getting lighter.

Dinner, particularly in the city, tends to be eaten late at night and is a fairly large, heavy meal. Every meal is accompanied by copious amounts of bread, called 'aysh – which, fittingly, is similar to 'āsh, meaning 'to live life', and to 'ayesh, 'living'.

THROUGH THE DAY أثناء النهار

breakfast	fiṭār	فطار
to eat breakfast	fiṭir, yifṭar	فطر
lunch	ghada	غدا
to eat lunch	itghadda, yitghadda	إتغدّى
dinner	'asha	عشاء
to eat dinner	it'ashsha, yit'ashsha	إتعشّى
meal	wagba	وجبة

VEGETARIAN & SPECIAL MEALS وجبات نباتيّة و خاصّة

Although there are a wide number of dishes that don't contain meat in Egyptian cuisine, vegetarianism isn't widespread. You may sometimes need to explain that even if a dish contains mostly vegetables, it still isn't vegetarian if it contains one or two pieces of meat. Keep in mind that most soup stocks will be beef-or chicken-based.

While Egypt doesn't have kosher restaurants, all meat is Halāl, which means that it's slaughtered according to Muslim law (whereby the animal is killed swiftly and with minimum pain, and its blood is drained from its body). Pork is rarely offered and will always be specified if it's in a dish, so, unless it says otherwise, even the bacon and ham in hotel breakfast buffets will really be beef.

I'm a vegetarian.		
ana nabaatee/yya	(m/f)	أنا نباتي.
I don't eat meat.		
ma bakulsh laHma		أنا مباكلش لحمة.
I don't eat chicken, fish or ham.		
ma bakulsh firaakh aw samak aw khanzeer		أنا مباكلش فراخ أو سمك أو خنزير.
I can't eat dairy products.		
ma bakulsh il albaan		مباكلش الألبان.
Do you have any vegetarian dishes?		
'andak akla nabaatiyya?		عندك أكلة نباتيّة؟
Does this dish have meat?		
il akla dee feeha laHma?		الأكلة دي فيها لحمة؟
Can I get this without meat?		
mumkin tideeni dee bidoon laHma?		ممكن تدّيني دي بدون لحمة؟
Does it contain eggs?		
feeha bayḍ?		فيها بيض؟
I'm allergic to ...		
'andi Hasasiyya lil ...		عندي حساسيّة ل
Is this organic?		
da min ghayr mubidaat?		ده من غير مبيدات؟

MUNCHIES TO GO

Egypt has a variety of traditional street food and snacks that remain popular despite a recent flood of Western-style fast food. Seeds and beans are especially popular.

Depending on the season, small carts with tiny ovens serve roasted corn on the cob or sweet potatoes. Some of the more substantial snacks are meals in themselves, although they often appear in menus as appetisers.

BREAKFAST الفطار

Fool, fava beans cooked slowly in a huge pot called a fawwāla, is often called Egypt's national dish and is the breakfast of choice of most Egyptians. Filling and highly nutritious, fool is a vehicle for vegetables, olive oil, spices, eggs, tahina or tuna – whatever takes your fancy. Most people have their own family combo that they swear by. Ta'miyya, falafel made with fava beans, is a popular accompaniment. Bread, yogurt, white cheese (similar to Greek feta), tea or coffee and olives often complete the meal. Hotels usually offer a Western-style breakfast that includes a leavened bread (often called feeno), with butter, jam, cheese and eggs.

bread	'aysh	عيش
butter	zibda	زبدة
eggs	bayḍ	بيض
fried eggs	bayḍ maʿli	بيض مقلي
boiled eggs	bayḍ maslooʿ	بيض مسلوق
jam	mirabba	مربة
omelette	umlett	أومليت
olives	zaytoon	زيتون
olive oil	zayt zaytoon	زيت زيتون
tahina	ṭiHina	طحينة
toast	tost	توست
tomatoes	ṭamāṭim	طماطم
white cheese	gibna bayḍa	جبنة بيضة
yogurt	zabaadi	زبادي

EATING OUT المطعم

Table for (five), please.
tarabayza li (khamsa) low samaHt — ترابيزة (لخمسة) لو سمحت.

May we see the menu?
mumkin nishoof il minay? — ممكن نشوف المينى؟

Do I get it myself or do they bring it to us?
Hangib il akl binafsina walla humma Haygibooh lina? — حانجيب الأكل بنفسنا ولاّ هم حايجيبو لنا؟

FOOD

Please bring us ...	low samaHt hatlina ...	لو سمحت هات لنا ...
an ashtray	ṭaffāya	طفّاية
the bill	il Hisaab	الحساب
a glass of water	kubbaayyit maya	كبّاية ميّة
with/without ice	ma'/bidoon talg	مع/بدون تلج

Is service included in the bill?
il Hisaab shaamil il khidma? الحساب شامل الخدمة؟

Utensils أدوات

cup	fingaan	فنجان
fork	shōka	شوكة
glass	kubbaaya	كبّاية
knife	sikeena	سكّينة
napkin	fooṭit sufra	فوطة سفرة
plate	ṭaba^c	طبق
spoon	ma'la^ca	معلقة
toothpick	khilla	خلّة

USEFUL CULINARY ADJECTIVES

boiled	masloo^c	مسلوق
delicious	lazeez	لزيز
foul	ṭa'mu mish kwayyis	طعمه مش كويّس
fresh	ṭāẓa	طاظة
fried	ma'li	مقلي
grilled	meshwi	مشوي
raw	nayy	نيّ
roasted	rustu	رستو
spicy (flavourful)	mitabbil	متبّل
spicy (hot)	Haami	حامي
stale/spoiled	mi'affin	معفّن
stuffed	maHshi	محشي
sweet	Hilu	حلو

TYPICAL DISHES آطباق صميمة

Appetisers مقبلات

Salaṭāt are small plates of appetisers consisting of dips, cold vegetables or pickles.

baba ghanoog بابا غنّوج
dip made of roasted eggplant and tahini (ground sesame paste)

bitingaan mukhallil بتنجان مخلّل
pickled eggplant

Hummuṣ حمّص
dip made of ground chickpeas and tahini

kibda كبدة
fried liver, usually chicken

labna لبنة
thick, creamy dip made of strained yogurt

mukh مخ
sheep's brain, usually fried and sprinkled with lemon juice

salaṭa khaḍra سلطة خضرة
salad of chopped tomato, cucumber and onion

taboola تبّولة
the famous Lebanese salad of parsley, tomato and bulgur (dried cracked) wheat

ṭiHeena طحينة
dip made of tahini, lemon and sometimes yogurt

ṭurshi طرشي
pickles (usually cucumber) carrot and turnip

wara^c 'inab ورق عنب
vine leaves stuffed with rice, meat (though not always) and spices. Sometimes served with a yogurt sauce on the side.

zabaadi زبادي
yogurt and cucumber dip

Soups شوربة

mulukhiyya ملوخيّة
often translated unappetisingly as 'Jew's Mallow', this is a quintessentially Egyptian soup made of a green leaf that turns glutinous (like okra) when cooked. The broth is made with either chicken or rabbit stock. You'll either love it or hate it.

shurbat 'ads شربة عدس
lentil soup which is usually flavoured with lots of cumin

shurbat firaakh شربة فراخ
chicken soup

shurbat khuḍār شربة خضار
vegetable soup

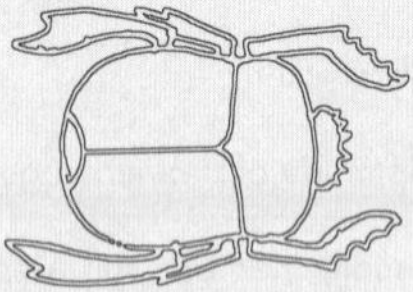

Main Courses أطباق رئيسية

escalōb banay إسكلوب بانيه
pan-fried veal fillets (not the least bit Egyptian but an ubiquitous item on Egyptian menus)

fatta فتّة
rice with a topping of broken bread and (sometimes) chicken, all covered in a rich broth, usually with yogurt added

Hamaam maHshi حمام محشي
stuffed pigeon, filled either with rice or wheat (called fireek)

kafta كفتة
ground meat (usually lamb) mixed with spices, which is skewered, grilled and then served on a bed of greens

makarōna bil beshamel مكرونة بالبشاميل
macaroni or other pasta baked in a bechamel sauce

shawarma شاورمة
pieces of lamb roasted on a spit and served in pita bread with tomato and parsley

sheesh kebab شيش كباب
grilled, skewered chunks of meat (usually lamb). In most restaurants, this dish is ordered by weight.

sheesh ṭaowook شيش طاووك
grilled chunks of chicken

ṭāgen طاجن
stew

torli تورلي
mixed vegetable casserole with meat

Side & Vegetable Dishes أطباق جانبية

bamya بامية
okra, usually served in a rich tomato sauce

baṭāṭis bilṭamāṭim بطاطس بالطماطم
potato baked in a tomato sauce

maHshi koosa محشي كوسة
stuffed zucchini, usually filled with rice and meat

maHshi kurumb محشي كرنب
stuffed cabbage leaves, usually filled with rice and lots of dill

moosa[c]'a مسقّعة
eggplant baked in tomato sauce, often with meat

ruzz bil sha'riyya رز بالشعريّة
rice cooked with browned vermicelli noodles. Accompanies most meals.

Sweets & Desserts حلويّات/حلو

Traditional Egyptian desserts, hilu, and sweets, halawiyyat, can be broadly divided into milk puddings and pastries. Neither appear widely on restaurant menus, but can be bought ready-made in pastry and pudding shops.

balooẓa بالوظة
: pudding of ground rice, cornflour and sugar

baqlawa بقلاوة
: filo pastry with nuts drenched in a sugar syrup

basboosa بسبوسة
: cake made of semolina and soaked in syrup

baskuweet بسكويت
: biscuits

bileela بليلة
: wheat, nuts and raisins cooked in milk and sugar

kaHk كحك
: biscuits made with butter and flour and rolled in icing sugar

kunaafa كنافة
: pastry that looks a little like shredded wheat but is much, much sweeter

mahalabiyya مهلّبيّة
: sweet milk pudding with rosewater, thickened with cornflour and rice

malban ملبن
: Turkish delight

ruzz bil laban رز باللبن
: rice pudding

umm 'ali أم علي
: filo pastry, butter, raisins and nuts baked in milk

zhelaati جلاتي
: ice cream

Snacks	وجبات صغيرة

baṭāṭa meshwiyya — بطاطا مشويّة
roasted sweet potato

baṭāṭis muHammara — بطاطس محمّرة
french fries

dura meshwiyya — درة مشويّة
roasted corn on the cob

fiṭeer — فطير
a kind of pizza made of flaky pastry and topped or stuffed with sweet or savoury mixtures such as honey or cheese

fool — فول
broad (or fava) beans served in semi-circles of 'aysh baladi with tomatoes or salad

fool sudaani — فول سوداني
Sudanese beans

kushari — كشري
a carbohydrate extravaganza of rice, macaroni, and lentils topped with fried onions and a spicy tomato sauce. This is more of a meal than a snack, but is often sold on carts as well as in kushari restaurants.

libb — لبّ
roasted sunflower or melon seeds

shakshooka — شكشوكة
a mixture of meat and tomato sauce with an egg on top

ṭa'miya — طعمية
mashed, deep-fried fava beans – the Egyptian equivalent of falafel

tirmus — ترمس
round, yellow lupin seeds with a thin, translucent skin that's removed before eating

FOOD

A kushari restaurant serves large bowls of noodles, rice, lentils, onion and tomato sauce.

SELF-CATERING التبضّع بالنفس

In Cairo, large supermarkets can supply all of your self-catering needs. But if you want to be more adventurous, or if you find yourself outside the metropolis, the neighbourhood grocer, or baᶜāl , is the place to go. Tell the proprietor what you want and he or she will get it for you – self-service is only for supermarkets. Most of these shops have a small deli section at the back which serves cheese and other dairy products, olives, pickles and processed meats.

At the Grocer's عند البقّال

How much is (a kilo of cheese)?
(kilo ig gibna) bikam? (كيلو الجبنة) بكم؟

Do you have anything cheaper?
'andak Haaga arkhaṣ? عندك حاجة أرخص؟

Give me (half) a kilo please.
iddeeni (nuṣṣ) إدّيني (نصّ)
kilu, min faḍlak كيلو من فضلك.

I'd like (six slices of ham).
'aayiz/'ayza عايز
(sitta transhāt zhamboon) (m/f) (ستّة ترنشات جمبون).

Can I taste it?
mumkin adooᶜuh/ha? (m/f) ممكن أدوقه؟

It tastes good/bad.
ṭa'mu kwayyis/wiHish طعمه كويّس/وحش.

ARABIC CONSTRICTONS

The 'ayn sound (') is made by constricting the throat. The glottal stop (ᶜ) is made by a break in the voice, like the sound made between the words in 'uh-oh'.

Making Your Own Meals شراء حاجات الطبخ

Where can I find the ...?
fayn il ...? فين ال ...؟

I'd like some ...	'aayiz/'ayza ... (m/f)	عايز ...
... bread/pita	'aysh ...	عيش ...
light-coloured (sold in bags)	shaami	شامي
pale brown (sold on street)	baladi	بلدي
butter	zibda	زبدة
cereal	korn fliks (or brand name)	كورن فليكس
cheese	gibna	جبنة
Edam	felamenk	فلمنك
hard, yellow (local)	gibna roomi	جبنة رومي
white (like feta)	gibna bayḍa	جبنة بيضة
chocolate	shikōlāta	شيكولاتة
eggs	bayḍ	بيض
flour	di^{c}ee^c	دقيق
ham	zhamboon	جمبون
honey	'asal	عسل
milk	laban	لبن
full cream	kaamil id desm	كامل الدّسم
half cream	nuṣṣ id desm	نصف الدّسم
skim	khaali id desm	خالي الدّسم
molasses	'asal iswid	عسل إسود
... oil	zayt	زيت ...
corn	dora	درة
olive	zaytoon	زيتون
olives	zaytoon	زيتون
pasta	makarōna	مكرونة
pepper	filfil iswid	فلفل إسود
pickles	ṭurshi	طرشي
salt	malH	ملح
sugar	sukkar	سكّر
vermicelli	sha'riyya	شعريّة
yogurt	zabaadi	زبادي

AT THE MARKET في السوق

Egyptian markets are chaotic and colourful and a fun place to buy fruit and vegetables. Most neighbourhoods also have a khoḍari, 'vegetable seller', or fakahaani, 'fruitier'. All produce is sold by the kilo.

Baladi eggs, which are tiny, free-range and locally produced, are brought to some markets by peasants. If you can find them, they're far better than the usual battery type. Poultry is usually sold live, along with pigeons and rabbits, so unless you're into slaughtering your own meat, you're better off buying from a shop.

Meat is bought from a gazzār, 'butcher', and is often cut differently than in the West. Outside of Cairo and large cities, chunks of meat are simply hacked off the carcass, with little regard to cut.

Meat & Poultry اللحوم والطيور

beef	laHma kandooz	لحمة كندوز
chicken	firaakh	فراخ
cured ham	zhamboon	جمبون
hamburger (mince)	laHma mafrooma	لحمة مفرومة
lamb	laHma ḍāni	لحمة ضاني
liver	kibda	كبدة
kidney	kilwa	كلوة
meat	laHma	لحمة
pigeon	Hamaam	حمام
pork	khanzeer	خنزير
rabbit	arnab	أرنب
sausage	sugu^c	سجق
sheep	kharoof	خروف
steak	filay	فيليه
turkey	deek roomi	ديك رومي
veal	bitillo	بتلو

SWEAT THE BASTURMA!

Basturma is a cold, sliced meat cured with fenugreek, a pungent spice which is so strong that you'll sweat it and smell it on your skin long after consuming it.

Seafood — أسماك البحر

fish	samak	سمك
lobster	istakōza	إستاكوزة
mullet	boori	بوري
Nile perch	ishr bayadi	قشر بياضي
sea bass	waʿār	وقّار
sea bream	morgaan	مرجان
shrimp	gambari	جمبرى
smoked herring	ringa	رنجة
sole	moosa	موسى
squid	kalamaari	كلماري

Vegetables — الخضار

artichoke	kharshoof	خرشوف
asparagus	kishkalmaaz	كشكلماز
(green) beans	faṣoolya	فاصولية
beetroot	bangar	بنجر
cabbage	kurumb	كرنب
carrot	gazar	جزر
red/green capsicum	filfil aHmar/akhḍar	فلفل أخضر/أحمر
cauliflower	arnabeeṭ	قرنبيط
celery	karafs	كرفس
cucumber	khiyār	خيار
eggplant	bitingaan	بتنجان
garlic	tōm	توم
leeks	kurāt	كرّات
lettuce	khass	خس
mushrooms	'aysh ghurāb	عيش الغراب
onion	baṣal	بصل
peas	bisilla	بسلّة
potato	baṭāṭis	بطاطس
radish	figl	فجل
spinach	sabaanikh	سبانخ
sweet potato	baṭāṭa	بطاطة
tomato	ṭamāṭim	طماطم
vegetables	khudār	خضار
zucchini	koosa	كوسة

Pulses الحبوب

black eyed beans	lubia	لوبيا
broad (fava) beans	fool	فول
cereal (grain)	burghul	برغل
chickpeas	Hummuṣ	حمص
lentils	'ads	عدس
rice	ruzz	رز

Fruit & Nuts الفواكه والمكسّرات

apples	tuffaaH	تفّاح
apricots	mishmish	مشمش
avocado	'abukaadu	أبكادو
banana	mooz	موز
coconut	gōz hind	جوز هند
dates	balaH	بلح
fig	teen	تين
grapes	'inab	عنب
seedless grapes	inab banaati	عنب بناتي
grapefruit	giribfiroot	جريب فروت
guava	gawaafa	جوافة
lemon	limoon	ليمون
mango	manga	منجه
melon	shamaam	شمّام
orange	burtu^{c}ān	برتقال
peach	khōkh	خوخ
pear	kummitra	كمّترى
plum	bar^{c}oo^c	برقوق
pomegranate	rumān	رمان
strawberry	farawla	فراولة
watermelon	baṭṭeekh	بطّيخ
almonds	lōz	لوز
hazelnut	bundu^c	بندق
pinenuts	ṣinōbar	صنوبر
pistachio	fuzdu^c	فسدق
walnuts	'ayn gamal	عين جمل

Spices & Condiments — العطارة

anis	yansoon	ينسون
basil	riHaan	ريحان
bay leaves	wara^c lawra	ورق لورة
chillies	shatta	شطّة
cinnamon	^cirfa	قرفة
clove	^curunfil	قرنفل
coriander (fresh)	kuzbara khadra	كزبرة خضرة
coriander (ground)	kuzbara nashfa	كزبرة نا شفة
cumin	kamoon	كمّون
dill	shabat	شبت
fenugreek	Hilba	حلبة
garlic	toom	توم
ginger	ganzabil	جنزبيل
oregano	za'tar	زعتر
parsley	ba'doonis	بقدونس
pepper	filfil iswid	فلفل إسود
salt	malH	ملح
sesame	simsim	سمسم
thyme	za'tar	زعتر
turmeric	kurkum	كركم

DRINKS — المشروبات

Non-Alcoholic — غير الروحيّة

juice	'aseer	عصير
soft drink	Haaga sa^c'a (lit: something cold)	حاجة ساقعة
... water	mayya ...	ميّة ...
boiled	maghliyya	مغليّة
mineral	ma'daniyya	معدنيّة

Fruit Juices — عصير الفاكهة

Juice stands are found in every neighbourhood in Egyptian towns and cities, and are a great place to quench your thirst on a hot day. You stand and watch the fruit being pressed and then down it in front of the 'bar'.

FOOD

I'd like a/an ... juice	ana 'aayiz/ 'ayza 'aṣeer ...	أريد عصير ...
banana	mooz	موز
guava	gawaafa	جوّافة
lemon	limoon	ليمون
mango	manga	منجه
orange	burtuʿān	برتقال
pomegranate	rumān	رمّان
sugar cane	ʿaṣab	قصب سكّر
strawberry	farawla	فراولة
tamarind	tamr hindi	تمر هندي

Coffee & Tea

الشاي والقهوة

coffee	ahwa	قهوة
instant coffee	neskafay	نسكافيه
filter coffee	ahwa amrikāni; ahwa firansawi	قهوة أمريكاني / قهوة فرنساوي

SMELLING SWEET

Coffee is always the Turkish variety and can be ordered in a variety of ways:

unsweetened	saada
slightly sweetened	'ar reeHa (lit: the smell of sweetness)
sweet	mazboot
very sweet	ziyaada

Tea is usually served very strong and sweet, but you can specify if you want it differently.

(cup of) tea	(kubbayit) shay	(كبايّة) شاي
with/without ...	bi/bidoon ...	ب/بدون ...
milk	laban	لبن
mint	na'na'	نعناع
sugar	sukkar	سكّر

Your choice of the following can be added to your tea:

anis	yansoon	ينسون
caraway	karaawya	كراوية
carob	kharub	خروب
cinnamon	ᶜirfa	قرفة
cocoa	kakaw	كاكاو
fenugreek	Hilba	حلبة
hibiscus	karkaday	كركديه
licorice	'irqisoos	عرق السهوس

SMOKING THE SHEESHA تدخين الشيشة

Give me a puff.
iddeeni nafas — إدّيني نفس.

I'd like more tobacco, please.
ghayarlee il Hagar low samaHt — غيّرلي الحجر، لو سمحت.

banuura — بانورة
glass where water sits

faHm — فحم
coal

froot koktayl — فروت كوكتيل
fruit-flavoured ma'assal

Hagar — حجر
tobacco with clay holder

kirayz — كريز
cherry flavoured ma'assal

kursi — كرسي
clay holder (without tobacco)

layy — لاي
long tube/pipe

THE SHEESHA

Smoking a sheesha isn't like smoking a cigarette. Tobacco is drawn through water and inhaled through a long pipe. The days of finding a chunk of hashish on top of your tobacco are long gone, but you can choose between a wide variety of tumbak (regular tobacco), or ma'assal (tobacco sweetened with molasses, usually with fruit flavouring). The sound of the bubbling water soothes the nerves, and it's a relaxing way to spend half an hour, even if you're not normally a smoker.

When you order a sheesha, make sure that you get a mabsam, a disposable plastic mouthpiece for each smoker, to protect you from contagious germs.

mabsam مبسم
mouthpiece
ma'assal معسّل
flavoured tobacco
mishmish مشمش
apricot-flavoured ma'assal
na'na' نعناع
mint-flavoured ma'assal
sheesha شيشة
water pipe
ṭāsa طاسة
metal ring under the Hagar
tufaaH ma'assal تفّاح معسّل
apple-flavoured
tufaaH bahreini تفّاح بحريني
apple with anis
tumbak تمباك
tobacco

AHWA LIFE

The ahwa, 'cafe', is where Egyptian men (but rarely women) go to meet their friends for coffee or tea, watch the soccer on TV, play a game of ṭawla, 'backgammon', or simply relax while pulling on a sheesha or waterpipe. Alcohol isn't on offer, with the exception of one or two cafes in Cairo that serve beer.

ALCOHOL الخمور

Egypt is a Muslim country, and the majority of Egyptians don't drink alcohol. Most of the country's 26 governorates are also dry. The good news is that the ban does not apply to tourist establishments, which include most large restaurants and pretty well all hotels with a star rating.

Spirits are less widely available than beer and wine, but almost all four- and five-star hotels and restaurants in Cairo have a wide selection on offer. Avoid the funky labels of local produced brands and stick to the imports. You'll save your head and perhaps your life. Meanwhile, keep in mind that wandering the streets inebriated isn't going to win you any friends, and in some areas, may even result in hostility.

beer	beera	بيرة
brandy	birandi	براندي
champagne	shambanya	شمبانيا
gin & tonic	zhin tōnik	جين و تونيك
rum	rum	رم
whisky	wiski	وسكي
a bottle of ... wine	izaazit nibeet ...	قزازة نبيت ...
a glass of ... wine	kaas nibeet ...	كاس نبيت ...
red	aHmar	أحمر
rosé	wardi	وردي
white	abyaḍ	أبيض
a glass of beer	kubbaayit beera	كبّاية بيرة
a ... bottle	izaaza ...	قزازة ...
large	kabeera	كبيرة
small	sughayyara	صغيرة

في الرّيف IN THE COUNTRY

The Egyptian countryside has charmed visitors for millenia. The bustling farm life of the lush band of green hugging the Nile contrasts with the vastness of the desert beyond. The pharaohs built their tombs and temples on the arid fringes of the Nile flood plain, and these are the most common tourist destinations. More recently, people have begun to venture further into the desert, exploring remote oases and camping amid the dunes. Others ignore the interior of the country entirely and head for the Mediterranean to the north and the Red Sea, with its world-famous reefs, to the east.

CAMPING التّخييم

While most major tourist centres have a municipal campground, they may be less than inviting. For real camping, Egyptians and visitors get in their four-wheel drives or, less frequently, mount a camel and head out to the Western Desert, or the rocky interior of the Sinai Peninsula.

Is there a campsite nearby?
fee mu'askar urayyib min hina? فيه معسكر قريّب من هنا؟

Where's the nearest campsite?
fayn a^c^rab mu'askar? فين أقرب معسكر؟

How much is it per ...?	**bikam lil ...?**	بكم ...؟
person	**nafar**	للنفر
tent	**khayma**	للخيمة
vehicle	**'arabiyya**	للعربيّة

Where can I hire a tent?
a^c^aggar khayma minayn? أأجّر خيمة منين؟

Who owns this land?
il arḍ di bitaa'it meen? الأرض دي بتاعت مين؟

Can I talk to him/her?
mumkin akallimu/ha? ممكن أكلّمه؟

Can we camp here?
mumkin ni'askar hina? ممكن نعسكر هنا؟

campfire	rakiya	راكية
camping	kamping/'askara	كامبنج/عسكرة
campsite	mu'askar	معسكر
firewood	Haṭb	حطب
matches	kibreet	كبريت
rope	Habl	حبل
tent	khayma	خيمة
torch	baṭṭariyya	بطّارية

THEY MAY SAY ...

il arḍ dee mayit'askarsh feeha
Camping isn't allowed on this land.

THE DESERT الصحراء

Ninety-seven percent of Egyptian land is desert, and the vast, sandy expanses are becoming increasingly popular for people who want to get away from the crowded tourist sites of the Nile Valley.

Apart from the austere beauty of the landscape, Egypt's deserts are dotted with Pharaonic and Roman ruins, making a trip there even more rewarding. But even with all the technology of GPS (Global Positioning Systems) and the latest four-wheel drives, the desert can be a dangerous place. Apart from the very real risk of getting lost, Egypt still has thousands of unexploded mines from WWII and wars with Israel. Guides are therefore necessary to go almost anywhere off-road, and permits are required to visit sites throughout the Western Desert.

Bedouin (nomadic people who traditionally come from the Western and Eastern Deserts and Sinai)	bedu	بدو

the desert	iṣṣaHara	الصّحرة
four-wheel drive	'arabiyyit gharz	عربيّة غرز
guide	murshid	مرشد
mine	laghm	لغم
mined	il arḍ malghooma	الأرض ملغومة
oasis	waaHa	واحة
permit	taṣreeH	تصريح
quicksand	rimāl mutaHarrika	رمال متحرّكة
salt marshes	sabakha	سبخة
sand	raml	رمل
soft sand	nitaya	نتاية
sand dunes	ghard rimāl	غرد رمال
barchan (convex on windward side, concave on leeward side)	barkān	بركان
crescent	sayf	سيف
star	areg	عرج
sand mats	Husr gharz	حصر غرز
shovel	garoof	جاروف
(hot) spring	beer (sukhn)	بير (سخن)
to get stuck	yighriz	يغرز
to dig out a car	ṭila' il 'arabiyya	طلع العربيّة

OASES الواحات

Egypt's vast Western Desert has five oases – Kharga, Dakhla, Farafra, Bahariyya and Siwa. All have long and fascinating histories. Dakhla and Farafra both have medieval mudbrick towns called El Qasr, which literally means 'the palace' but here is used to mean fortress.

All five oasis settlements date back to antiquity and, in Roman times, most were famed for their production of wheat and wine. They were also used as way stations on caravan routes from Africa and across the Sahar. The most famous of these was the darb el arba'yeen, or forty-days road, which brought slaves and, later, camels from Sudan to Egypt.

HIKING — التسلّق

Hiking isn't widely practised in Egypt. There are a few set trails in the mountains around St Katherine's monastery in Sinai, but they are designed to be walked in a day or two, and with Bedouin guides (see page 164) to help.

Getting Information — الحصول على المعلومات

Where can I find out about hiking trails in the region?	minayn 'araf ṭuru^c ṭulu' il gebel hina?	منين أعرف طرق طلوع الجبل هنا؟
Where's the nearest village?	fayn a^{c}rab qarya?	فين أقرب قرية؟
Is it safe to climb this mountain?	ṭuloo' il gebel amaan?	طلوع الجبل أمان؟
Is there a hut up there?	fee kōkh hinak?	فيه كوخ هناك؟
Do we need a guide?	iHna miHtageen murshid?	إحنا محتاجين مرشد؟
I'd like to talk to someone who knows this area.	ana 'aayiz/'ayza akallim had 'ārif il manṭi^{c}a kuwayyis	أنا عايز أكلّم حدّ عارف المنطقة كويّس.
How high is the climb?	irtifa'u addi ey?	إرتفاعه قد إيه؟
Which is the easiest route?	ey as-hal ṭaree^c?	إيه أسهل طريق؟
When does it get dark?	imta id dinya bitḍallim?	إمتى الدنيا بتضلّم؟
Where can we buy supplies?	minayn ni^{c}dar nishtiri Hagaat?	منين نقدر نشتري حاجات؟

On the Path على الطريق

Where have you come from?
inta gayt minayn? أنت جيت منين ؟

How long did it take you?
akhadt wa'ct 'caddi ey? أخدت وقت قد إيه ؟

Does this path go to ...?
is sikka di tiwaddi li ...? السكّة دي تودّي ل ... ؟

Are there any tourist attractions near here?
fee Hagaat tagzib is suyāH hina? فيه حاجات تجذب السيّاح هنا؟

Can I leave some things here for a while?
mumkin 'caseeb Hagaati hina shuwayya? ممكن أسيب حاجاتي هنا شويّة؟

Can we go through here?
mumkin numur min hina? ممكن نمر من هنا؟

Is the water OK to drink?
il mayya hina tuṣliH lil shurb? الميّة هنا تصلح للشرب ؟

I'm lost.
ana toht أنا تهت.

altitude	irtifaa'	إرتفاع
backpack	shanṭit ḍahr	شنطة ضهر
binoculars	naḍārat mu'aẓama	نضّارة معظّمة
candles	shama'	شمع
to climb	ṭila'	طلع
compass	buṣla	بوصلة
downhill	asfal il gebel	أسفل الجبل
first-aid kit	il is'aafaat il uliyya	الإسعافات الأوليّة
gloves	gawant	جونت
guide	murshid	مرشد
hiking	tasalluq	تسلّق
map	khareeṭa	خريطة
rope	Habl	حبل
steep	mitdaHdar	متدحدر
uphill	'ca'la ig gebel	أعلى الجبل
to walk	yimshi	يمشي

IN THE COUNTRY

AT THE BEACH — على الشاطيء

Can we swim here?
mumkin n'oom hina? — ممكن نعوم هنا؟

Is it safe to swim here?
il 'oom hina amaan? — العوم هنا أمان؟

What time is high/low tide?
ey awʿaat il madd wil gazr? — إيه أوقات المدّ و الجزر؟

Is there a (public) beach near here?
fee bilaazh ('aam) urayyib min hina? — فيه بلاج (عام) قريّب من هنا؟

Do we have to pay?
laazim nidfa'? — لازم ندفع؟

How much for ...?	bikam li ...?	بكم ل ...؟
a chair	kursi	كرسي
an umbrella	shamsiyya	شمسيّة
coral	murgaan	مرجان
fishing	ṣayd is samak	صيد السّمك
the Mediterranean	il baHr il abyaḍ il mutawassiṭ	البحر الأبيض المتوسّط
ocean	muHeeṭ	المحيط
the Red Sea	il baHr il aHmar	البحر الأحمر
reef	shi'ba	شعبة
rock	ṣakhr	صخر
sand	raml	رمل
sea	il baHr	البحر
sunblock	kireem ḍid ish shams	كريم ضد الشمس
sunglasses	naḍḍārat shams	نضّارة شمس
swimming	is sibāHa	السّباحة
towel	fooṭa	فوطة
waves	amwāg	أمواج

Aquatic Creatures / كائنات مائيّة

crab	kabōriya	كا بوريّا
dolphin	darfeel	درفيل
eel	t'abeen	تعابين
fish (pl)	samak	سمك
lobster	istakōza	أستاكوزا
ray	Hidaya	حداية
seagull	nooras	نورس
sea urchin	unfud il baHr	قنفذ البحر
shark	'irsh	قرش
shellfish	wada'	ودع
turtle	zuHlifa	زحلفة

WEATHER / الجوّ

What's the weather like?
ig gaw shakluh ay?
الجو شكله إيه؟

It's raining.	biyitmaṭṭar	بيتمطّر.
Today it's ...	innaharda ...	النهارده ...
cloudy	mighayyim	مغيّم
cold	bard	بردّ
hot	Harr	حر
warm	daafi	دافي
wet	riṭib	رطب
windy	fee hawa	فيه هواء
mist/fog	shaboora	شبورة
sandstorm	'āṣifat raml	عاصفة رمل
storm	'āṣifa	عاصفة
sun	shams	شمس
temperature	Harāra	حرارة

SEASONS / المواسم

summer	iṣ ṣayf	الصيف
autumn	il khareef	الخريف
winter	ish shitaᶜ	الشّتاء
spring	ir rabee'	الرّبيع

GEOGRAPHICAL TERMS إصطلاحات جغرافيّة

area	manti^c^a	منطقة
beach	bilaazh	بلاج
bridge	kubri	كوبري
cave	kahf	كهف
cliff	Hāfit il gebel	حافة الجبل
desert	ṣaHara	صحرة
district (administrative)	markaz	مركز
earthquake	zilzaal	زلزال
farm	'izba	عزبة
forest	ghaaba	غابة
harbour	meena	ميناء
hill	tell	تل
hot spring	beer sukhn	بير سخن

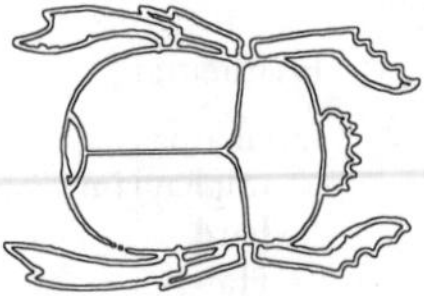

inlet	sharm	شرم
island	gizeera	جزيرة
lake	biHeyra	بحيرة
mountain	gebel	جبل
oasis	waaHa	واحة
path	mumar	ممر
peak	qimma	قمة
point	ra^c^s	رأس
province	muHāfza	محا فظة
river	nahr	نهر
spring	beer	بير
sea	baHr	بحر
valley	waadi	وادي
village	qarya	قرية

FAUNA حيوانات

Domestic Creatures الخلائق البيتيّة

What animal is that? ey il Hayawaan da? إيه الحيوان ده؟

calf	'egel	عجل
cat	ᶜuṭṭa	قطّة
chicken	farkha	فرخة
cow	baᶜara	بقرة
dog	kelb	كلب
donkey	Humaar	حمار
duck	baṭṭa	بطّة
goat	mi'aza	معزة
goose	wizza	وزّة
horse	faras	فرس
pig	khanzeer	خنزير
pigeon	Hamāma	حمامة
rabbit	arnab	أرنب
sheep	kharoof	خروف
water buffalo	gamoosa	جاموسة

Birds عصافير

egret	abu qurdān	أبو قردان
hoopoe (pinkish-brown bird with black and white wings)	hudhud	هدهد
kestrel	ṣaqr al garād	صقر الجراد
quail	sammān	سمّان
swallow	'aṣfoor il genna	عصفور الجنّة
turtle dove	Hamaam	حمام
white stork	laqlaq abyaḍ	لقلق أبيض

Wildlife الحياة البريّة

ant	namla	نملة
bee	naHla	نحلة
bird	'aṣfoora	عصفورة
butterfly	farāsha	فراشة
cockroach	ṣirṣār	صرصار
crocodile	timsaaH	تمساح
fish	samak	سمك
fly	dibbān	دبّان
fox	ta'leb	ثعلب
frog	ḍufda'	ضفدع
gerbil	gerbō'	جربوع
lizard	saHliyya	سحلية
monitor lizard	waran	ورن
mosquito	namoosa	ناموسة
mouse/rat	fār	فار
scorpion	'aᶜrab	عقرب
snake	ti'bān	تعبان
spider	'ankaboot	عنكبوت

FLORA & AGRICULTURE نباتات وزراعة

What plant is that?
ey iz zar'a da? إيه الزرع ده؟
What's it used for?
bitusta'mil fee ey? بتستعمل في إيه؟
Can you eat the fruit?
il fak-ha dee mumkin tit'akkil? الفاكهة دي ممكن تتّاكل؟

acacia	akaasya	أكاسيا
date palm	nakhl	نخل
doum palm	dom	دوم
eucalyptus	kafoor	كافور
olive tree	zaytoona	زيتونة
pine	ṣinōbir	صنوبر

DID YOU KNOW ...

The khamaseen is a hot, dust-laden wind that blows from the south each spring between March and May. It resembles a raging sandstorm – the air is invaded by fine dust that penetrates the smallest of openings and settles into a thick layer on everything it can, including the mouth, throat and nostrils.
It takes its name from the number fifty (khamseen), because it usually occurs over a fifty-day period.

Herbs, Flowers & Crops أعشاب، أزهار و حصاد

agriculture	zaraa'a	زراعة
basil	riHān	ريحان
bougainvillea	guhanamiyya	جهنّميّة
corn	durra	درة
crops	zar'	زرع
flower	warda	وردة
grapevine	karmit 'inab	كرمة عنب
harvest (a)	Haṣād	حصاد
irrigation	rayy	ري
irrigation canal	tir'a	ترعة
jasmine	yasmeen	ياسمين
leaf	waraʿa	ورقة
lemon tree	shagarat limoon	شجرة ليمون
orange tree	shagarat burtu'ān	شجرة برتقال
orchard	bustān	بستان
parsley	ba'doonis	بقدونس
planting/sowing	zara'	زرع
rosemary	Haṣalbān	حصالبان
sugar cane	ʿaṣab	قصب
sunflower	'abād ish shams	عبّاد الشمس
thyme	za'tar	زعتر
tree	shagara	شجرة
vineyard	mazra'at 'inab	مزرعة عنب
wheat	'amH	قمح

المهرجانات و الإجازات

FESTIVALS & HOLIDAYS

The ancient Egyptians were great lovers of life, which is why they devoted so much time to ensuring that life in the hereafter was well-supplied with such necessities as beer, wine, food, jewellery and luxurious clothing.

Their modern descendants have retained their sense of fun too, even if Islamic propriety precludes alcohol from most occasions. Apart from countrywide holidays to celebrate religious feasts, **moulids**, 'saints' festivals', are a popular excuse for a celebration. Much like a country fair, they come complete with a parade, candy and rides for the kids, and displays of local folk customs. **Moulids** apply to both Muslim and Christian saints. Another ancient festival, Sham il-Nesseem, takes place on the first Monday after Easter.

BIRTHDAYS
أعياد الميلاد

When's your birthday?
'eed milaadak/milaadik imta? (m/f) — عيد ميلادك إمتى؟

My birthday is on (25 January).
'eed milaadi (khamsa wa 'ishreen yanayir) — عيد ميلادي (خمسة و عشرين يناير).

Happy Birthday!
Kull sana wa inta/inti ṭayyib/a! (m/f) — كل سنة و إنت طيّب!

Response:
wa inta/inti tayyib/a (m/f) — وإنت طيّب.

Blow out the candles!
itfee ish shama'! — إطفي الشمع!

birthday cake	turtit 'eed il milaad	تورتة عيد الميلاد
candles	shama'	شمع
to exchange gifts	yatabadil il hidaaya	يتبادل الهدايا
gift	hidaaya	هدايّة
party	Hafla	حفلة

WEDDINGS الزواج

Marriage for most Egyptians is a two- or three-step affair. First, there's the engagement, il khuṭooba, where the groom gives the bride-to-be a shabka, or 'gift of jewellery'. The actual wedding consists of the signing of the contract, katb ik kitāb, which can be separate from the wedding celebration, faraH, itself. Although the couple is technically married after signing the contract, they don't live together until they've had the faraH celebration, which could be the same day or several months later.

Congratulations!
mabrook! مبروك!
Response: allah yibaarik feek/i (m/f) الله يبارك فيك.

A thousand congratulations!
alf mabrook! ألف مبروك!
Response: allah yibaarik feek/i (m/f) ألله يبارك فيك.

contract signing	katb ik kitāb	كتب الكتاب
engagement	khuṭooba	خطوبة
honeymoon	shahr il 'asal	شهر العسل
wedding	faraH	فرح
wedding anniversary	'eed gawaaz	عيد جواز
wedding cake	turtit gawaaz	تورتة جواز

TOASTS & CONDOLENCES الشرب للصّحة والعزاء

Bon appetit!
bil hana wish shifa^c! بالهنا و الشفاء!
Response: allah yihanneek/i! (m/f) الله يهنّيك!

Bon voyage!
tirooH wa tigi bis salaama! تروح و تيجي بالسّلامة!
Response: allah yisallimak/yisallimik (m/f) الله يسلّمك!

Cheers!
fee ṣaHitak/ṣaHitik/ṣaHitku! (m/f/pl) في صحّتك!
(lit: to your health)

Good luck!	Hazz sa'eed!	حظ سعيد!
Never mind.	ma'lish.	معلش.

Get well soon.
salaamtak/salaamtik (m/f) سلامتك.
Response: allah yisallimak/yisallimik (m/f) الله يسلّمك.

I'm very sorry.
il baᶜiya fee Hayaatak البقيّة في حياتك.
Response: Hayaatak il baᶜiya حياتك البقيّة.

HOLIDAYS & FESTIVALS اجازات ومهرجانات

il arba'een الأربعين

This gathering of friends and relatives takes place 40 days after the death of a loved one. Held by both Christians and Muslims, the practice is thought to have originated in Pharaonic times.

'eed il adHa or 'eed il kibeer عيد الأضحى

This feast, usually lasting three days, commemorates Abraham's willingness to sacrifice his son, and marking the end of pilgrimage to Mecca. Many families buy a sheep which they slaughter on the first morning of the holiday.

il moolid المولد

A moolid is a cross between a religious festival and a fun fair, and is held to commemorate the birthday of a local saint or holy person. The festivities usually focus on the saint's tomb and can last for as long as a week, culminating in the layla il kibeera, or 'big night'. Apart from carnival-like rides and games, sufis hold zikrs, usually ceremonies in which they chant the word allah until they fall into a trance-like state. Although moolids are an important part of Egyptian folk culture, they are frowned upon by the religious purists in the Islamist movement.

Ramaḍān رمضان

Ramaḍān is the Muslim month of fasting, in which neither food nor water can pass the lips from sunrise to sunset. In Egypt, Ramaḍān is also a month of night-time revelry, with special programs on television, intense socialising with friends and relatives, and plenty of rich food. The month ends with a three-day holiday, called 'eed il fitr.

sham in nessim — شمّ النّسيم

This holiday has Pharaonic origins, and falls on the first Monday after Easter each year. The name literally means 'the smell of the breeze', and Egyptians celebrate by having picnics and family outings.

is suboo' — السّبوع

This ceremony is held seven days after a birth. Children are invited, candles lit, and small presents of sweets are distributed.

Season's Greetings! (for all religious festivities)

kulli sana wa inta/inti ṭayyib/a! (m/f) — كل سنة و إنت طيّب!

response: wa inta/inti ṭayyib/a (m/f) — وأنت طيّب.

to celebrate (in general)	yiHtifil	يحتفل
to celebrate the (Muslim feast)	eid yi'ayid	يعيّد
holiday	agaaza	إجازة

CHRISTIAN CELEBRATIONS إحتفالات مسيحيّة

Egyptian Christians are referred to as Coptic Christians. The term 'Copt' comes from the Greek word 'Aegyptios', meaning 'Egypt', and the term was used to differentiate between Egyptian Christianity and the Orthodox Church of the Byzantine Empire. The Greek word was borrowed by the Arabs and eventually shortened to Copt.

baptism/christening	ma'moodiyya	معموديّة
Christmas	kireesmas	كريسماس
Easter	'eed il qiyāma	عيد القيامة
New Year's Eve	laylat rās is sana	ليلة رأس السّنة

HEALTH

While the quality of health care provided by private clinics is high, state facilities suffer from severe shortages of even the most basic medicines. Outside Cairo and one or two other large cities, visitors have little choice but to use state facilities in emergencies, and ensure that they have insurance that will get them transferred to private clinics or airlifted abroad.

Egypt has a surplus of doctors, all of whom receive at least part of their training in English. So even if their conversational skills are rusty, they'll know the English for almost all medical terms. Outside large private hospitals, other health professionals are likely to speak only Arabic.

AT THE DOCTOR عند الدكتور

I'm sick.
ana 'ayyān/a (m/f) أنا عيّان.

My friend is sick.
ṣadeeq/ati 'ayyaan/a (m/f) صديقي عيّان.

I need someone who speaks English.
ana miHtaag/a Had biyitkallim ingileezi (m/f) أنا محتاج حدّ بيتكلّم إنجليزي.

Could the doctor come here?
mumkin il duktoor yeegi hina? ممكن الدّكتور ييجي هنا؟

Where's the nearest ...?	fayn aʿrab ...?	فين أقرب ...؟
chemist	ṣaydaliyya	صيدليّة
clinic	'iyaada	عيادة
dentist	duktoor asnaan	دكتور أسنان
doctor	duktoor	دكتور
hospital	mustashfa	مستشفى

Can I have a receipt for my insurance?
mumkin waṣl 'ashaan il taʿmeen? ممكن وصل علشان التأمين؟

THE DOCTOR MAY SAY …

fee ey? — فيه إيه؟
What's the matter?

Hāsis/a bi waga'? (m/f) — حاسس بوجع؟
Do you feel any pain?

biyuwga'ak/biyuwga'ik fayn? (m/f) — بيوجعك فين؟
Where does it hurt?

'andik id dawra? — عندك الدّورة؟
Are you menstruating?

'andak/andik sukhuniyya? (m/f) — عندك سخونيّة؟
Do you have a temperature?

min ᶜimta wa inta/ inti kida? (m/f) — من إمتى و أنت كده؟
How long have you been like this?

gaalak/gaalik da ᶜabl kida? (m/f) — جالك ده قبل كده؟
Have you had this before?

bitakhud/i ᶜadwiya? (m/f) — بتاخد أدوية؟
Are you on medication?

bitidakhkhan/i? (m/f) — بتدخّن؟
Do you smoke?

bitishrab/i khamra? (m/f) — بتشرب خمرة؟
Do you drink?

bitakhud/i mukhaddarāt? (m/f) — بتاخد مخدّرات؟
Do you take drugs?

'andak/'andik Hasasiyya min ayya Haaga? (m/f) — عندك حساسيّة من أي حاجة؟
Are you allergic to anything?

inti Haamil? — أنت حامل؟
Are you pregnant?

AILMENTS — الأمراض

I'm ill.
ana 'ayyaan/a (m/f) — أنا عيّان.

I've been vomiting.
ana ragga't — أنا رجّعت.

I feel nauseated.
'aayiz/'ayza aragga' — عايز أرجّع.

I can't sleep.
mish aadir/a anaam (m/f) — مش قادر أنام.

I'm dizzy.
'andi dōkha — عندي دوخة.

I feel weak.
Haasis inni ḍa'eef/a — حاسس إنّي ضعيف.

It hurts there.	biyuwga'ni hina	بيوجعني هنا.
I feel better/worse.	ana aHsan/awHash	أنا أحسن/أوحش.

I have (a/an) ...	'andi ...	عندي ...
I've had (a/an) ...	kaan 'andi ...	كان عندي ...
allergy	Hasaasiyya	حساسيّة
anaemia	faᶜr damm/aneemiya	فقر دم/أنيمية
blister	buᶜaasha	بوقاشة
bronchitis	iltihaab fiṣṣidr	إلتهاب في الصّدر
burn	Harq	حرق
cancer	saraṭān	سرطان
chicken pox	gudiri	جديري
cold	bard	برد
constipation	'imsaak	إمساك
cough	kuHHa	كُحّة
cystitis	iltihaab fil masaana	إلتهاب في المثانة
diarrhoea	ᶜis haal	إسهال
fever	Humma	حمّة
gastroenteritis	nazla ma'awiyya	نزلة معويّة
glandular fever	mununukliōsis	مونونوكليوسيس
hayfever	Hasaasiyya	حساسيّة
headache	ṣudā'	صداع
heart condition	Haga fil ᶜalb	حاجة في القلب

hepatitis	iṣ ṣafra	الصفرة
indigestion	ṣu'ooba fi haḍm	صعوبة في الهضم
infection	iltihaab	إلتهاب
inflammation	iltihaab	إلتهاب
influenza	anfilwanza	إنفلونزا
injury	garH	جرح
lice	'aml	قمل
lump	waram	ورم
migraine	ṣudā' nuṣfi	صداع نصفي
pain	waga'	وجع
rash	ṭafH	طفح
sore throat	ʿiltihaab fiz zōr	إلتهاب في الزّور
sprain	gaz'a	جزع
stomachache	maghaṣ	مغص
sunburn	itHarra't min ish shams	إتحرّقت من الشمس
sunstroke	ḍarbit shams	ضربة شمس
thrush	iltihaab fiṭri	إلتهاب فطري
toothache	waga' fid ḍirs	وجع في الضرس
travel sickness	dōkha	دوخة
urinary tract infection	iltihaab fil bool	إلتهاب في البول
venereal disease	amrāḍ tanasuliyya	أمراض تناسليّة
worms	dood	دود
wound	garaH	جرح

WOMEN'S HEALTH صحّة المرأة

Could I see a ...?	'ayza ashoof ...	عايزة أشوف ...
female doctor	duktura	دكتورة
gyneacologist	duktoor amrāḍ nisa	دكتور أمراض نسا

I'm pregnant.
ana Haamil
أنا حامل.

I think I'm pregnant.
aftikir ana Haamil
أفتكر أنا حامل.

I'm on the Pill.
bakhud Huboob — باخد حبوب.

I haven't had my period for ... weeks.
makansh 'andi iddawra min ... asabee' — مكنش عندي الدورة من ... أسابيع.

I'd like to use contraception.
'ayza Haaga li mana' il Haml — عايزة حاجة لمنع الحمل.

I'd like to have a pregnancy test.
'ayza taHleel Haml — عايزة تحليل حمل.

abortion	'ighāḍ	إجهاض
cystitis	iltihāb fil masaana	ألتهاب في المثانة
diaphragm	il haagiz il mihbali	الحاجز المهبلي
IUD	lawleb	لولب
mammogram	mamoogram	أشعّة على الثّدي
menstruation	id dawra	الدورة
miscarriage	ighāḍ	إجهاض
pap smear	pap smeer	مسح على عنق الرحم
period pain	alam id dawra	ألم الدورة
the Pill	Huboob mana' al Haml	حبوب منع الحمل
thrush	iltihaab fiṭri	إلتهاب فطري
ultrasound	sonār	سونار

THEY MAY SAY ...

yirHamkum allah!
Bless you! (after sneezing)

SPECIAL HEALTH NEEDS

إحتياجات صحية خاصة

I'm ...

anaemic	'andi aneemiya	عندي أنيميا
asthmatic	'andi azmit raboo	عندي أزمة ربو
diabetic	'andi is sukkar	عندي السّكر

I'm allergic to ..	andi Hasaasiyya min ...	عندي حساسيّة من ...
antibiotics	muḍāḍ Hayawi	مضاد حيوي
aspirin	asbireen	أسبرين
bees	naHl	نحل
codeine	kudayeen	كدايين
dairy products	il ᶜalbaan	الألبان
dust	it turāb	التراب
penicillin	penisileen	بنسلين
pollen	Huboob il luqāH	حبوب اللقاح

I have a skin allergy.
'andi Hasaasiyya gildiyya — عندي حساسيّة جلديّة.

I have high/low blood pressure.
'andi ḍaghṭ id dam 'aali/wāṭi — عندي ضغط الدم عالي/واطي.

I have a weak heart.
albi ḍa'eef — قلبي ضعيف.

I've had my vaccinations.
ana iṭ'amt — أنا إتطّعمت.

I have my own syringe.
'andi is siringa bitaa'ti — عندي السرنجة بتاعتي.

I don't want a blood transfusion.
ana mish 'aayiz/'ayza na'l id damm (m/f) — أنا مش عايز نقل الدم.

This is my usual medicine.
da il dawa illi ana bakhuduh — ده الدوا اللي أنا باخده.

I'm on medication for ...
ana baᶜkhud dawa 'ashaan ... أنا بأخد دوا علشان ...
I'm on a special diet.
ana maashi 'ala rezheem mu'ayyan أنا ماشي على رجيم معيّن.
I need a new pair of glasses.
ana miHtaag/miHtaaga naḍḍāra gideeda (m/f) أنا محتاج نضارة جديدة.

addiction	idmān	إدمان
bite	ᶜarṣ	قرص
blood test	taHleel id damm	تحليل الدمّ
contraceptive	mana' il Haml	منع الحمل
cure	'ilaag	علاج
inhaler	bakhaakha	بخّاخة
injection	Hu'na	حقنة
pacemaker	manaẓẓim li ḍarabāt il ᶜalb	منظّم لضربات القلب
treatment	'ilaag	علاج
x-ray	isha'a	أشعّة

ALTERNATIVE TREATMENTS علاج بديل

acupuncture	ibar ṣiniyya	إبر صينيّة
herbalist	'aṭṭār	عطّار
massage	masaazh	مسّاج
yoga	yōga	يوجا

PARTS OF THE BODY أعضاء الجسم

My (chest) hurts.
(ṣidr)i biyuwga'ni (صد)ري بيوجعني.
I have a pain in my ...
'andi waga' fil ... عندي وجع في ال ...
I can't move my ...
mish ᶜaadir/'adra aHarrak ... (m/f) مش قادر أحرّك ...

ankle	rigl	رجل
appendix	iz zayda	الزايدة الدودية
arm	dirā'	دراع
back	ḍahr	ضهر
bladder	masaana	مثانة
blood	damm	دم
bone	'aḍm	عضم
chest	ṣidr	صدر
ears	widaan	ودان
eye	'ayn	عين
two eyes	'inayn	عينين
finger	ṣubā'	صباع
foot	rigl	رجل
hand	'eed	يد
head	raᶜs	رأس
heart	alb	قلب
jaw	fakk	فكّ
kidney	kilya	كلية
knee	rukba	ركبة
leg	rigl	رجل
liver	kibd	كبد
lungs	riᶜa	رئة
mouth	buᶜ	بق
muscle	'aḍala	عضلة
nose	manakheer	مناخير
ribs	ḍulu'	ضلوع
shoulders	kitf	كتف
skin	gild	جلد
spine	'amood faqri	عمود فقري
stomach	mi'da	معدة
teeth	sinān	أسنان
tooth	sinna	سنّة
molar	ḍirs	ضرس
throat	zoor	زور
vein	'irᶜ	عرق

AT THE CHEMIST في الصيدليّة

Almost all drugs (including antibiotics) are available without prescription in Egypt, and chemists can be very helpful if you can't find a doctor. All drugs come with leaflets or descriptions in English as well as Arabic.

Is there an all-night chemist nearby?
fee ṣaydaliyya shaghaala arba'a wi 'ishreen saa'a urayyeba min hina? — فيه صيدليّة شغّالة أربعة وعشرين ساعة قريبة من هنا؟

I need something for ...
ana miHtaag/a Haaga li ... — أنا محتاج حاجة ل ...

How many times a day?
kam marra fil yōm? — كم مرّة في اليوم؟

Twice a day.
marratayn fil yōm — مرّتين في اليوم.

with food
ma' il ᶜakl — مع الأكل

Can I drive on this medication?
aᶜdar asooᶜ wana waakhud il dawa da? — أقدر أسوق وانا واخد الدوا ده؟

Will it make me drowsy?
id dawa da biynayyim? — الدوا ده بينيّم؟

antibiotics	muḍād Hayawi	مضاد حيوي
antiseptic	muṭahir	مطهّر
aspirin	asbireen	أسبرين
bandage	rubāṭ	رباط
Band-aids	bilastar	بلستر
cotton balls	uṭn ṭibbi	قطن طبّي
cough medicine	dawa lil kuHHa	دوا للكحّة
gauze	shaash	شاش
laxatives	mulayyin	مليّن
painkillers	Haaga lil ᶜalam	حاجة للألم
sleeping pills	Huboob munawwima	حبوب منوّمة
vitamins	fitameenaat	فيتامينات

See Shopping chapter (page 138) for general toiletries.

AT THE DENTIST عند دكتور الأسنان

Note that most Egyptian dentists speak English.

I have a toothache.
'andi ḍirs biyuwga'ni عندي ضرس بيوجعني.

I have a cavity.
ḍirsi misawwis ضرسي مسوّس.

I've lost a filling.
il Hashw wi'i' الحشو وقع.

I've broken my tooth.
ḍirsi itkassar ضرسي إتكسّر.

My gums hurt.
lisa bituga'ni لسّة بيوجعني.

I don't want it extracted.
ana mish 'aayiz/'ayza asheeloo أنا مش عايز أشيلوه.

Please give me an anaesthetic.
iddeeni bing, min faḍlak إدّيني بنج من فضلك.

Ouch!
'ayyy! أيي!

إحتياجات خاصّة SPECIFIC NEEDS

Egypt is a low-income country with huge unemployment, so finding work isn't easy, but nor is it impossible. English teachers, diving instructors, copy-editors and journalists may be able to carve out a position, but a work permit is required and these are usually only given to those hired abroad by foreign companies.

DISABLED TRAVELLERS مسافرين معوقين

There are very few facilities for disabled travellers in Egypt, and while people are usually willing to help, they're unlikely to anticipate your needs.

I'm disabled/handicapped.
ana mu'awwaq — أنا معوّق.

I need assistance.
ana miHtaag/a musaa'da — أنا محتاج مساعدة.

What services do you have for disabled people?
ey il khadimaat illi bit'addimuha lil mu'awwaqeen? — إيه الخدمات اللي بتقدّموها للمعوّقين؟

Is there wheelchair access?
fee madkhal li kursi mutaHarrak? — فيه مدخل لكرسي متحرّك؟

I'm deaf.
ana aṭrash/ṭarsha. — أنا أطرش/طرشة.

I have a hearing aid.
'andi samaa'a fee widni — عندي سمّاعة في ودني.

Speak more loudly, please.
itkallim fee ṣōt 'aali, min faḍlak — إتكلّم بصوت عالي، من فضلك.

disabled person	shakhs mu'awwaq	شخص معوّق
wheelchair	kursi mutaHarrik	كرسي متحرّك

GAY TRAVELLERS المسافرون اللوطيّون

Sexuality isn't a topic for open discussion in Egypt, and gay consciousness on a general level doesn't exist, even though homosexuality may be acknowledged behind closed doors. Even finding a non-pejorative word meaning 'gay' is difficult.

The two most commonly used terms, khawal and shaaz literally mean 'sodomite' and 'deviant'. Egyptian homosexuals say they prefer the following classical Arabic words, even though they aren't widely used:

gay man	lootee	لوطي
lesbian	suHaqiyya	سحاقيّة

Where are the gay hangouts?
fayn il amākin illi il luwāti yoon biyruHuha? — فين الأماكن اللي اللواطيّون بيروحوها؟

Are we/am I likely to be harassed here?
mumkin Hadd yidayi'ni hina? — ممكن حد يضايقني هنا؟

TRAVELLING WITH THE FAMILY السفر مع العائلة

Are there facilities for babies?
fee ista^c^dadaat khāṣa lil aṭfāl? — فيه إستعدادات خاصّة للأطفال؟

Do you have a child-minding service?
fee khidmat ra'ayit ṭifl? — فيه خدمة رعاية طفل؟

Where can I find an English-speaking babysitter?
mumkin alaa^c^ee galisat ^c^aṭfāl bititkallim ingileezi fayn? — ممكن ألاقي جليسة أطفال بتتكلّم إنجليزي فين؟

Can you put an (extra) bed/cot in the room?
mumkin tiHuṭṭu sireer lil aṭfāl (ziyāda) fil ghurfa? — ممكن تحطّوا سرير للأطفال (زيادة) في الغرفة؟

I need a car with a child seat.
'aayiz/'ayza 'arabiyya bikursi lil ṭifl (m/f) — عايز عربيّة بكرسي للطّفل.

Is it suitable for children?		
da munaasib lil aṭfāl?	ده منا سب للأطفال ؟
Is there a family discount?	
fee takhfiḍ lil usra?	فيه تخفيض للأسرة ؟
Are children allowed?	
masmooH bisṭHaab il aṭfāl?	مسموح بأ صطحاب الأطفال ؟
Do you have a children's menu?	
fee menay lil aṭfāl?	فيه مني للأطفال ؟
Are there any activities for children?	
fee anshiṭa lil aṭfāl?	فيه أنشطة للأطفال ؟
Is there a playground nearby?	
fee mal'ab urayyib?	فيه ملعب قريّب؟

LOOKING FOR A JOB البحث عن عمل

Where can I find local job advertisements?	
fayn a'dar alaa'i i'lanaat shughl?	فين أقدر ألاقي إعلانات شغل؟
Do I need a work permit?	
laazim aakhud taṣreeH 'amal?	لازم آخد تصريح عمل؟
I've had experience.	
'andi khibra	عندي خبرة.
I've come about the position advertised.	
ana gayt 'ashaan i'laan il wazeefa	أنا جيت علشان إعلان الوظيفة.
I'm ringing about the position advertised.	
ana bataṣil 'ashaan i'laan il wazeefa	أنا بتّصل علشان إعلان الوظيفة.
What's the wage?	
il murattab kam?	المرتّب كم؟
Do I have to pay tax?	
laazim adfa' ḍarāyib?	لازم أدفع ضرايب؟

SPECIFIC NEEDS

I can start ...	mumkin abtidi ...	ممكن أبتدي ...
today	innaharda	النهارده
tomorrow	bukra	بكرة
next week	lusboo' illi gayy	الأسبوع اللي جاي

casual	ghayr munaẓẓam/a	غير منظّم
employee	muwaẓẓaf	موظّف
employer	ṣāHib/it 'amal	صاحب عمل
full-time	kull il wa't	كل الوقت
job	waẓeefa	وظيفة
occupation/trade	mihna	مهنة
part-time	ba'ḍ il wa^ct	بعض الوقت
résumé/CV	seevee	سي في
traineeship	tadreeb	تدريب
work experience	khibrit 'amal	خبرة عمل

ON BUSINESS رحلات العمل

We're attending a ...	iHna biniHḍar ...	إحنا بنحضّر ...
conference	mu'tamar	مؤتمر
meeting	igtimaa'	إجتماع
trade fair	ma'raḍ tugāri	معرض تجاري

I'm on a course.
ana bakhud kurs — أنا باخد كورس.

I have an appointment with ...
'andi mi'aad ma'... — عندي ميعاد مع ...

Here's my business card.
da il kart bitaa'i — ده الكرت بتاعي.

I need an interpreter.
ana 'aayiz/'ayza mitargim (m/f) — أنا عايز مترجم.

I need to use a computer.
ana miHtaag/a istakhdam il kumputir (m/f) — أنا محتاج إستخدم الكمبيوتر.

I need to send a fax/an email.
ana 'aayiz/'ayza aba'at faks/eemayl (m/f) — أنا عايز أبعت فاكس/إيميل.

client	'ameel/a	عميل
colleague	zameel/a	زميل
distributor	muwazza'	موزّع
email	eemayl	إيميل
exhibition	ma'raḍ	معرض
manager	mudeer	مدير
mobile phone	maHmool	محمول
profit	ribH	ربح
proposal	iqtirāH	إقتراح

ON TOUR على الطريق

We're part of a group.
iHna ma'na magmoo'a — إحنا معا نا مجموعة.

We're on tour.
iHna fee gawla — إحنا في جولة.

We're taking a break of ... days.
iHna 'andina fatrit rāHa ... ayaam — إحنا عندنا فترة راحة ... أيّام.

Please speak with our manager.
itkallim ma' mudeerna, min faḍlak — إتكلّم مع مديرنا، من فضلك.

We've lost our equipment.
aghizitna ḍā'it — أجهزتنا ضاعت.

We're playing on ...	bin'azzif 'ala ...	بنعزف على ...
I'm with the ...	ana ma'a il ...	أنا مع ...
band	fir'a musiqiya	فرقة موسيقيّة
crew	ṭa'm	طقم
group	magmoo'a	مجموعة
team	faree'	فريق
We sent equipment on this ...	ba'tna il aghiza 'ala ... dee/da	بعتنا الأجهزة على ... دي
bus	il utubees	الأوتوبيس
flight	il riHla	الرحلة
train	il 'aṭr	القطر

SPECIFIC NEEDS

FILM & TV CREWS فريق التصوير

We're on location.
iHna fee makaan it taṣweer — إحنا في مكان التصوير.

We're filming!
ihna binṣawwar! — إحنا بنصوّر!

May we film here?
ni'dar niṣawwar hina? — نقدر نصور هنا؟

We're making a ...	iHna bin'amal ...	إحنا بنعمل ...
documentary	film tasgeeli	فيلم تسجيلي
film	film	فيلم
TV series	musalsal	مسلسل

PILGRIMAGE & RELIGION الحج والدين

While the concept of agnostism is understood in Egypt, people are considered to be either believers or non-believers.

What's your religion?
diyaantak ey? — ديانتك إيه؟

I'm ...	ana ...	أنا ...
Buddhist	boodi/yya	بوذي
Christian	misiHi/yya	مسيحي
Hindu	hindoosi/yya	هندوسي
Jewish	yehoodi/yya	يهودي
Muslim	muslim/a	مسلم

I'm not religious.
ana mish mutadayyin/a (m/f) — أنا مش متديّن.

I'm (Catholic), but not practising.
ana (kathōleeki) bass mish mutadayyin/a — أنا (كاثوليكي) بس مش متدين.

I believe in God.
ana u^{c}min billah — أنا أؤمن بالله.

I believe in destiny/fate.
ana u^{c}min bilqadr — أنا أؤمن بالقدر.

I'm interested in astrology/philosophy.
ana muhtamm bil tangeem/falsafa — أنا مهتم بالتنجيم/فلسفة.

I'm an atheist.
ana mulHid/a (m/f) — أنا ملحد.

Can I pray here?
mumkin aṣalli hina? — ممكن أصلّي هنا؟

Where can I pray/worship?
mumkin aṣalli/at'abid fayn? — ممكن إتعبّد فين؟

Where can I make confession (in English)?
fayn mumkin a'tarif (bil ingileezi)? — فين ممكن أعترف (بالإنجليزي)؟

church	kineesa	كنيسة
confession	i'tirāf	إعتراف
funeral	ginaaza	جنازة
God	allah	الله
god	ilaah	اله
monk	rāhib	راهب
prayer	muṣalli	مصلّي
priest	ᶜasees	قسّيس
relic	asar muqaddis	أثر مقدّس
sabbath	sabt il yehood	سبّت اليهود
saint (Christian)	qiddees	قدّيس
saint (Muslim)	sayyid/a	سيد
shrine	ḍareeH	ضريح
temple	ma'bad	معبد

TRACING ROOTS & HISTORY

البحث عن الأصل والتاريخ

(I think) my ancestors came from this area.
(aftikir) inn agdaadi kaanu min il manti^{c}a dee
(أفتكر) أن أجدادي كانوا من المنطقة دي.

I'm looking for my relatives.
ana badawwar 'ala araybi
أنا بدوّر على قرايبى.

I have (had) a relative who lives around here.
ana (kaan) 'andi areeb 'ayesh hina
أنا (كان) عندي قريب عايش هنا.

Is there anyone here by the name of ...?
fee Hadd hina ismuh/ ismaha ...? (m/f)
فيه حد هنا إسمه ...؟

I'd like to go to the cemetary/ burial ground.
'aayiz/'ayza arooH il gabbāna (m/f)
عايز أروح الجبّانة.

I think he fought/died near here.
aftikir innu Haarib/ itwaffa hina
أفتكر أنه حارب/ إتوفّى هنا.

My (father) fought/died here in WWII.
(waldi) Haarib/ itwaffa hina fil Harb il 'alamiyya il tanya
(والدي) حارب/ إتوفّى هنا في الحرب العالميّة الثانية.

My (grandmother) nursed here in WWII.
(giditi) kaanit mumarrida hina fil Harb il 'alamiyya il tanya
(جدّتي) كانت ممرّضة هنا في الحرب العالميّة الثانية.

الوقت و التواريخ

TIME & DATES

TELLING THE TIME معرفة الوقت

Because the Arabic equivalent of the English 'o'clock' (is saa'a) is feminine, the numbers used in telling the time are in the feminine form.

When specifying am or pm, the words 'morning', 'afternoon', or 'night' are used.

8 am	**is saa'a tamanya ṣabaHan** (lit: o'clock eight morning)	الساعةثمانية صباحاً
3 pm	**is saa'a talāta ba'd iḍ ḍuhr** (lit: o'clock three afternoon)	الساعة ثلاثة بعد الظهر
8 pm	**is saa'a tamanya bil layl** (lit: o'clock eight night)	الساعة ثمانية بالليل

o'clock	**is saa'a**	الساعة
half past	**wi nuṣ**	ونص
quarter to/past	**illa/wi rub'**	الاّ/وربع
twenty to/past	**illa/wi tilt**	الاّ/وثلث
twenty-five to/past	**wi nuṣ illa/wi khamsa**	ونص الاّ/وخمسة

What time is it?	**is saa'a kam?**	السّاعة كم؟
(It's) one o'clock.	**is saa'a waHida** (lit: o'clock one)	السّاعة واحدة.

Half past one.
is saa'a waHida wi nuṣ السّاعة واحدة و نصّ.
(lit: o'clock one past half)

Quarter past one.
is saa'a waHida wi rub' السّاعة واحدة و ربع.
(lit: o'clock one past quarter)

Twenty-five past three.
is saa'a talaata wi nuṣ illa khamsa السّاعة تلاتة و نصّ الاّ خمسة.
(lit: o'clock three half past to five)

TIME & DATES

DAYS الأيام

Monday	yōm il itnayn	يوم الإثنين
Tuesday	yōm il talaat	يوم الثلاثاء
Wednesday	yōm il arbā'	يوم الأربعاء
Thursday	yōm il khamees	يوم الخميس
Friday	yōm il guma'	يوم الجمعة
Saturday	yōm il sabt	يوم السبت
Sunday	yōm il Hadd	يوم الأحد

MONTHS الشهور

January	yanayir	يناير
February	fibrayir	فبراير
March	maaris	مارس
April	abreel	إبريل
May	mayu	مايو
June	yoonyu	يونيو
July	yoolyu	يوليو
August	ughusṭus	أغسطس
September	sibtambir	سبتمبر
October	uktoobir	أكتوبر
November	nufembir	نوفمبر
December	disembir	ديسمبر

DATES التواريخ

What date it is today?	innaharda kam?	النهارده كم؟
It's 18 October.	tamantāshar uktoobar	١٨أكتوبر.

PRESENT الحاضر

now	dilwa'ti	دلوقتي
right now (immediately)	Haalan	حالاً
today	innaharda	النهارده
this morning	innaharda is subH	النهارده الصّبح
this afternoon	innaharda ba'd iḍ ḍuhr	النهارده بعد الضّهر

TIME & DATES

tonight	il layla dee	الليلة دي
this week	il usboo^c da	الأسبوع ده
this month	ish shahr da	الشهر ده
this year	is sana dee	السنة دي

PAST — الماضي

yesterday	imbaariH	إمبارح
yesterday morning	imbaariH iṣ ṣubH	إمبارح الصبح
yesterday afternoon/ evening	imbaariH ba'd iḍ ḍuhr/bil layl	إمبارح بعد الضهر/بالليل
last night	imbaariH bil layl	إمبارح بالليل
day before yesterday	awwil imbaariH	أوّل إمبارح
last week	il usboo' illi faat	الأسبوع اللي فات
last month	ish shahr illi faat	الشهر اللي فات
last year	is sana illi faat	السنة اللي فاتت
(half an hour) ago	min (nuṣ saa'a)	من (نصّ ساعة)
(three) days ago	min (talaat) ayaam	من (ثلاثة) أيام
(five) years ago	min (khamas) sineen	من (خمس) سنين
a while ago	min shiwayya	من شويّة
since (May)	min (mayu)	من (مايو)

FUTURE — المستقبل

tomorrow	bukra	بكرة
tomorrow morning	bukra iṣ ṣubH	بكرة الصبح
tomorrow afternoon	bukra ba'd iḍ ḍuhr	بكرة بعد الضهر
tomorrow evening	bukra bil layl	بكرة بالليل
day after tomorrow	ba'd bukra	بعدبكرة
next week	il usboo' illi gayy	الأسبوع اللي جا ي
next month	ish shahr illi gayy	الشهر اللي جا ى
next year	is sana gayya	السنة اللي جاية
in (five) minutes	ba'd (khamas) da^cayi^c	بعد (خمس) دقائق
in (six) days	ba'd (sittat) ayyām	بعد (ستة) أيام
until (June)	lighāyit (yoonyu)	لغاية (يونيو)

DURING THE DAY — أثناء النهار

It's early.	lissa badri	لسّه بدري.
It's late.	kida mit[c]akhkhir	كده متأخّر.
afternoon	ba'd iḍ ḍuhr	بعد الضّهر
dawn	il fagr	الفجر
day	yōm	يوم
early	badri	بدري
evening	misā[c]	مساء
lunchtime	wa[c]t il ghada	وقت الغدا
midday	iḍ ḍuhr	الضهر
midnight	nuṣ il layl	نصّ الليل
morning	iṣ ṣubH	االصّبح
night	il layl	الليل
setting of the sun	ghuroob ish shams	غروب الشمس
sunrise	shuru[c] ish shams	شروق الشمس
sunset	il maghreb	المغرب

الأرقام والكمّيات NUMBERS & AMOUNTS

Cardinal numbers between two and ten have both a long and a short form in Egyptian Arabic. The long form is followed by a singular noun and is used when counting, using money, ordering food or measuring:

three pounds	talata ginay	ثلاثة جنيه
four soups	arb'a shorba	أربعة شوربة

On all other occasions, numbers between two and 10 are given in the short form, followed by a plural noun:

three books	talat kutub	ثلاثة كتب
five months	khamas shuhoor	خمسة أشهر

Most nouns also have a dual form with the ending -ayn, or -tayn for the feminine (see Grammar, page 19):

two books	kitabayn	كتابين
two months	shahrayn	شهرين

CARDINAL NUMBERS أعداد أصليّة

		LONG	SHORT	
0	٠	sifr/zeero	–	صفر
1	١	waaHid (m)	waHda (f)	واحد
2	٢	itnayn	–	إثنين
3	٣	talaata	talat	ثلاثة
4	٤	arba'a	arba'	أربعة
5	٥	khamsa	khamas	خمسة
6	٦	sitta	sitt	ستة
7	٧	saba'a	saba'	سبعة
8	٨	tamanya	taman	ثمانية
9	٩	tis'a	tis'	تسعة
10	١٠	'ashara	'ashar	عشرة

Numbers above 11 have only one form, and are followed by singular nouns.

11	١١	Hadāshar	أحدعشر
12	١٢	itnāshar	إثني عشر
13	١٣	talatāshar	ثلاثة عشر
14	١٤	arba'tāshar	أربعة عشر
15	١٥	khamastāshar	خمسة عشر
16	١٦	sittāshar	ستّة عشر
17	١٧	saba'tāshar	سبعة عشر
18	١٨	tamantāshar	ثمانية عشر
19	١٩	tisa'tāshar	تسعة عشر
20	٢٠	'ishreen	عشرين
21	٢١	wāHid wi 'ishreen	أحد وعشرين
22	٢٢	itnayn wi 'ishreen	إثني وعشرين
30	٣٠	talateen	ثلاثين
40	٤٠	arbi'een	أربعين
50	٥٠	khamseen	خمسين
60	٦٠	sitteen	ستّين
70	٧٠	saba'een	سبعين
80	٨٠	tamaneen	ثمانين
90	٩٠	tisa'een	تسعين

When followed by a noun, the pronunciation of 100 and the numbers 300-900 changes from miyya to meet. The noun is always singular:

300 kgs	tultumeet keelu	ثلاثمئة كيلو

Two hundred uses the dual form, so 200 books is mitayn kitaab.

100	١٠٠	miyya	مئّة
200	٢٠٠	mitayn	مئتين
300	٣٠٠	tultumiyya	ثلاثمئة
400	٤٠٠	rub'umiyya	أربعةمئّة
500	٥٠٠	khumsumiyya	خمس مئّة
600	٦٠٠	suttumiyya	ستّ مئّة

700	٧٠٠	sub'umiyya	سبعميّة
800	٨٠٠	tumnumiyya	ثمانميّة
900	٩٠٠	tus'umiyya	تسعميّة
1000	١٠٠٠	alf	ألف
one million		milyoon	مليون

ORDINAL NUMBERS أعداد ترتيبيّة

Ordinal numbers under 11 coming before the subject always use the masculine form; those coming after the subject vary according to the gender.

the third girl — tālit bint or il bint it talta

After 10, only the latter form is possible:

the 11th girl — il bint il Hidāshar

	Masculine		Feminine	
1st	awwil	أوّل	oola	أولى
2nd	taani	ثاني	tanya	ثانية
3rd	taalit	ثالث	talta	ثالثة
4th	raabi'	رابع	rab^ca	رابعة
5th	khaamis	خامس	khamsa	خامسة

FRACTIONS كسور

quarter	rub'	ربع
half	nuṣ	نصّ
third	tilt	ثلث
three-quarters	talat tirba'	ثلاثة أرباع

USEFUL AMOUNTS كميّات مفيدة

How many?
kam waaHid? كم واحد ؟

Could you please give me ...?
mumkin tideeni ...? (m/f) ممكن تدّيني ...؟

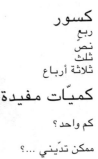

I need ...
ana miHtaag/miHtaaga ... (m/f) أنا محتاج ...

all	kull	كلّ
double (twice)	ḍ'if	ضعف
double (adj)	muzdawag	مزدوج
a dozen	dasta; disat (pl)	دستة
enough	kifaaya	كفاية
few	shiwayya	شويّة
less	a'all	أقل
(just) a little; some	shiwayya	شويّة
many/much/a lot	kiteer	كثير
more	aktar min	أكثر من
none	mafeesh	مفيش
once	marra	مرّة
a pair	itnayn	إثنين
some	ba'ḍ	بعض
some of them	ba'ḍuhum	بعضهم
too many/much	aktar min il laazim	أكثر من اللازم
twice	marratayn	مرّتين

a bottle of ...	'izaazat ...	قزازة ...
half a kilogram of ...	nuṣ keelu ...	نصف كيلو ...
half a dozen ...	nuṣ dasta ...	نصّف دستة ...
100 grams of ...	meet garam ...	مئة جرام ...
a jar of ...	barṭamān ...	برطمان ...
a kilogram of ...	keelu ...	كيلو ...
a packet of ...	baaku ...	باكو ...
a slice of ...	taransh ...	ترنش ...
a tin of ...	'ilbat ...	علبة ...

EMERGENCIES الطوارئ

GENERAL عام

Help!	ilHa'ni!	إلحقني!
Stop!	u'af!	أقف!
Go away!	imshi!	إمشي!
Thief!	Harāmi!	حرامي!
Fire!	Haree'!	حريق!
Watch out!	khalli baalak/baalik! (m/f)	خلّي بالك!
It's an emergency.	fee ṭawāri'	فية طوارىء.
I'm lost.	ana tayih/tuht (m/f)	أنا تايه.

Could you help us, please?
mumkin tisa'dna low samaHt? ممكن تساعدنا لو سمحت؟

Could I please use the telephone?
mumkin atkallim fit tilifoon? ممكن أتكلّم في التليفون؟

Where are the toilets?
fayn il tawaleet? فين التواليت؟

Call the police!
itaṣṣal bil bulees! إتّصل بالبوليس!

Where's the police station?
fayn 'ism il bulees? فين قسم البوليس؟

POLICE الشرطة

Egypt has several police forces. Most important for foreigners are the Tourist Police, who wear an armband with an insignia in Arabic and English. Note that although the word **bulees** is widely used for police, the formal word is **shurṭa**.

Airport Police	shurṭat il maṭār	شرطة المطار
Military Police	shurṭat 'askariyya	شرطة عسكريّة
Traffic Police	shurṭat il muroor	شرطة المرور
Tourist Police	shurṭat is siyaaHa	شرطة السياحة
Railway Police	shurṭat il maHaṭa	شرطة المحطّة
River Police	shurṭat il nahr	شرطة االنهر
Central Security Forces	il amn il markazi	الأمن المركزي

We want to report an offence.
'ayzeen niballagh il bulees — عايزين نبلّغ البوليس.

I've been raped/assaulted.
ana mughtaṣaba — أنا مغتصبة.

I've been robbed.
ana itsara^c^t — أنا إتسرقت.

My ... was/were stolen.	il ... bitaa'i itsara^c^ (m)	ال... بتاعي اتسرق.
My ... was/were stolen.	il ... bitaa'ti itsara^c^it (f; pl)	أل... بتاعي إتسرقت.
backpack	shanṭit ḍahr (f)	شنطة ضهر
bags	shunat (f, pl)	شنط
handbag	shanṭa (f)	شنطة
money	filoos (f, pl)	فلوس
papers	awrā^c^ (f, pl)	أوراق
passport	gawaaz is safar (m)	جواز السفر
travellers cheques	sheekaat siyaHiyya (f, pl)	شيكات سياحية
wallet	maHfaẓa (f)	محفظة

My possessions are insured.
Haagti mit'ammina — حاجتي متأمّنة.

I'm sorry/I apologise.
ana aasif/a (m/f) — أنا آسف.

I didn't realise I was doing anything wrong.
ma 'arafsh inna da ghalaṭ — معرفش أنّ ده غلط.

I didn't do it.	ma 'amaltuhoosh	معملتهوش.
We're innocent.	iHna abriyā^c^	إحنا أبرياء.
We're foreigners.	ihna agaanib	إحنا أجانب.

I want to contact my embassy/consulate.
'aayiz/'ayza attaṣal bi ^c^unsuliyyati/safaarati (m/f) — عايز أتّصل بقنصليّتي/ سفارتي.

Can I call someone?
mumkin attaṣal bi Hadd? — ممكن إتّصل بحدّ؟

Can I have a lawyer who speaks English?
mumkin tidooni muHaami biyitkallim ingileezi?
ممكن تدّوني محامي بيتكلّم إنجليزي؟

Is there a fine we can pay to clear this?
mumkin nidfa' gharāma wi'nkhalaṣ il mawḍu'?
ممكن ندفع غرامة و نخلّص الموضوع؟

I (don't) understand.
ana (mish) faahim/fahma (m/f)
أنا (مش) فاهم.

I know my rights.
ana 'aarif/'arfa Huᶜuᶜi (m/f)
أنا عارف حقوقي.

arrested	'abaḍu 'aley	قبضوا عليه
cell	zinzaana	زنزانة
embassy/consulate	safāra/unṣuliyya	سفارة/قنصليّة
fine (payment)	gharāma	غرامة
guilty	muznib	مذنب
lawyer	muHaami	محامي
not guilty	baree'	بريء
police officer	zābit il bulees	ضابط البوليس
police station	ism il bulees	قسم البوليس
prison	sigin	سجن
trial	maHakma	محكمة

What am I accused of?
ana mutahim bi ey?
أنا متّهم بإيه؟

You'll be charged with ...	inta mutahim bi ...	إنت متّهم ب ...
She/He will be charged with ...	huwa/hiyya mutahim/a bi ... (m/f)	هو متّهم ب ...

anti-government activity	nashāṭ ḍid il Hukooma	نشاط ضدّ الحكومة
assault	i'tidāᶜ	إعتداء
disturbing the peace	'amal iz'aag	عمل إزعاج
illegal entry	dukhool bi shakl ghayr mashru'	دخول بشكل غير مشروع
murder	qatl	قتل

not having a visa	mafeesh feeza	مفيش فيزا
overstaying your visa	wa't il feeza khilis	وقت الفيزا خلص
possession (of illegal substances)	Hayaazit mamnu'aat	إزعاج حيازة ممنوعات
rape	ightiṣāb	إغتصاب
robbery/theft	sirᶜa	سرقة
traffic violation	kharaq ishārat il muroor	خرق إشارة المرور
working without a permit	shughl min ghayr taṣreeH	شغل من غير تصريح

HEALTH الصحّة

Call a doctor!
itaṣal/i bi duktoor! (m/f) إتّصل بدكتور!

Call an ambulance!
ittaṣal/i bil is'aaf! (m/f) اتّصل بالإسعاف!

I'm ill.
ana 'ayyaan/a (m/f) أنا عيّان.

My friend is ill.
ṣaHbi 'ayyaan/ṣaHbiti 'ayyaana (m/f) صاحبي عيّان.

I have medical insurance.
'andi taᶜmeen ṭibee عندي تأمين طبي.

ENGLISH - ARABIC

This dictionary includes transliterations of both present and past tense forms of verbs, which are separated by a comma. Only the Arabic script of past tense forms has been given. The infinitive form doesn't exist in Egyptian Arabic – the 'to' preceeding certain words thus indicates that they are verbs, not that they are infinitives.

to carry	sh**a**al, yisheel	شال

Nouns and adjectives have been given in the masculine and feminine form where applicable, separated by a forward slash (/). Both feminine endings and whole words are shown after the slash. All words in Arabic script indicate the masculine form only.

artist	fanaan/a	فنّان
empty	fāḍi/fāḍya	فاضي

Where a word has several alternative meanings, these are listed separated by a bullet.

centimetre	santimitr • santi	سنتي

A

able (to be)	idir, yi^{c}dar	قدر
abortion	ig-haaḍ	إجهاض
above	fu^c	فوق
abroad	barra	برّة
to accept	abal	قبل
accident	Hadsa	حادثة
accom-modation	sakan	سكن
across	'abr	عبر

across the road
'abr il shāri' عبر الشارع

activist	nāshiṭ/a	ناشط
adaptor	adaptar	أدابتر
addiction	idmān	إدمان
address	'inwaan	عنوان
admission	dukhool	دخول
to admit	'itaraf, yi'tarif	يعترف
adult	kibeer/a	كبير
advantage	meeza	ميزة
advice	naṣeeHa	نصيحة
aeroplane	ṭayyāra	طيّارة

to be afraid of	khayif/a min	خايف من
after	ba'd	بعد
(in the) afternoon	ba'd iḍ ḍuhr	بعد الضّهر
(this) afternoon	ba'd iḍ ḍuhr innahārda	بعد الضّهر النّهارده
again	taani	تاني
against	ḍidd	ضدّ
age	sinn	سنّ
aggressive	udwaani/yya	عدواني
(a while) ago	min shuwayya	من شويّة
(half an hour ago)	min nuṣ saa'a	من نص ساعة
(three days) ago	min talaat ayyaam	من ثلاثة أيّام

to agree (with)
ittafa^c,yittifi^c (ma'a) إتّفق مع وافق
to agree (on)
waafi^c, yiwaafi^c ('ala) وافق على

I don't agree.
ana mish muwaafi^c/a أنا غير موافق.

Agreed!
muwaafa^c! موافق!

agriculture	ziraa' a	زراعة
ahead	illi ^cudaam	اللي قدّام
aid (help)	musa'da	مساعدة
AIDS	aydz	إيدز
air	hawa	هوا
air-conditioned	mukayyif	مكيّف
air mail	bareed gawwi	بريد جوّي
airport	maṭār	مطار
alarm clock	minabbih	منبّه
all	kull	كلّ
all day	ṭool in nahār	طول النّهار
an allergy	Hasasiyya	حساسيّة
to allow	samaH, yismaH	سمح،

You're allowed.
masmuHlak/lik مسموح لك.

It's (not) allowed.
(mish) masmuH (مش) مسموح.

almost	ta^creeban	تقريباً
alone	li waHid	لواحد
already	khalaṣ	خلاص

I already paid.
dafa't khalaṣ دفعت خلاص.

also	kamaan	كمان
altitude	irtifā'	إرتفاع
always	dayman	دايماً
amateur	haawi	هاوي
ambassador	safeer	سفير
among	ḍimn	ضمن
anarchist	fawḍawi/yya	فوضوي
ancient	adeem/udaam	قديم
and	wi	و
angry (at)	za'laan/a min	زعلان من
animal	Hayawaan	حيوان
annual	sanawi	سنوي
answer	radd	ردّ
ant	namla	نملة
antibiotics	muḍād Hayawi	مضاد حيوي
antinuclear	ḍidd il asliHa in nawawiya	ضدّ الأسلحة النوويّة
antiques	'aadiyaat	عاديّات
antiquities	asār	آثار
antiseptic	muṭahir	مطهّر
any	ayy	أي
anyone	ayy Hadd	أي حدّ
appointment	mi'aad	ميعاد
archaeological	khāṣ bil Hafriyaat	خاص بالحفريّات
architect	muhandis mi'maari	مهندس معماري
to argue	gaadil, yigaadil	جادل
arm	dirā'	دراع
to arrive	wiṣil, yiwṣil	وصل
arrivals (airport)	wuṣool	وصول
art	fann	فنّ
art gallery	ṣālit 'arḍ il funoon	صالة عرض الفنون
artist	fanaan/a	فنّان
artwork	'amal fanni	عمل فنّي
ashtray	ṭaffāya	طفّاية
to ask (for something)	ṭalab, yuṭlub	طلب
to ask (a question)	sa^cal, yis^cal	سأل

aspirin	asbireen	أسبرين

(He's) asthmatic.
('andu) Hasasiyya fiș șidr
(عنده) حساسيّة في الصّدر.

atmosphere (weather)	gaww	جوّ
atmosphere (mood)	manaakh	مناخ
aunt (maternal)	khaala	خالة
aunt (paternal)	'amma	عمّة
automatic teller machine (ATM)	makanit filoos	مكنة فلوس
autumn	il khareef	الخريف
awful	fazee'	فظيع

B

baby	baybi	بيبي
baby food	akli lil baybi	أكل للبيبي
baby powder	budrat baybi	بودرة بيبي
babysitter	daada	دادة
back (body)	ḍahr	ظهر
at the back (behind)	wara	ورا
backpack	shanțit ḍahr	شنطة ظهر
bad	wiHish/ wiHsha	وحش
bag	shanța	شنطة
baggage	shunaț	شنط
baggage claim	akhd il Hiqayib	أخذ الحقائب
bakery	furn	فرن
balcony	balakōna	بلكونة
ball	kōra	كرة
ballet	balay	باليه
band (music)	fir^c^a musiqiya	فرقة موسيقيّة
bandage (plaster)	bilaster	بلاستر
bank	bank	بنك
baptism	ma'mudiyya	معموديّة
bar • cafe	ahwa	قهوة
basket	sabat	سبت
bath	Hammaam	حمام
bathtub	banyu	بنيو
bathing suit	mayō	مايوه
bathroom	Hammaam	حمام
battery	bațțariyya	بطّارية
to be	kaan, yikoon	كان
beach	bilaazh	بلاج
beautiful	gameel/a	جميل
because	'ashaan	علشان
bed	sireer	سرير
bedroom	ōḍit nōm	أوضة نوم
before	abl	قبل
beggar	shaHHaat/a	شحات
to begin	ibtada, yibtidi	إبتدا
behind	wara	ورا
belly dancing	ra^c^ș shar'i	رقص شرقي
below	taHt	تحت
beside	gamb	جنب
best	aHsan	أحسن
bet	rahaan	رهان
better (than)	aHsan min	أحسن من
between	bayn	بين
Bible	il ingeel	الإنجيل
bicycle	'agala	عجلة
big	kibeer/a	كبير
bike	'agala	عجلة
bill (account)	Hisaab	حساب
binoculars	naḍāra ma'zzama	نظّارة معظّمة

biography	seera	سيرة
bird	'aṣfoor	عصفور
birth certificate	shihaadit milaad	شهادة ميلاد
birthday	'eed milaad	عيد ميلاد
birthday cake	turtit 'eed il milaad	تورتة عيد الميلاد
bite (dog)	'aḍḍa	عضة
bite (insect)	^{c}arṣ	قرص
black	iswid/sōda	إسود
B&W (film)	film abyaḍ wi ^{c}iswid	فيلم أبيض و إسود
blanket	baṭṭaneeya	بطّانية
to bleed	nazaf, yinzif	نزف
to bless	baarik, yibaarik	بارك

God bless you.
allāh yibaarik feek/i
الله يبارك فيك.

blind	a'ma/'amya	أعمى
blood	damm	دم
blood group	magmu'it id damm	مجموعة الدم
blood pressure	ḍaghṭ id damm	ضغط الدّم
blood test	taHleel id damm	تحليل الدّم
blue	azra^c/zar^{c}a	أزرق
to board (ship, etc)	rikib, yirkab	ركب
boat	markib	مركب
body	gism	جسم

Bon appetit!
bil hana wa shifa! بالهنا والشفا!

Bon voyage!
tiruH/ieewa tigieebis salaama!
تروح و تيجي بالسلامة!

response: allah yisallimak/mik
الله يسلّمك.

bone	'aḍm	عظم
book	kitaab	كتاب
to book	Hagaz, yiHgiz	حجز
bookshop	maktaba	مكتبة
boots	boot	بوت
border	Hudood	حدود
bored	zihiq	زهق
boring	mumill/a	ممل
to borrow	istalaf, yistilif	إستلف
both	il itnayn	الإثنين

both of you
intu il itnayn إنتوا الإتنين

bottle	izaaza	قزازة
bottle opener	miftaH izaaz	مفتاح قزاز
(at the) bottom	(fil)^{c}a'r	(في)القعر
box	'ilba	علبة
boxing	mulaakama	ملاكمة
boy	walad	ولد
boyfriend	ṣadeeq	صديق

my boyfriend
ṣadeeqi صديقي

branch	fara'	فرع
brave	shugā'/a	شجاع
bread	'aysh	عيش
to break	kasar, yiksar	كسر
breakfast	fiṭār	فطار
to breathe	itnaffas, yitnaffis	اتنفّس
bribe	rashwa	رشوة
to bribe	rasha, yirshi	رشى
bridge	kubri	كوبري
brilliant (intelligent)	zaki/ya giddan	زكي جدًا

brilliant	laama'/a	لامع
to bring	gaab, yigeeb	جاب

Bring it!
haat/i! هات!

broken	maksoor	مكسور
brother	akh	أخ
brown	bunni	بني
bruise	kadma	كدمة
bucket	gardal	جردل
Buddhist	booḍi	بوذي
bug	Hashara	حشرة
to build	bana, yibni	بنى
building	'imāra	عمارة
bus (large)	utubees	أوتوبيس
bus (minibus)	minibaṣ	ميني باص
bus station	maw'if utubees	موقف أوتوبيس
bus stop	maHaṭṭit utubees	محطّة أوتوبيس
business	shughl	شغل
business-man	rāgil a'maal	رجل أعمال
business-woman	sayyidit a'maal	سيّدة أعمال
busy	mashghool/a	مشغول
but	bas • laakin	بس • لكن
butterfly	farāsha	فراشة
buttons	zurār	زرار
to buy	ishtara, yishtiri	إشترى

I'd like to buy ...
ana 'aayiz/'ayza ashtiri ...
أنا عايز أشتري ...

Where can I buy a ticket?
mumkin ashtiri tazkara minayn?
ممكن أشتري تذكرة منين؟

C

calendar	nateega	نتيجة
can (may)	mumkin	ممكن

May I take your photo?
mumkin aṣawwarak? ممكن أصوّرك؟

camera	kamira	كاميرا
camera operator	muṣaw-warāti/ya	مصوّراتي
camera shop	maHall kamirāt	محل كاميرات
to camp	'askar, yi'askar	عسكر

Can we camp here?
mumkin ni'askar hina?
ممكن نعسكر هنا؟

campsite	mu'askar	معسكر
can (to be able)	idar, yi^c^dar	قدر

We can do it.
ni^c^dar na'milu نقدر نعمله.
I can't do it.
ma^c^darsh a'milu/ha مقدرش أعمله.

can (aluminium)	'ilba	علبة
can opener	fataaHa	فتّاحة
to cancel	lagha, yilghi	لغى

to cancel an appointment
lagha il mi'aad لغى المعاد

candle	shama'	شمع
car	'arabiyya	عربية
car registration	rukhsit 'arabiyya	رخصة عربية
to care (about)	ihtamm, yihtamm bi	إهتم ب

C

DICTIONARY

to care for (look after)
akhad, yakhud baal min — أخد بال من

card	kart	كرت
playing cards	kutsheena	كتشينة

Careful!
Haasib! — حاسب!
Be careful!
khalli baalak/ik! — خلّي بالك!

to carry	shaal, yisheel	شال
carton	kartōna	كرتونة
cartoons	aflaam kartoon	أفلام كارتون
cash register	khazna	خزنة
cashier	ṣarrāf/a	صرّاف
cassette	shireeṭ	شريط
cassette recorder	kasitt	كا سيت
castle	al'a	قلعة
cat	^{c}uṭṭa	قطّة
cathedral	katedriyya	كاتدرائيّة
Catholic	katoleek	كاثوليك
cave	kahf	كهف
CD	seedee (CD)	سي دي
to celebrate	iHtafal, yiHtifil (bi)	إحتفل (ب)
centimetre	santi • santimitr	سنتي
ceramic	khazafi	خزفي
certificate	shahāda	شهادة
chair	kursi	كرسي
champagne	shambanya	شمبانيا
championship	buṭoola	بطولة
chance	furṣa	فرصة
change	fakka	فكّة
to change	ghayyar, yighayyar	غيّر
to make change	fakk, yifukk	فكّ
changing rooms	ghorfit tighyeer il malaabis	غرفة تغيير الملابس
charming	ẓareef/a	ظريف
to chat up	'aakis, yi'aakis	عاكس
cheap	rikheeṣ/a	رخيص
cheap hotel	fundu^{c} rikheeṣ	فندق رخيص
cheat	ghashaash/a	غشّاش
to check (inspect)	tammim, yitammim 'ala	تمّم على

Checkmate!
kish maat! — كش مات!

checkpoint	kameen	كمين
cheese	gibna	جبنة
chemist	ṣaydaliyya	صيدليّة
chess	shaṭarang	شطرنج
chessboard	la'bit shaṭarang	لعبة شطرنج
chest	ṣidr	صدر
chewing gum	libaan	لبان
chicken (to eat)	firaakh	فراخ
chicken (live)	farkha	فرخة
child	'ayyil	عيّل
chocolate	shikōlāta	شيكولاته
to choose	ikhtār, yikhtār	إختار، يختار
Christian	maseeHi/ya	مسيحي
Christmas	kirismas	كريسماس
church	kineesa	كنيسة
cigarette papers	wara' bafra	ورق بفرة
cigarettes	sagaayir	سجاير
cinema	seenima	سينما
circus	sirk	سيرك
citizenship	ginseeyya	جنسية
city	medina	مدينة

city centre	wusṭ il balad	وسط البلد
class (school)	faṣl	فصل
class (social)	ṭabaᶜa	طبقة
classical theatre	il maṣraH il klasseeki	المسرح الكلاسيكي
clean	naḍeef/a	نظيف
clean hotel	funduᶜ naḍeef	فندق نظيف
cleaning	tanḍeef	تنظيف
client (customer)	ziboon	زبون
to climb	ṭili', yitla'	طلع، يطلع
cloak	'abaaya	عباية
clock	saa'a	ساعة
to close	afal, yiᶜfil	قفل، يقفل
closed	maᶜfool/a	مقفول
clothing	hudoom • malaabis	هدوم • ملابس
clothing store	maHall malaabis	محل ملابس
cloud	siHaab	سحاب
cloudy	mighayyim	مغيم
clown	muharrig	مهرج
coast	saaHil	سا حل
coat	balṭu	بالطو
cocaine	kukayeen	كوكايين
coins	'umla ma'daniyya	عملة معدنية
a cold	bard	برد
cold (adj)	bard	برد

It's cold.
id dinya bard — الدنيا برد.

I have a cold.
'andi bard — عندي برد.

cold (for drinks or food)	saaᶜa	ساقع
cold water	mayya saaᶜa	مية ساقعة
colleague	zameel/a	زميل
college	kulliyya	كلية
colour	lōn	لون
comb	mishṭ	مشط
to come (here)	ga, yeegi	جاء، يجي

Come! — ta'aala/i! — تعالى!

to come (arrive)	waṣal yuwṣil	وصل
comedy	kumidya	كوميديا
comfortable	muriH/a	مريح

to feel comfortable
mistirayyaH/a — مستريح

comics	magallaat hazliyya	مجلات هزلية
communion	minawla	مناولة
communist	shiyoo'i/yya	شيوعية
company	shirka	شركة
compass	buṣla	بوصلة
computer	kumbiyootar	كمبيوتر
computer games	atāri	أتاري
concert	Hafla musiqiyya	حفلة موسيقية
confession (religious)	i'tirāf	إعتراف
to confirm (a booking)	ᶜakkid, yi'akkid	أكد

Congratulations!
mabrook! — مبروك!
response:
allah yibaarik — الله يبارك فيك.

conservative	muHāfiẓ/a	محافظ
constipation	imsaak	إمساك
to be constipated	'anduh imsāk	عنده إمساك
construction work	insha'aat	إنشاءات

D

consulate	unṣuliyya	قنصليّة
consul	unṣul	قنصل
contact lenses	adasaat laṣ'a	عدسات لاصقة
contraception	mana' il Haml	منع الحمل
contraceptives	wasaa'il mana' il Haml	وسائل منع الحمل
contract	'a^c^d	عقد
convent	dayr	دير
to cook	ṭabakh, yuṭbukh	طبخ، يطبخ
cool	ishṭa	قشطة
corner (of room)	rukn	ركن
corner (of street)	naṣya	نا صية
corrupt	faasid	فاسد
corruption	fasaad	فساد
to cost	kallif, yikallif	كلّف

How much is it?
bikam?
بكم؟
It costs a lot.
yikallif kiteer
يكلّف كتير.

cotton	uṭn	قطن
cotton wool	uṭn ṭibbi	قطن طبّي
country	balad	بلد
countryside	reef	ريف
cough	kuHHa	قحّة
to count	'add, yi'idd	عدّ، يعدّ
court (legal)	maHkama	محكمة
court (tennis)	mal'ab	ملعب
cow	ba^c^ara	بقرة
crafts	muntigaat yadawiyya	منتجات يدويّة
crafty	makkār	مكّار
crazy	magnoon	مجنون
credit card	kredit kārd	كريدت كارد

Can I pay by credit card?
mumkin adfa' bi kredit kārd visa?
ممكن أدفع بكريدت كارد؟

creep (slang)	la^c^eem	لئيم
cross (angry)	za'laan/a	زعلان
cross (religious)	ṣaleeb	صليب
cuddle	Haḍn	حضن
cup	fingaan	فنجان
cup (trophy)	kaas	كاس
cupboard	dulaab	دولاب
current affairs	moogiz il anbā^c^	موجز الأنباء
customs	gumruk	جمرك
to cut up	aṭṭa', yi^c^aṭṭa'	قطّع
to cut with scissors	^c^aṣ, yi^c^uṣ	قصّ
to cycle	rakib, yirkab 'agala	ركب عجلة
cyclist	raakib 'agala	راكب عجلة
cystitis	iltihaab fil masaana	إلتهاب في المثانة

D

dad	bāba	بابا
daily	yōmi	يومي
dairy products	il albaan	الألبان
to dance	ra^c^aṣ, yir^c^uṣ	رقص
dancing	ra^c^ṣ	رقص
dangerous	khaṭeer	خطير
dark (colour)	ghami^c^	غامق
dark (no light)	ḍalma	ظلمة

DICTIONARY

date (appointment) — mi'aad — ميعاد
date (time) — tareekh — تاريخ
to date (someone) — maashi ma' — ماشي مع
date of birth — tarikh il milaad — تاريخ الميلاد
daughter — bint — بنت
dawn — fagr — فجر
day — yōm — يوم
day after tomorrow — ba'di bukra — بعد بكرة
day before yesterday — awwil imbaariH — أوّل إمبارح

in (six) days
ba'di (sittat) ayaam — بعد (ست) أيام

dead — mayyit/a — ميّت
deaf — aṭrash/ṭarsha — أطرش
death — mōt — موت
to decide — qarrar, yiqarrar — قرر
deck (of cards) — kutsheena — كتشينة
deep (water) — gharee^c — غريق
deer (gazelle) — ghazaal — غزال
degree (temperature) — daraga — درجة
(diploma) — diblōm — دبلوم
delay — ta^ckheer — تأخير
delirious — bihalwis — بيهلوس
democracy — dimuqrāṭiyya — ديموقراطية
demonstration (political) — muẓahra — مظاهرة
dental floss — khayṭ il asnān — خيط أسنان
dentist — duktōr il asnaan — دكتور الأسنان

to deny — nafa, yinfi — نفى، ينفي
deodorant — muzeel li reeHit il' ara^c — مزيل لريحة العرق
to depart (leave) — mishi, yimshi — مشي، يمشي
department store — maHall — محل
departure — zihaab — ذهاب
descendent — nasl/a — نسل
desert — ṣaHra — صحرا
design — taṣmeem — تصميم
destination — ittigaah — إتّجاه
to destroy — dammar, yidammar — دمّر
diabetes — maraḍ is sukkar — مرض السّكر
dial tone — Harāra — حرارة
diarrhoea — is-haal — إسهال
diary (agenda) — azhenda — أجندة
dictionary — qāmoos — قاموس
die (dice) — zahr — زهر
to die — maat, yimoot — مات
different (from) — mukhtalif/a ('an) — مختلف (عن)
difficult — ṣa'b/a — صعب
dining car — 'arabiyat akl — عربية أكل
dinner — 'asha — عشاء

to eat dinner
it'ashsha, yit'ashsha — إتعشّى

direct — mubaashir/a — مباشر
director — mudeer/a — مدير
dirty — wisikh/a — وسخ
disabled — mu'āq — معاق
disadvantage — 'eeb — عيب

discount	takhfeeḍ	تخفيض
to discover	iktashaf, yiktishif	إكتشف
discrimination (racial)	tafri^{c}a 'unṣuriyya	تفرقة عنصريّة
discrimination (sexual)	tafri^{c}a ginsiyya	تفرقة جنسيّة
disease	maraḍ	مرض
distributor (car)	asbirateer	أسبيراتور
diving	ghaṭs	غطس
diving equipment	ag-hizat ghaṭs	أجهزة غطس
dizzy	daayikh/ daaykha	دايخ
to do	'amal, yi'mil	عمل
doctor	duktōr/a	دكتور
documentary film	film tasgeeli	فيلم تسجيلي
dog	kalb	كلب
doll	'aroosa	عروسة
door	baab	باب
double	muzdawag	مزدوج
double bed	sireer muzdawag	سرير مزدوج
double room	ghurfa li itnayn	غرفة لإثنين
a dozen	dasta	دستة
drama	dirāma	دراما
dramatic	dirāmi	درامي
to dream	Hilim, yiHlam	حلم
dress	fustaan	فستان
drink	mashroob	مشروب
to drink	shirib, yishrab	شرب
to drive	saa^c, yisoo^c	ساق
driver	sawaa'	سوّاق
driver's licence	rukhṣit siwaa^{c}a	رخصة سواقة
drugs (pharmaceutical)	dawa	دواء
(recreational)	mukhaḍḍarāt	مخدّرات
drums	ṭabl	طبل
to be drunk	sakrān/a	سكران
to dry (clothes)	nishif, yinshaf	نشف
dummy	titeena	تيتّينة

E

each	kull	كل
ear	widn	ودن
early	badri	بدري

It's early.
lissa badri
لسّه بدري.

to earn	kisib, yiksab	كسب
earrings	Hala^c	حلق
Earth	il 'aalam	العالم
earth (soil)	arḍ	أرض
earthquake	zilzaal	زلزال
east	shar^c	شرق
the Middle East	ish sharq il awsaṭ	الشرق الأوسط
Easter	'eed il qiyāma	عيد القيامة
easy	sahl/a	سهل
to eat	akal, yaakul	أكل
to eat breakfast	fiṭir, yifṭar	فطر
to eat lunch	itghadda, yitghadda	إتغدّى
to eat dinner	it'ashsha, yit'ashsha	إتعشّى
economy	iqtiṣād	إقتصاد
editor	muHarrir/a	محرر
education	ta'leem	تعليم

Egypt	maṣr/miṣr	مصر
Egyptian	maṣri/yya	مصري
elections	intikhabaat	إنتخاب
electricity	kahraba	كهرباء
elevator	asanseer	أسانسير
embarrassed	muHarrag/a	محرج
embarrassment	iHrāg	إحراج
embassy	sifāra	سفارة
emergency	tawāri[c]	طوارئ
employee	muwaẓẓaf/a	موظف
employer	ṣāHib/ it 'amal	صا حب عمل
empty	fāḍi/fāḍya	فاضي
end	nihaaya	نهاية
to end	intaha, yintihi	إنتهى
endangered species	kaa'inaat munqarriḍa	كائنات منقرضة
engagement	khuṭooba	خطوبة

We're engaged.
ihna makhṭubeen liba'ḍ
إحنا مخطوبين لبعض.

engine	mutor	موتور
engineer	muhandis/a	مهندس
engineering	handasa	هندسة
English	ingileezi	إنجليزي
to enjoy (oneself)	inbasaṭ, yinbisiṭ	إنبسط
enough	kifaaya	كفاية

Enough!
kifaaya!
كفاية!

to enter	dakhal, yudkhul	دخل
entertaining	musalli/ya	مسلّي
envelope	ẓarf	ظرف
environment	bee[c]a	بيئة
epileptic	'anduh/' andaha ṣara'	عنده صرع
equality	musawaah	مساواه
equipment	ag-hiza	أجهزة
European	[c]urubbi/ya	أوروبي
evening	misa	مساء
every day	kull yōm	كل يوم
example	masal	مثل

For example ...
masalan ...
مثلاً ...

excellent	mumtaaz/a	ممتاز
exchange	tabdeel	تبديل
to exchange	ghayyar, yighayyar	غيّر
exchange rate	nisbit ittaHweel	نسبة التّحويل

Excuse me. (to call attention)
low samaHt/i
لو سمحت.
Excuse me. (to get past)
'an iznak/ik
عن إذنك.
Excuse me. (apology)
ma'lish
معلش.

to exhibit	'araḍ, yi'riḍ	عرض
exhibition	ma'raḍ	معرض
exit	khuroog	خروج
expensive	ghaali/ ghaalya	غالي
exploitation	istaghlaal	إستغلال
express	saree'	سريع
express letter	gawaab mista'gil	جواب مستعجل
eye	'ayn	عين
eyes	'uyoon	عيون

F

face	wish	وجه
factory	maṣna'	مصنع
factory worker	'aamil fee maṣna'	عا مل في مصنع
fall (autumn)	il khareef	الخريف

F

DICTIONARY

F

family	'ayla	عائلة
famous	mashhoor/a	مشهور
fan	marwaHa	مروحة
fan (of a team)	mu'gab	معجب
far	ba'eed	بعيد
farm	'izba	عزبة
farmer	muzāri'	مزارع
fast (quick)	saree'/a	سريع
fat	tikheen/a	تخين
father	abb	أب
father-in-law	Hama	حمى
fault (someone's)	ghalṭa	غلطة
faulty	'aṭlān	عطلان
fear	khōf	خوف
to feel	Hass, yiHiss (bi)	حسّ (ب)
feelings	mashaa'ir	مشاعر
fence	soor	سور
festival	mahragaan	مهرجان
fever	Humma	حمّة
few	shiwayya	شويّة
fiance/ fiancee	khaṭeeb/a	خطيب/ خطيبة
fiction	khayaal	خيال
field	gheet	غيط
fight	khinaa^{c}a	خناقة
to fight	itkhaani^c, yitkhaani^c ma'a	إتخانق مع
to fill	mala, yimla	ملأ
film	film	فيلم
film speed	sur'at il film	سرعة الفيلم
films (movies)	^{c}aflaam	أفلام
to find	la^{c}a, yilaa^{c}i	لاقى
a fine	gharāma	غرامة
finger	ṣubā'	إصبع

fire	nār	نار
fire (accident)	Haree'a	حريقة
firewood	Haṭb	حطب
first	awwil	أوّل
first-aid	is'aafaat uliyya	إسعافات أوليّة
fish	samak	سمك
fish shop	sammaak	سمّاك
flag	'alam	علم
flat (land, etc)	musaṭṭaH	مسطّح
flea	barghoot	برغوت
flashlight	baṭṭariyya	بطّاريّة
flight	riHla	رحلة
floor	^{c}arḍ	أرض
floor (storey)	dōr	دور
flour	di^{c}ee^c	دقيق
flower	zahr	زهر
flower seller	maHall zuhoor	محل زهور
fly	dibbaan	دبّان
to follow	taba', yitba'	تبع
food	akl	أكل
foot (body)	rigl	رجل

two feet
riglayn رجلين

foot (measurement)	adam	قدم
football (soccer)	kōrat qadam	كرة قدم
footpath	sikka	سكّة
foreign	khaarigi	خارجي
foreigner	khawaaga	خواجة
forest	ghaaba	غابة
forever	ṭool il 'umr	طول العمر
to forget	nisi, yinsa	نسي

I forget.
ana bansa أنا أنسى.

Forget about it! • Don't worry!		
insa/insi il mawdoo'!		إنسى الموضوع!
to forgive	saamiH, yisaamiH	سامح
fortnight	usbu'ayn	أسبوعين
foyer	madkhal	مدخل
free (not bound)	Hurr/a	حرّ
free (of charge)	bi balaash	ببلاش
to freeze	gammid, yigammid	جمّد
Friday	yōm ig guma'	يوم الجمعة
friend	ṣaaHib/ṣaHba	صاحب
frozen foods	akl migammid	أكل مجمّد
full	malyaan/a	مليان
fun	mut'a	متعة
for fun	lil mut'a	للمتعة
to have fun		
ᶜinbasaṭ, yinbisiṭ		إنبسط
to make fun of (laugh at)		
ḍaHak, yiḍHak 'ala		ضحك على
funeral	ganaaza	جنازة
future	mustaᶜbal	مستقبل

G

game	li'ba	لعبة
garage (repairs)	warsha	ورشة
garage (parking)	garaazh	جراج
garbage	zibaala	زبالة
garden	gineena	جنينة
gas bottle (butane)	amboobit butagaaz	أمبوبة بوتا جاز
gate	bawwaaba	بوّابة
gay	looṭee	لوطي
general	'umoomi	عمومي
Get lost!		
iw'a!		إوعى!
gift	hadiyya	هديّة
girl	bint	بنت
girlfriend	ṣadeeqa	صديقة
to give	idda, yiddi	ادّى
Could you give me ...?		
mumkin tiddeeni ...?		ممكن تدّيني ...؟
glass	izaaz	قزاز
glass (for drinking)	kubāya	كباية
glasses (eyes)	naḍḍāra	نظّارة
to go	rāH, yirooH	راح
Let's go.		
yalla beena		يالاّ بيبا.
We'd like to go to ...		
ayzeen nirooH ...		عايزين نروح ...
Go straight ahead.		
imshi 'ala ṭool		إمشي على طول.
to go out with		
kharag, yikhrag ma'a		خرج مع
goal	gōl	جول
goalkeeper	Haaris il marma	حارس المرمى
goat	mi'za	معزة
God	allāh	الله
of gold	dahabi	ذهبي
Good afternoon/evening.		
masaaᶜ il khayr		مساء الخير.

Goodbye.
ma'is salaama مع السّلامة.

Good health! • Cheers!
fee saHitkum! في صحتكم!

Good morning.
ṣabaH il khayr صباح الخير.

Good night.
tiṣbaH/i 'ala khayr تصبح على خير.

government	Hukooma	حكومة
gram	gram	جرام
grandchild	Hafeed	حفيد
grandfather	gidd	جدّ
grandmother	gidda	جدّة
grapes	'inab	عنب
graphic art	fann il grafeek	فنّ الجرافيك
grass	nigeel	نجيل
grave	ma^{c}bara	مقبرة
great	'aẓeem	عظيم
green	akhḍar/ khaḍra	أخضر
greengrocer	khuḍari	خضري
grey	rumādi	رمادي
to guess	Hazzar, yiHazzar	حزّر
guide (person)	murshid/a	مرشد
guidebook	daleel	دليل
guitar	geetār	جيتار
gym	zhim	جيم
gymnastics	zhimnaas-teek	جمناستيك

H

hair	sha'r	شعر
hairbrush	fursha	فرشة
half	nuṣ	نصّ
half a litre	nuṣ litr	نصّ لتر
hammer	shakoosh	شاكوش
hand	eed	إيد
handbag	shanṭa	شنطة
handicrafts	muntagaat yadawiyya	منتجات يدويّة
handmade	shughl yadawi	شغل يدوي
handsome	waseem	وسيم
happy	mabsooṭ	مبسوط
harbour	meena	ميناء
hard (difficult)	ṣa'b/a	صعب
hard (surface)	gaamid/a	جامد
harrassment	taḍyee^c	تضييق
hash	Hashish	حشيش
to have	'and	عند

Do you have ...?
'andak ...? عندك ؟

I have ...
'andi... عندي ...

he	huwwa	هو
head	ra^{c}s	رأس
headache	ṣudā'	صداع
health	ṣiHHa	صحّة
to hear	simi', yisma'	سمع
hearing aid	samaa'a	سمّاعة
heart	alb	قلب
heat	Harāra	حرارة
heater	daffaaya	دفّاية
heater (hot water)	sakhkhaan	سخّان
heavy	ti^{c}eel/a	ثقيل

Hello.
ahlan أهلاً.

Hello! (answering telephone)
alō ألو

helmet	khōza	خوذة

Help! ilhaᶜni!		إلحقني!
to help	saa'id, yisaa'id	ساعد
herbs	'ushb	عشب
herbalist	'aṭṭār	عطّار
here	hina	هنا
high	'aalee/ya	عالي
high blood pressure	ḍaghṭ damm 'āli	ضغط دمّ عالي
high school	madrassa sanawiya	مدرسة ثانوية
hill	tal	تل
Hindu	hindusi	هندوسي
to hire	ᶜaggar, yiᶜaggar	أجّر
holiday (or festival)	'eed	عيد
holidays	ᶜagaaza	أجازة
homeless	musharadeen	مشردين
homosexual	suHāqiyya (f)	سحاقيّة
	looṭee (m)	لوطي
honey	'asal	عسل
honeymoon	shahr il 'asal	شهر العسل
horrible	faẓee'	فظيع
horse	faras	فرس
horse riding	rukoob il khayl	ركوب الخيل
hospital	mustashfa	مستشفى
hot	sukhn/a	سخن
It's hot. (weather) ig gaw Harr		الجو حار.
to be hot	harrān/a	حرّان
hot water	mayya sukhna	ميّة سخنة
house	bayt	بيت
housework	shughl il bayt	شغل البيت
how	izzay	إزّاي
How do I get to ...? aruH il ... izzay?		أروح ال... إزّاي؟
How do you say ...? bitᶜool ... izzay?		بتقول ... إزاي؟
hug	Huḍn	حضن
human rights	Huᶜooᶜ il insaan	حقوق الإنسان
a hundred	miyya	ميّة
to be hungry	ga'aan/a	جعان
husband	gōz	جوز

I

I	ana	أنا
ice	talg	ثلج
ice pick	kassārit talg	كسارة ثلج
ice cream	zhelaati •	جلاتي •
	ays kireem	أيس كريم
identification	baṭāᶜa	بطاقة
idiot	'abeeṭ/a	عبيط
if	iza	إذا
ill	'ayyaan/a	عيّان
immigration	higra	هجرة
important	muhimm	مهم
It's (not) important. huwa (mish) muhimm		هو (مش) مهم.
in a hurry	mista'gil/a	مستعجل
in front of	ᶜuddaam	قدّام
included	shaamil	شامل
income tax	ḍareeba	ضريبة
incomprehensible	ghayr mafhoom	غير مفهوم
indicator (car)	ishāra	إشارة
indigestion	'asir haḍm	عسر هضم

I

DICTIONARY

industry	ṣinā'a	صناعة
inequality	it tafaawit	التفاوت
to inject	Haᶜan, yiHᶜin	حقن
injection	Huᶜna	حقنة
injury	garH	جرح
inside	guwwa	جوة
instructor	mudarris/a	مدرس
insurance	taᶜmeen	تأمين
interesting	ẓarif	ظريف
intermission	istirāHa	إستراحة
international	dawli	دولي
interview	muᶜabla	مقابلة
island	gazeera	جزيرة
itch	harsh	هرش
itinerary	burnaamig ir riHla	برنامج الرحلة

J

jail	sigin	سجن
jar	barṭamān	برطمان
jealous	ghayraan/a	غيران
jeans	zheens	جينز
jeep	'arabiyit zheep	عربية جيب
jewellery	migaw harāt	مجوهرات
Jewish	yihoodi/yya	يهودي
job	waẓeefa	وظيفة
job advertisement	i'laan waẓeefa	إعلان وظيفة
joke	nukta	نكتة
to joke (with)	hazzar, yihazzar (ma'a)	هزّر (مع)
journalist	ṣuHafi/yya	صحفي
journey	riHla	رحلة
judge	qaḍi	قاضي
juice	'aṣeer	عصير
to jump	naṭ, yinuṭ	نطّ
jumper	buloofar	بلوفر
justice	'adaala	عدالة

K

key	muftaaH	مفتاح
to kill	mawwit, yimawwit	موت
kilogram	keelu	كيلو
kilometre	kilumitr	كيلومتر
kind	ṭayyib/a	طيب
kindergarten	Haḍāna	حضانة
king	malik	ملك
kiss	bōsa	بوسة
to kiss	baas, yiboos	باس
kitchen	maṭbakh	مطبخ
kitten	ᶜuṭṭa	قطّة
knapsack	shanṭit ḍahr	شنطة ظهر
knee	rukba	ركبة
knife	sikeena	سكينة
to know	'irif, yi'raf	عرف

I don't know.
ma'arafsh. معرفش.

L

lace	dantilla	دانتيلا
lake	buHeera	بحيرة
land	arḍ	أرض
language	lugha	لغة
large	kibeer/a	كبير
last	aakhir	آخر
last night	imbaariH bil layl	امبارح بالليل
late	mit'akhkhir/a	متأخر
laugh	ḍiHik, yiḍHak	ضحك
launderette	tanturleeh	تنتورليه
law	qanoon	قانون
lawyer	muHaami	محامي
laxatives	mulayyin	مليّن
lazy	kaslaan/a	كسلان
leader	qāᶜid	قائد
to learn	ᶜit'allim, yit'allim	إتعلّم

DICTIONARY

leather	gild	جلد
to be left (behind/over)	fiḍil, yifḍal	فضل
left (not right)	shimaal	شمال
left-wing	yasāri/yya	يساري
leg	rigl	رجل
leg (in race)	marHala	مرحلة
legislation	tashree'	تشريع
lens	'adasa	عدسة
less (than)	a^call (min)	أقلّ (من)
letter	gawaab	جواب
liar	kaddaab	كذّاب
library	maktaba	مكتبة
lice	aml	قمل
to lie	kidib, yikdib	كذب
life	Hayaa	حياة
lift (elevator)	asanseer	أسانسير
to light	walla^c, yiwalla^c	ولّع
light (sun/ lamp)	noor	نور
light (adj)	khafeef	خفيف
light (colour)	faatiH/a	فاتح
light bulb	lamba	لمبة
lighter	wallaa'a	ولّاعة
to like	Habb, yiHibb	حب
line	khaṭ	خط
lip	shiffa	شفّة
lipstick	aHmar shafaayif	أحمر شفايف
to listen	simi', yisma'	سمع
little (small)	ṣughayyir/a	صغير
a little (amount)	shiwayya	شوية
to live (life)	'aash, yi'eesh	عاش
to live (some-where)	sikin, yuskun	سكن
local	maHalli	محلّي
location	makaan	مكان
lock	kalōn	كالون
to lock	sakk, yisukk	سك
long	ṭaweel	طويل
long distance (phone call)	tarank	ترنك
to look	baṣṣ, yibuṣṣ	بصّ
to look after	khad, yaakhud baal min	أخذ باله من
to look for	dawwar, yidawwar ('ala)	دور على
loose change	fakka	فكّة
to lose	ḍayya', yiḍayya'	ضيع
loser	khasrān/a	خسران
loss	khusāra	خسارة
a lot	kiteer	كتير
loud	'aali/ya	عالي
to love	Habb, yiHibb	حب
lover	Habeeb	حبيب
low	wāṭi	واطي
low	ḍaghṭ	ضغط
blood pressure	damm wāṭi	دم واطي
loyal	mukhliṣa	مخلص
luck	Haẓẓ	حظ
lucky	maHẓooẓ/a	محظوظ
luggage	shunat	شنط
lump	waram	ورم
lunch	ghada	غدا
luxuries	kamaliyyaat	كماليات

M

machine	makana/aat	مكنة
mad	magnoon/a	مجنون
made (of)	ma'mool/a (min)	معمول (من)
magazine	magalla	مجلّة
magician	sāHir	ساحر
mail	busta	بوستة
mailbox	ṣandoo^c busta	صندوق بوستة
main road	ṭaree^c ra^ceesi	طريق رئيسى

main square	maydaan ra^{c}eesi	ميدان رئيسي
majority	aghlabiyya	أغلبيّة
to make	'amal, yi'mil	عمل
make-up	makyāzh	ماكياج
man	rāgil, riggaala	راجل
manager	mudeer/a	مدير
manual worker	'aamil	عامل
many	kiteer	كتير
map	khareeṭa	خريطة

Can you show me on the map?
mumkin tiwareeni 'alil khariṭa?
ممكن تورّيني على الخريطة؟

marijuana	bango	بانجو
marital status	il Haala il igtima-'iyya	الحالة الإجتماعية
market	soo^c	سوق
marriage	gawaaz	جواز
to marry	^{c}itgawwiz, yitgawwiz	إتجوز

I'm married.
ana mitgawwiz/a
انا متجوّز.

marvellous	haayyil	هايل
mass (Catholic)	^{c}uddaas	قدّاس
massage	masāzh	مسّاج
mat	Haṣeera	حصيرة
matches	kibreet	كبريت
mattress	martaba	مرتبة
maybe	yimkin	يمكن
mayor	muHāfiz • 'umda	محافظ • عمدة
mechanic	mikaneeki/yya	ميكانيكي
medal	midalya	ميداليّة
medicine	dawa	دواء
Mediterranean	il baHr il abyaḍ il mutawassiṭ	البحر الأبيض المتوسط
to meet	it^{c}aabil, yit^{c}aabil (ma'a)	اتقابل (مع)
member	'uḍw/a	عضو
menstruation	id dawra	الدورة
menu	minay • kart	كرت • ميني
message	risaala	رسالة
metal	ma'dan	معدن
meteor	shuhub	شهب
metre	mitr	متر
midnight	is saa'a itnāshir bil layl	الساعة اتنا عشر بالليل
migraine	ṣudā' niṣfi	صداع نصفي
military service	khidma 'askariyya	خدمة عسكريّة
milk	laban	لبن
millimetre	milli	ملّي
million	milyōn	مليون
mind	'a^{c}l	عقل
mineral water	mayya ma'daniyya	ميّة معدنية
minute	di^{c}ee^{c}a	دقيقة
mirror	miraaya	مراية
miscarriage	ig-haaḍ	إجهاض
to miss (someone)	waHash, yiwHash	وحش
mistake	ghalṭa	غلطة
to mix	khalaṭ, yikhliṭ	خلط
mobile phone	maHmool	محمول
modem	mōdem	مودم
moisturiser	kireem	كريم
monastery	dayr	دير
money	filoos	فلوس
monk	raahib	راهب

month	shahr	شهر
monument (antiquities)	asār	آثار
moon	amar	قمر
more	aktar	أكثر
morning	ṣubH	صبح
mosque	gāmi'	جامع
mosquito coil	ṭārid in namoos	طارد النا موس
mosquito net	namoosiyya	نا موسيّة
mother	umm	أم
mother-in-law	Hama	حماة
motorboat	lansh	لانش
motorcycle	mutusikl	موتوسيكل
mountain	gabal	جبل
mouse	fār	فار
mouth	bu^{c}	بق
movie	film	فيلم
mud	ṭeen	طين
Mum	mama	ما ما
muscle	'adala	عضلة
museum	matHaf	متحف
music	museeqa	موسيقى
musician	museeqi	موسيقي
Muslim	muslim/a	مسلم

N

name	ism	إسم
nappy	kafoola	كفولة
nappy rash	tasallukh	تسلّخ
nationality	ginsiyya	جنسيّة
nature	iṭ ṭabee'a	الطبيعة
nausea	dōkha	دوخة
near	urayyib/a (min)	قريّب (من)
necessary	laazim	لازم
necklace	'u^{c}d	عقد
to need	iHtaag, yiHtaag	إحتاج
needle (sewing)	ibra	إبرة
net	shabaka	شبكة
never (after negative statement)	abadan	أبداً
new	gideed/a	جديد
news	khabar	خبر
newsagency	wikaalat anba^{c}	وكالة أنباء
newspaper	gurnāl	جرنال
newspapers	garaayid	جرايد
New Year	ras is sana	رأس السنة
next	illi gayy/a	اللي جاي
next to	gamb	جنب
next week	il usboo' illi gayy	الأسبوع اللي جاي
nice	laṭeef/a	لطيف
nickname	ism id dala'	إسم الدلع
night	layl/a	ليلة
tonight	il layla dee	الليلة دي
no	la^{c}	لأ
noise	dawsha	دوشة
noisy	dawsha	دوشة
non-direct	gheyr mubāshir	غير مبا شر
none	mafeesh	مفيش
noon	ḍuhr	ظهر
north	shimaal	شمال
nose	manakheer	مناخير
notebook	kurrāsa	كرّاسة
nothing	wala Haaga	ولا حاجة
not yet	lissa	لسّه
novel (book)	riwaaya	رواية
now	dilwa^{c}ti	دلوقتي
nuclear energy	iṭṭāqa in nawawiyya	الطاقة النووية
nun	rāhiba	راهبة
nurse	mumarriḍ/a	ممرّضة

O

obvious	wāḍiH	واضح
ocean	muHeeṭ	محيط
offence	tahma	تهمة
office	maktab	مكتب
office worker	muwaẓẓaf	موظّف
offside	tasallul	تسلّل
often	kiteer	كتير
oil (cooking/ crude)	zayt	زيت

OK.
maashi
ماشي.
It's OK.
mish baṭāl
مش بطّال.

old (thing)	adeem	قديم
old (not young)	kibeer	كبير
old person	kibeer fis sinn	كبير في السن
olive oil	zayt zaytoon	زيت زيتون
olives	zaytoon	زيتون
Olympic Games	il al'aab il ulimbiyya	الألعاب الأوليمبيّة
on	'ala	على
on time	fil mi'aad	في الميعاد
once • one time	marra	مرة
only	bas	بسّ
open	maftooH	مفتوح
to open	fataH, yiftaH	فتح
opening	iftitaaH	إفتتاح
opera	ubira	أوبرا
opera house	dār il ubira	دار الأوبرا
operation	'amaliyya	عمليّة
operator	'aamil/a tilifōnaat	عامل تليفونات
opinion	raᶜy	رأي
opposite	ᶜuṣād	قصاد
or	ow	أو
orange (colour)	burtuᶜāli	برتقالي
orchestra	urkistra	أوركسترا
order	amr	أمر
to order (request)	ṭalab, yuṭlub	طلب
ordinary	'aadi	عادي
organise	naẓam, yinaẓam	نظّم
original	asli	أصلي
other	taani/taanya	تاني
outgoing	munṭaliq/a	منطلق
outside	barra	برّة
over	fuᶜ	فوق
overcoat	balṭu	بالطو
overdose	gar'a ziyaada	جرعة زيادة
to owe	'alay	عليه
owner	ṣāHib/a	صاحب
oxygen	uksizheen	أكسجين
ozone layer	ṭabaqat il ōzōn	طبقة الأوزون

P

pacifier (dummy)	titeena	تيتّينة
package	laffa	لفّة
packet (general)	baaku	باكو
packet (of cigarettes)	'ilbit (sagayyir)	علبة سجاير
padlock	afl	قفل
page	ṣafHa	صفحة
pain	waga'	وجع
painful	biyuwaga'	بيوجع
to paint (not art)	dahan, yidhin	دهن
to paint (art)	rasam, yirsim	رسم
painter (of pictures)	rassaam/a	رسّام

paintings	luHaat	لوحات
pair (a couple)	gōz	جوز
palace	qaṣr	قصر
pan	Halla	حلّة
frying pan	ṭāsa	طاسة
pap smear	pap smeer • masaH 'ala 'unq ir raHm	مسح علي عنق الرّحم
paper	wara^c	ورق
(sheet of)	wara^{c}a	ورقة
parcel	ṭard	طرد
parents	ahl	أهل
a park	gineyna	جنينة
to park	rakan, yirkin	ركن
parliament	barlamān	برلمان
part	guz^c	جزء
party	Hafla	حفلة
party (political)	Hizb	حزب
to pass	faat, yifoot	فات
passenger	raakib/a	راكب
passive	maghool	مغول
passport	basboor • gawaz is safr	جواز السفر
passport number	raqam gawaz is safr	رقم جواز السفر
past	māḍi	ماضي
path	mamsha	ممشى
patient (adj)	ṣaboor	صبور
to pay	dafa', yidfa'	دفع
payment	daf'	دفع
peace	salaam	سلام
peak	qimma	قمّة
pedestrians	mushā	مشاة
pen (ballpoint)	alam	قلم
pencil	alam ruṣāṣ	قلم رصاص
penknife	moos	موس

people	naas	ناس
pepper	filfil	فلفل
percent	fil miyya	في الميّة
performance	'arḍ	عرض
permanent	daayim/a	دايم
permission	^{c}izn	إذن
permit	taṣreeH	تصريح
person	shakhs	شخص
personality	shakhṣiyya	شخصيّة
to perspire	'iri^c, ya'ra^c	عرق
petition	iltimaas	إلتماس
petrol	banzeen	بنزين
pharmacy	ṣaydaliyya	صيدلية
phonecard	kārt tilifōn	كارت تليفون
photo	ṣoora	صورة

Can I take a photo?
mumkin aṣawwar? ممكن أصوّر ؟

photographer	musaw-warāti/yya	مصوّراتي
photography	taṣweer	تصوير
to pick up (carry)	shaal, yisheel	شال
piece	Hitta	حتّة
pig	khanzeer	خنزير
pill	Habbaaya	حبّاية
the Pill	Huboob mana' il Haml	حبوب منع الحمل
pillow	makhadda	مخدّة
pillowcase	kees makhadda	كيس مخدّة
pine	ṣinōbar	صنوبر
pink	bambi	بمبي
pipe (plumbing)	masoora	ماسورة
place	makaan	مكان
place of birth	maHal il milaad	محل الميلاد
plain (unadorned)	saada	سادة

plane	ṭayyāra	طيّارة
planet	kawkab	كوكب
plant	zara'	زرع
to plant	zara', yizra'	زرع
plastic	bilastik	بلاستيك
plate	ṭabaᶜ	طبق
platform	raṣeef	رصيف
play (theatre)	masraHiyya	مسرحيّة
to play cards	yila'ib kutsheena	لعب كتشينة
to play (a game)	li'ib, yil'ab	لعب
to play (music)	'azaf, yi'zif	عزف
player (sports)	laa'ib	لاعب
playing cards	kutsheena	كتشينة
plug (bath)	saddaada	سدّادة
plug (electricity)	feesha	فيشة
pocket	geeb	جيب
poetry	shi'r	شعر
to point (to)	shaawir, yishaawir ('ala)	شاور (على)
poker	bookir	بوكر
police	bulees	بوليس
politics	siyaasa	سيا سة
political speech	khuṭba siyaasiyya	خطبة سيا سيّة
politicians	siyaasi-yiyeen	سياسيّين
pollen	Huboob il luqāH	حبوب اللقاح
pollution	talawwus	تلوّث
pool (game)	bilyardu	بلياردو
pool (swimming)	Hammaam is sibaaHa	حمام السبا حة
poor	faᶜeer/a	فقير
popular	maHboob/a	محبوب
port	meena	ميناء
possible	mumkin	ممكن

It's (not) possible.
(mish) mumkin (مش) ممكن.

postcard	kart bustaal	كرت بوستال
postcode	raqm bareed	رقم بريد
postage (stamp)	ṭābi'	طابع
poster	mulṣaᶜa	ملصقة
post office	il busṭa	البوستة
pot (ceramic)	aṣriyya	قصريّة
pot (dope)	bango	بانجو
pottery	fukhār	فخّار
poverty	faᶜr	فقر
power (strength)	quwwa	قوّة
prayer	muṣalli	مصلّي
to prefer	faḍḍal, yifaḍḍal	فضّل
pregnant	Haamil	حامل
to prepare	gahhiz, yigahhiz	جهّز
present (gift)	hidiyya	هديّة
present (time)	il mawgood	الموجود
presentation	taᶜdeem	تقديم
presenter (TV, etc)	muzee'	مذيع
president	raᶜees	رئيس
pressure	ḍaght	ضغط
pretty	Hilw	حلو
prevent	mana'	منع
price	taman	تمن
pride	ghuroor	غرور
priest	assees	قسيس
prime minister	raᶜees il wuzara	رئيس الوزارة
prison	sigin	سجن
prisoner	masgoon	مسجون
private	khāṣṣ	خاص
private hospital	mustashfa khāṣṣ	مستشفى خاص

P DICTIONARY

privatisation	khaṣkhaṣa	خصخصة
to produce	antag, yintig	أنتج
producer	muntig/a	منتج
profession	mihna	مهنة
profit	ribH	ربح
profitability	ribHiyya	ربحيّة
program	birnaamig	برنامج
projector	pruzhektoor	بروجكتور
promise	wa'd	وعد
proposal	iqtirāH	إقتراح
to protect	Hama, yiHmi	حمى
protected species	kaa^cinat maHmiyya	كائنة محميّة
protest	iHtigaag	إحتجاج
to protest	iHtag, yaHtag	إحتج
public toilet	durit mayya 'aama	دورة مياه عامّة
to pull	saHab, yisHab	سحب
pump	ṭurumba	طرمبة
puncture	khurm	خرم
to punish	'aaqib, yi'aaqib	عاقب
puppy	kalba	كلبة
pure	ṭāhir	طاهر
purple	banafsigi	بنفسجي
to push	za^c, yizu^c	زقّ
to put	Haṭṭ, yiHuṭṭ	حطّ

Q

qualifications	mu^cahilaat	مؤهّلات
quality	gooda	جودة
quarantine	karanteena	كرنتينة
quarrel	khinā^ca	خناقة
quarter	rub'	ربع
queen	malika	ملكة
question	su^caal	سؤال
question (topic)	mas'aala	مسألة
to question	sa'al, yis'al	سأل
queue	ṭaboor	طابور
quick	saree'	سريع
quiet	haadi/ya	هادي
to quit	baṭṭal, yibaṭṭal	بطّل

R

rabbit	arnab	أرنب
race (biological)	ṣanf	صنف
race (sport)	saba^c	سبق
racism	tafri^ca 'unṣuriyya	تفرقة عنصريّة
racquet	maḍrab	مضرب
radiator (car)	radiyateer	ردياتير
railroad	sikkat Hadeed	سكّة حديد
railway station	maHaṭṭit ^caṭr	محطّة قطر
rain	maṭar	مطر

It's raining.
bitmaṭṭar
بتمطر.

rally (political)	muzahra	مظا هرة
rape	ightiṣāb	إغتصاب
rare	naadir	نادر
rash	ṭafH	طفح
rat	fār	فار
raw	nayy/a	ني
razor (blades)	moos	موس
to read	^cara, yi'ra	قرأ
ready (for)	musta'idd/a (li)	مستعد (ل)
to realise	'araf	عرف
reason	sabab	سبب
receipt	waṣl	وصل
to receive (someone)	ista^cbil, yista^cbil	إستقبل
to receive (something)	istalam, yistilim	إستلم
recent	urayyib	قريّب
recently	min urayyib	من قريّب

R

DICTIONARY

to recognise	'irif, yi'raf	عرف
to recommend	^{c}iqtaraH, yaqtariH	إقترح
recording	tasgeel	تسجيل
red	aHmar/Hamra	أحمر
referee	Hakam	حكم
reference (letter)	shahaadit seer wi sulook	شهادة سير وسلوك
reflection (mirror)	in'akaas	إنعكاس
reflection (thinking)	ta^{c}mul	تأمّل
refrigerator	tallaaga	ثلاّجة
refugee	laagi^c	لاجيء
refund	istirdaad	إسترداد
to refund	istarid, yistirid	إسترد
to refuse	rafaḍ, yirfuḍ	رفض
regional	iqleemi	إقليمي
registered letter	gawaab misaggil	جواب مسجّل
to regret	nidim, yindam	ندم
relationship	'ilāqa	علاقة
to relax	irtaH, yirtaH	إرتاح
religion	deen	دين
religious (of religion)	deenee	ديني
religious (person)	mutadayyin/a	متديّن
to remember	iftakar, yiftikir	إفتكر
remote	ba'eed	بعيد
remote control	il reemōt	الريموت
rent	^{c}igār	إيجار
to rent	^{c}aggar, yi^{c}aggar	أجّر
to repeat	karrar, yikarrar	كرر
republic	gumhuriyya	جمهوريّة
reservation	Hagz	حجز
to reserve	Hagaz, yiHgiz	حجز
resignation	istiqāla	إستقالة

respect	iHtirām	إحترام
rest (relaxation)	^{c}istirāHa	إستراحة
rest (what's left)	baa'i	باقي
to rest	istirayyaH, yistirayyaH	إستريّح
restaurant	maṭ'am	مطعم
résumé	seevee	سي في
retired	mutaqā'ad/a	متقاعد
return (ticket)	tazkara zihaab wi 'awda	تذكرة ذهاب و عودة
to return	rigi', yirga'	رجع
review	murag'a	مرجع
rhythm	ritm	رتم
rice	ruzz	رز
rich (food)	dasim	دسم
rich (wealthy)	ghani/yya	غني
to ride (a horse)	rikib, yirkab	ركب
right (correct)	maẓbooṭ	مظبوط
right (not left)	yimeen	يمين
to be right	ṣaH, yiṣaH	صح

You're right.
'andak Ha^c
عندك حق.

civil rights	Hu^{c}oo^c madaniyya	حقوق مدنية
right now	Haalan	حالاً
right-wing	il yimeen	اليمين
ring (on finger)	khaatim	خاتم
ring (of phone)	garas	جرس

I'll give you a ring.
Hataṣṣal beek/i
حاتّصل بيك.

ring (sound)	garas	جرس
rip off	naṣb	نصب

risk	mukhatra	مخاطرة
river	nahr	نهر
road (main)	ṭaree^c	طريق
to rob	sara^c, yisra^c	سرق
rock	ṣakhr	صخر
romance	rumansi	رومانسي
room	ōḍa •	أوضة •
	ghurfa	غرفة
room number	raqam il ghurfa	رقم الغرفة
rope	Habl	حبل
round	midawwar/a	مدور
(at the) roundabout	ṣaniyya	صنيّة
rowing	tagdeef	تجديف
rubbish	zabaala	زبالة
rug	siggaada	سجّادة
ruins	asār	آثار
rules	qawā'id	قواعد
to run	giri, yigri	جري

S

sad	Hazeen/a	حزين
safe (adj)	amaan	أمان
safe (n)	khazna	خزنة
saint (Muslim)	sayyid/sayyida	سيد
saint (Christian)	qiddees	قديس
salary	murattab	مرتّب
(on) sale	ukazyōn	أوكّازيون
sales department	qism il mabi'aat	قسم المبيعات
salt	malH	ملح
same	nafs	نفس
sand	raml	رمل
sanitary napkins	fooṭa ṣiHHiya	فوطة صحيّة
Saturday	yōm il sabt	يوم السبت
to save (time, money, etc)	waffar, yiwaffar	وفّر
to say	aal, yi^{c}ool	قال
to scale (climb)	ṭal'a, yiṭla'	طلع
scarf (neck)	kufiyya	كوفيّة
scarf (women's silk)	isharb	إيشارب
school	madrasa	مدرسة
science	'ilm	علم
scientist	'aalim	عالم
scissors	ma^{c}aṣ	مقص
to score a goal	gaab gōl	جاب جول
scoreboard	il 'ārḍa	العارضة
screen (TV or film)	shaasha	شاشة
script	khaṭ	خط
sculpture	naHt	نحت
sea	baHr	بحر
seasick	duwār il baHr	دوار البحر
seaside	shāṭi il baHr	شاطيء البحر
seat	kursi	كرسي
seatbelt	Hizam amaan	حزام أمان
second (time)	sanya	ثانية
second	taani/ya	تاني
secretary	sikirteera	سكرتيرة
to see	shaaf, yishoof	شاف

See you later.
ashoofak ba'deen أشوفك بعدين.

See you tomorrow.
ashoofak bukra أشوفك بكرة.

selfish	anaani/ya	أناني
to sell	baa', yibee'	باع

to send	ba'at, yib'at	بعت
sensible	'āᶜil/a	عاقل
sentence (prison)	Hukm	حكم
sentence (words)	gumla	جملة
to separate	faṣal, yifṣil	فصل
series (TV)	musalsal	مسلسل
serious	gadd	جدّ
service (assistance)	khidma	خدمة
service (Orthodox or Catholic)	uddās	قدّاس
several	kiteer	كتير
to sew	khayyaṭ, yikhayyaṭ	خيّط
sex	gins	جنس
sexism	tafri'a ginsiyya	تفرقة جنسية
shade/ shadow	ẓill	ظلّ
shampoo	shaamboo	شامبو
shape	shakl	شكل
to share (with)	shaarik, yishaarik	شارك
to share a dorm	itᶜaasim ghurfa	إتقاسم غرفة
to shave	Hala', yiHla'	حلق
she	hiyya	هي
sheep	kharoof	خروف
sheet (bed)	milaaya	ملاية
sheet (of paper)	waraᶜa	ورقة
shelf	raff	رفّ
shell	ṣadaf	صدف
ship	markib	مركب
to ship	na'al, yin'il	نقل
shirt	amees	قميص
shoe shop	maHall gizam	محل جزم

shoes (pair)	gazma	جزمة
to shoot (someone)	ṭakhkh, yiṭukhkh	طخ، يطخ
to shoot at	ḍarab, yiḍrab nār	ضرب نار
shop	maHall	محل

to go shopping
tasawwuq yatsawwaq تسوّق

short	uṣayyar/a	قصير
short films	aflaam uṣayyara	أفلام قصيرة
short stories	qiṣaṣ uṣayyara	قصص قصيرة
shortage	naᶜs	نقص
shorts	shurt	شورت
shoulder	kitf	كتف
to shout	za'aᶜ, yiza'aᶜ	زعّق
show (stage)	'arḍ	عرض
to show	warra, yiwarri	ورى

Can you show me on the map?
mumkin tiwarrini 'alil khareeṭa?
ممكن تورّيني على الخريطة؟

shower	dush	دش
shrine	ḍareeH	ضريح
to shut	ᶜafal, yiᶜfil	قفل
shy	maksoof/a	مكسوف
sick	'ayyaan/a	عيّان
sickness	maraḍ	مرض
side	naHya	ناحية
sign	ishāra	إشارة
to sign	maḍa, yimḍi	مضى
signature	imḍa	إمضاء
silk	Hareer	حرير
of silver	faḍḍi	فضي
similar (to)	zayy	زي
simple	baseeṭ	بسيط
sin	ism	إثم
since (May)	min (Mayu)	من (مايو)

to sing	ghanna, yighanni	غنّى
singer	mughanni/yya	مغنّي
single (person)	'aazib/a	عازب
single (unique)	waHeed/a	وحيد
single room	ghurfa lishakhṣ waaHid	غرفة لشخص واحد
sister	ukht	أخت
to sit	a$^{c'}$ad, yu$^{c'}$ud	أقعد
size (clothes/ shoes)	ma^{c}aas	مقاس
size (of objects)	Hagm	حجم
skin	gild	جلد
sky	samaa	سما
sleep	nōm	نوم
to sleep	naam, yinaam	نام
sleeping bag	sleeping baag	سليبن باج
sleeping pills	Huboob munawwima	حبوب منومة
sleepy	na'saan/a	نعسان
slide (film)	shareeHa	شريحة
slow	baṭee^{c}	بطيء
slowly	bishweesh	بشويش
small	ṣughayyar/a	صغير
smell	reeHa	ريحة
to smell	shamm, yishimm	شم
to smile	ibtasam, yibtisim	إبتسم
to smoke	dakhkhan, yidakhkhan	د خّن
soap	ṣaboon/a	صابون
soap opera	tamsiliyya	تمثيلية
soccer	kōra	كرة
social sciences	'uloom il igtima'iyya	علوم الإجتماعية
social security	id ḍamān il igtimaa'i	الضمان الإجتماعى
socialist	ishtirā-ki/yya	إشتراكي
solid	gaamid/a	جامد
some	ba'ḍ	بعض
some of them	ba'ḍuhum	بعضهم
someone	Hadd	حد
something	Haaga	حاجة
sometimes	aHyaanan	أحياناً
son	ibn	ابن
song	ghinwa	غنوة
soon	^{c}urayyib	قريباً

I'm sorry.
aasif/asfa آسف.

sound	ṣōt	صوت
south	ganoob	جنوب
souvenir	tizkār	تذكار
space	faḍā^{c}	فضاء
to speak	kallim, yikallim	كلّم
special	khuṣooṣi	خصوصي
specialist	mutakhaṣ-ṣis/a	متخصّص
speed	sur'a	سرعة
speed limit	Hadd is sura'a	حد السرعة
spicy (hot)	Haami	حامي
sport	riyāḍa	رياضة
sportsperson	riyādi/ya	رياضي
sprain	gaz'a	جزع
spring (coil)	susta	سستة
spring (season)	ir rabee'	الربيع
square (shape)	murabba'	مربع
square (in town)	midaan	ميدان
stadium	istaad	الستاد
stage (theatre)	khashabit il masraH	خشبة المسرح
stairway	sillim	سلّم
stamps	ṭābi'	طابع

standard (usual)	'aadi/ya	عادي
star	nigma	نجمة
to start	bada^c, yibda^c	بدأ
station	maHaṭṭa	محطّة
stationers	maktaba	مكتبة
statue	timsaal	تمثال
to stay (remain)	a^{c}ad, yu$^{c'}$ud	قعد
to stay (somewhere)	nizil, yinzil (fee)	نزل (في)
to steal	sara^c, yisra^c	سرق
steam	bukhār	بخار
step (stair)	sillim	سلّم
stomach	mi'da	معدة
stomachache	maghaṣ	مغص
stone	Hagar	حجر
stop	maw^{c}if	موقف
to stop	wi^{c}if, yu^{c}af	وقف

Stop!
u^{c}af! أوقف!

storm	'āṣifa	عاصفة
story	Hikaaya	حكاية
stove	butagaaz	بوتجاز
straight (ahead)	dughri	دغري
strange	ghareeb/a	غريب
stranger	ghaarib/a	غارب
street	shaari'	شارع
strength	quwwa	قوّة
strike	iḍrāb	إضراب
string	dubāra	دبارة
strong	shideed/a	شديد
stubborn	'aneed/a	عنيد
student	ṭālib/a	طالب
stupid	ghabi/ya	غبي
style	usloob	أسلوب
suburb (district)	ḍāHiyya	ضاحية
subway station	maHatit mitru	محطة مترو
success	nagaaH	نجاح
to suffer	'aana, yi'aani	عانى
sugar	sukkar	سكّر
suitcase	shanṭa	شنطة
summer	iṣ ṣayf	الصيف
sun	shams	شمس
sunblock	kreym ḍid ish shams	كريم ضد الشمس
sunburn	lafHit shams	لفحة شمس
sunglasses	naḍḍārit shams	نظّارة شمس
sunny	mishamis	مشمّس
sunrise	il fagr	الفجر
sunset	il ghuroob	الغروب

Sure.
akeed أكيد.

surface mail	bareed 'aadi	بريد عادي
surname	ism il gadd	إسم الجد
surprise	mufag^{c}a	مفاجأة
to survive	'aash, yi'eesh	عاش
sweater	buloofar	بلوفر
sweet	Hilw/a	حلو
to swim	sabaH, yisbaH	سبح
swimming	sibāHa	سباحة
swimming pool	Hammaam is sibaaHa	حمّام السباحة
swimsuit	mayō	مايوه
sword	sayf	سيف
sympathetic	mit'āṭaf	متعاطف
synagogue	ma'bad yehoodi	معبد يهودي
synthetic	ilyaaf ṣinā'iyya	ألياف صناعيّة
syringe	siringa	سرينجة

T

table	tarabeeza	ترابيزة
table tennis	tinis iṭ ṭawla	تنس الطاولة
tail	deel	ديل
to take (away)	wadda, yiwaddi	ودى
to take (food, the train, etc)	khad, yakhud	أخد
to take photographs	ṣawwar, yiṣawwir	صوّر
to talk	kallim, yikallim	كلّم
tall	ṭaweel/a	طويل
tampons	tamboonaat	تمبونات
tasty	ṭa'amu kwayyis	طعمه كويّس
tax	ḍareeba	ضريبة
taxi	taksi	تاكس
teacher	mudarris/a	مدرّس
teaching	tadrees	تدريس
team	faree^c	فريق
tear (crying)	dam'	دمع
technique	tekneek	تكنيك
teeth	sinaan	أسنان
telegram	tillighrāf	تلّغراف
telephone	tilifoon	التليفون
to telephone	itkallim, yitkallim fee ttilifōn	إتكلّم في تليفون
telephone office	sintrāl	سنترال
telescope	teliskōp	تليسكوب
television	tilifizyōn	تليفزيون
to tell	aal, yi^cool	قال
temperature (fever)	sukhuniyya	سخونيّة
temperature (weather)	daragit il Harāra	درجة الحرارة
temple	ma'bad	معبد
tennis	tinis	تنس
tennis court	mal'ab tinis	ملعب تنس
tent	kheema	خيمة
tenth	'aashir	عاشر
terrible	faẓee'/a	فظيع
test (exam)	imtiHaan	إمتحان
test (medical)	taHleel	تحليل
to thank	shakar, yushkur	شكر

Thank you.
shukran
شكرًا.

theatre	tiyatru	تياترو
they (m)	humma	هم
they (f)	hiyya	هي
thick	tikheen/a	تخين
thief	Harāmi	حرامي
thin	rufayya'/a	رفيع
to think (about)	fakkar, yifakkar (fee)	فكّر (في)
to think (believe)	iftakar, yiftikir	إفتكر
third	taalit	تالت

one third
tilt
تلت

thirsty	'aṭshān/a	عطشان
this (one, m)	da	ده
this (one, f)	dee	دي
thought	fikra	فكرة
throat	zōr	زور
ticket	tazkara	تذكرة
ticket collector	kumsāri	كمساري
ticket office	shibaak it tazaakir	شباك التذاكر
tight	dayya^c/a	ديّق
time	wa^ct	وقت
timetable	gadwal	جدول
tin (can)	'ilba	علبة
tin opener	fattaaHit 'ilab	فتّاحة علب

tip (gratuity)	baksheesh	بكشيش
tired	ta'baan/a	تعبان
tissues	manadeel wara^c	مناديل ورق
toast	tōst	توست
tobacco	dukhaan	دخّان
tobacco kiosk	kushk dukhaan	كشك دخّان
today	innaharda	النهارده
together	ma'a ba'ḍ	مع بعض
toilet paper	wara^c tuwalit	ورق تواليت
toilets	tuwalit	تواليت
tomorrow	bukra	بكرة
tomorrow evening	bukra bil layl	بكرة بالليل
tomorrow morning	bukra iṣ ṣubH	بكرة الصبح
tonight	il layla dee	الليلة دي
too (as well)	kamaan	كمان
too expensive	ghaali giddan	غالي جداً
too much/many	kiteer	كتير
tooth (front)	sinn	سن
tooth (back)	ḍirs	ضرس
toothache	waga' fil ḍirs	وجع في الضرس
toothbrush	furshit sinaan	فرشة أسنان
toothpaste	ma'goon asnaan	معجون أسنان
torch (flash-light)	baṭṭariyya	بطّارية
to touch	lamas, yilmas	لمس
tour	riHla	رحلة
tourist	saayiH/saayHa	سايح
tourist information office	maktab is siyaaHa	مكتب السياحة

towards	naHyit	ناحية
towel	fooṭa	فوطة
tower	burg	برج
toxic waste	il nifayat is saama	النفايات السامة
track (foot, animal, car)	gurra	جره
track (path)	sikka	سكة
track (sports)	traak	تراك
trade union	niqāba	نقابة
traffic	muroor	مرور
traffic lights	ishārit muroor	إشارة مرور
train	aṭr	قطر
train station	maHaṭṭit aṭr	محطّة قطر
tram	turumaay	تروماي
transit lounge	taranseet	ترانسيت
to translate	targim, yitargim	ترجم
travel (books)	safar	سفر
to travel	saafir, yisaafir	سافر
travel agency	maktab siyaaHa	مكتب سياحة
travel sickness	dōkha	دوخة
travellers cheques	sheek siyaaHi	شيك سياحي
tree	shagara	شجرة
trendy (person)	hawaa^{c}i/yya	هوائي
trip	riHla	رحلة
trousers	banṭalōn	بنطلون
truck	loori	لوري
trust	siqa	ثقة
to trust	wasaq, yasiq (fee)	وثق (في)
truth	Ha^c	حق
to try (out)	garrab, yigarrab	جرب

to try (to attempt)	Haawil, yiHaawil	حاول
T-shirt	teeshirt	تي شيرت
tune	naghama	نغمة

Turn left.
khush shimaal | خش شمال.

Turn right.
khush yimeen | خش يمين.

TV	tilifizyōn	تليفزيون
twice	marratayn	مرتين
twin beds	sireerayn	سريرين
twins	tawā^{c}im	توائم
to type	ṭaba', yiṭba'	طبع
typical	'aada	عادي
tyres	kawitsh	كاوتش

U

umbrella	shamsiyya	شمسية
to under-stand	fihim, yifham	فهم
unemployed	'āṭil/a	عا طل
unemploy-ment	il biṭāla	البطالة
universe	il kōn	الكون
university	gaam'a	جامعة
unleaded	bidoon ruṣāṣ	بدون رصاص
unsafe	khaṭeer	خطير
until (June)	lighaayit (yoonyu)	لغاية (يونيو)
unusual	naadir/a	نادر
up	fō^{c}	فوق
uphill	a'la it tal	أعلى التل
urgent	mista'gil	مستعجل
useful	mufeed/a	مفيد

V

vacant	fāḍya	فاضي
vacation	agaaza	أجازة
vaccination	Hu^{c}na	حقنة
valley	wādi	وادي
Valley of the Kings	wadi il mulook	وادي الملوك
valuable (expensive)	ayyim	قيّم
value (price)	eema	قيمة
vegetables	khuḍār	خضار
vegetarian	nabaatee/yya	نباتي

I'm vegetarian.
ana nabaatee/yya | أنا نباتي.

vegetation	khaḍār	خضار
veil (head scarf)	Higaab	حجاب
veil (full face covering)	niqāb	نقاب
vein	'ir^{c}	عرق
venereal disease	amrāḍ tanasuliyya	أمراض تنا سلية
very	awi	قوي
video tape	shireeṭ vidyu	شريط فديو
view	manzar	منظر
village	qarya	قرية
virus	veerus	فيروس
visa	ta^{c}sheera	تأشيرة
to visit	zār, yizoor	زار
vitamins	vitameen	فيتامين
voice	ṣōt	صوت
volume (sound)	ṣōt	صوت
to vote	intakhab, yintikhib	إنتخب

W

Wait!
istanna! استنّى!

waiter	garsōn	جرسون
to walk	mishi, yimshi	مشي
wall (inside)	Heeṭa	حيطة
wall (outside)	soor	سور
to want	'aayiz/'ayza	عايز

I want
ana 'aayiz/'ayza عايز

war	Harb	حرب
wardrobe	dulaab	دولاب
warm	daafi/yya	دافي
to wash	ghasal, yighsil	غسل
wash cloth (flannel)	fooṭit wishsh	فوطة وش
washing machine	ghassaala	غسّالة
watch	saa'a	ساعة
to watch	itfarrag, yitfarrag	إتفرّج
water	mayya	ميّة
mineral water	mayya ma'daniyya	ميّة معدنيّة
waterfall	shalaal	شلاّل
watermelon	baṭṭeekh	بطّيخ
wave (sea)	mōg	موج
way	ṭareeᶜ	طريق

Please tell me the way to ...
min faḍlak, ooli iṭ ṭareeᶜ li ...
من فضلك قول لي الطريق ل ...

Which way?
ayy ṭareeᶜ? أي طريق؟

Way Out
khurug خروج

we	iHna	إحنا
weak	ḍa'eef/a	ضعيف
wealthy	ghani/yya	غني
to wear	libis, yilbis	لبس
weather	gaww	جو
wedding	faraH	فرح
wedding present	hidayyit il faraH	هدية الفرح
week	usboo'	أسبوع

this week
il usboo' da الأسبوع ده

weekend	nihaayit il usboo'	نهاية الأسبوع
to weigh	wazan, yiwzin	وزن
weight	wazn	وزن
welcome	ahlan wa sahlan	أهلاً وسهلاً
welfare	rifaaha	رفاهة
well (water)	beer	بير
west	gharb	غرب
wet	mablool/a	مبلول
what	ey	أيه

What's he saying?
biyᶜool ey? بيقول إيه؟

What time is it?
is sā'a kaam? الساعة كم؟

wheel	'agala	عجلة
wheelchair	kursi muta-Harrik	كرسي متحرك
when	imta	إمتى

When does it leave?
Hayimshi imta? حيمشي إمتى؟

where	fayn	فين

Where's the bank?
fayn il bank? فين البنك؟

white	abyaḍ	أبيض
who	meen	مين

Who is it?
meen da? مين ده ؟

Who are they?
meen dōl? مين دول ؟

whole	kull	كلّ
why	lay	ليه

Why is the museum closed?
il matHaf maᶜfool lay?
المتحف مقفول ليه؟

wide	waasi'/a	واسع
wife	mirāt	مرات
wild animal	Hayawaan	حيوان
to win	kisib, yiksab	كسب
wind	reeH	ريح
window	shibbaak	شبّاك
windscreen	barbireez	بربريز
wine	nibeet	نبيد
wings	igniHa	أجنحة
winner	faayiz/a	فايز
winter	ish shita	الشتاء
wire	silk	سلك
wise	'aaᶜil/a	عاقل
to wish	itmanna, yitmanna	اتمنّى
with	ma'a	مع
within	fee daakhil	في داخل

within an hour
khilaal saa'a خلال ساعة

without	min ghayr	من غير
without filter	min ghayr filtir	من غير فلتر
woman	sitt	ست
wonderful	haayil/a	هايل
wood	khashab	خشب
wool	ṣoof	صوف
word	kilma	كلمة
work	shughl	شغل
to work	ishtaghal, yishtaghal	اشتغل
work permit	taṣreeH 'amal	تصريح عمل
workshop	warsha	ورشة
the world	il 'aalam	العالم
World Cup	kas il 'aalam	كأس العالم
worms	dood	دود
worried	al'ᶜaan/a	قلقان
worship	it'abid, yit'abid	إتعبّد
worth	istaahil, yistaahil	إستاهل
wound	garH	جرح
to write	katab, yiktib	كتب
writer	kaatib/a	كاتب
wrong	ghalaṭ	غلط

I'm wrong.
ana ghalṭān/a أنا غلطان.

Y

year	sana	سنة

this year
il sana dee السنة دي

yellow	asfar	أصفر
yesterday	imbaariH	إمبارح
yesterday morning	imbaariH iṣ ṣubH	إمبارح الصّبح
yet	lissa	لسّة
you (m)	inta	إنت
you (f)	inti	إنت
you (pl)	intu	إنتوا
young	ṣugha-yyar/a	صغير
youth (collective)	shabaab	شباب
youth hostel	bayt ish shabaab	بيت الشّباب

Z

zebra	Humār mikhaṭaṭ	حمار مخطط
zoo	gineenit il Haya-wanaat	جنينة الحيوانات

ARABIC - ENGLISH

In the order of the Arabic English dictionary, no distinction is made between long and short vowels (a/ā o/ō), nor between emphatic and non-emphatic consonants (d/ḍ, s/ṣ, t/ṭ, z/ẓ). The presence of a glottal stop (ᶜ) or the sound known as 'ayn (') does not affect alphabetical order. The sound k appears before kh; g appears before gh; and h appears before H. (See Pronunciation, page 15, for an explanation of these sounds.)

A

aᶜ'ad, yuᶜ'ud	to sit • to stay	أقعد
'aadi	ordinary	عادي
'aadiyaat	antiques	عاديات
'aaᶜil/a	wise • sensible	عاقل
aakhir	last	آخر
'aakis, yi'aakis	to chat up	عاكس
aal, yiᶜool	to tell to say	قال
'aali/ya	loud	عالي
'aalim	scientist	عالم
'aaliya	high	عالية
aᶜall (min)	less (than)	أقل (من)
'aamil	manual worker	عامل
'aamil/a tilifōnaat	telephone operator	عامل تليفونات
'aana, yi'aani	to suffer	عانى
'aaqib, yi'aaqib	to punish	عاقب
'aash, yi'eesh	to live (life) • to survive	عاش
'aashir	tenth	عاشر

> 'aasif/'asfa آسف.
> I'm sorry.

'aayiz/'ayza	to want	عايز
'aazib/a	single (person)	عازب
'abaaya	cloak	عباية
abb	father	أب
'abeeṭ/a	idiot	عبيط
abl	before	قبل
abyaḍ	white	أبيض
'aᶜd	contract	عقد
'adaala	justice	عدالة
'aḍala	muscle	عضلة
adam	foot (measurement)	قدم
'adasa	lens	عدسة
adasaat laṣ'a	contact lenses	عدسات لاصقة
'add, yi'idd	to count	عدّ
'aḍḍa	bite (dog)	عضّة
adeem	old (thing)	قديم
adeem/udām	ancient	قديم
'aḍm	bone	عظم
ᶜafal, yiᶜfil	to shut • to close	قفل
afl	padlock	قفل
ᶜaflaam	films • movies	أفلام
ᶜaflaam kartoon	cartoons	أفلام كارتون
ᶜagaaza	vacation • holidays	أجازة
'agala	wheel • bicycle	عجلة
ᶜaggar, yiᶜaggar	to rent • to hire	أجّر
ag-hiza	equipment	أجهزة
ag-hizat ghaṭs	diving equipment	أجهزة غطس

aghlabiyya	majority	أغلبيّة
ahl	parents	أهل

ahlan — أهلاً.
Hello.

ahlan wa sahlan — أهلاً وسهلاً.
Welcome.

aHyaanan	sometimes	أحياناً
aHmar/ Hamra	red	أحمر
aHmar shafaayif	lipstick	أحمر شفايف
aHsan	best	أحسن
aHsan (min)	better (than)	أحسن من
ahwa	bar • cafe	قهوة
akal, yaakul	to eat	أكل

akeed — أكيد.
Sure.

akkid, yiᶜakkid	to confirm (a booking)	أكّد
akl	food	أكل
akli lil baybi	baby food	أكل للبيبي
akh	brother	أخ
akhad, yākhud	to take (the train/etc)	أخذ
akhad, yakhud baal min	to care for	أخذ بال من
akhḍar/ khaḍra	green	أخضر
akhd il Haqayib	baggage claim	أخذ الحقائب
aktar	more	أكثر
'aᶜl	mind	عقل
al'a	castle	قلعة
'ala	on	على
alᶜaan/a	worried	قلقان
a'la it tal	uphill	أعلى التّل
alam	pen (ballpoint)	قلم
'alam	flag	علم
alam ruṣāṣ	pencil	قلم رصاص
'alay	to owe	عليه
alb	heart	قلب
allāh	God	الله

allāh yibaarik feek/i — الله يبارك فيك.
God bless you.

alō — ألو!
Hello! (answering telephone)

a'ma/'amya	blind	أعمى
amaan	safe (adj)	أمان
'amal, yi'mil	to do • to make	عمل
'amal fanni	artwork	عمل فنّي
'amaliyya	operation	عمليّة
amar	moon	قمر
amboobit butagaaz	gas bottle (butane)	أمبوبة بوتاجاز
amees	shirt	قميص
aml	lice	قمل
'amma	aunt (paternal)	عمّة
amr	order	أمر
amrāḍ tanasuliyya	venereal disease	أمراض تناسليّة
ana	I	أنا

ana bansa — أنا أنسى.
I forget.

anaani/ya	selfish	أناني
'and	to have	عند

'andak Haᶜ — عندك حقّ.
You're right.

'anduh imsaak	to be constipated	عنده إمساك
'aneed/a	stubborn	عنيد

'an iznak/ik عن إذنك.
Excuse me. (to get past)

antag, yintig	to produce	أنتج
ara, yi'ra	to read	قرأ
'arabiyat akl	dining car	عربيّة أكل
'arabiyit zheep	jeep	عربيّة جيب
'arabiyya	car	سيّارة
'araḍ, yi'riḍ	to exhibit	عرض
'araf	to realise	عرف
arḍ	earth (soil) • land • floor	أرض
'arḍ	perfopmance • show	عرض
arnab	rabbit	أرنب
'aroosa	doll	عروسة
arṣ/a	bite (insect)	قرص
aṣ, yi^{c}uṣ	to cut with scissors	قصّ
asanseer	elevator	أسانسير
asār	ruins • monument	آثار
asbirateer	distributor (car)	أسبيراتور
asbireen	aspirin	أسبيرين
aṣfar	yellow	أصفر
'aṣfoor	bird	عصفور
'asha	dinner	عشاء
'ashān	because	علشان

ashoofak ba'deen أشوفك بعدين.
See you later.

ashoofak bukra أشوفك بكرة.
See you tomorrow.

'āṣifa	storm	عاصفة
'askar, yi'askar	to camp	عسكر
'asr haḍm	indigestion	عسر هضم
aṣli	original	أصليّ
aṣriyya	pot (ceramic)	قصريّة
assees	priest	قسّيس
atāri	computer games	أتاري
'āṭil/a	unemployed	عاطل
'aṭlān	faulty	عطلان
aṭr	train	قطر
aṭrash/ṭarsha	deaf	أطرش
'aṭshān/a	thirsty	عطشان
aṭṭa', yi^{c}aṭṭa'	to cut up	قطّع
'aṭṭār	herbalist	عطّار
awi	very	قوي
awwil	first	أوّل
'ayla	family	عيلة
'ayn	eye	عين
'ayntayn	two eyes	عينتين
'aysh	bread	عيش
ayy	any	أيّ
'ayyaan/a	ill	عيّان
ayy Hadd	anyone	أيّ أحد
'ayyil	child	عيّل
ayyim	valuable (expensive)	قيّم
'azaf, yi'zif	to play (music)	عزف
'aẓeem	great	عظيم
azhenda	diary (agenda)	أجندة
azra^c/zar^{c}a	blue	أزرق

B

baa', yibee'	to sell	باع
baab	door	باب
baaba	dad	بابا
baaku	packet (general)	باكو
ba^{c}ara	cow	بقرة
baarik, yibaarik	to bless	بارك

B

ba'at, yib'at	to send	بعت
ba'ḍ	some	بعض
badaᶜ, yibdaᶜ	to start	بدأ
badri	early	بدري
ba'ḍuhum	some of them	بعضهم
ba'eed	remote • far	بعيد
baHr	sea	بحر
baa'i	rest (what's left)	باقي
balad	country	بلد
balakōna	balcony	بلكونة
balay	ballet	باليه
balṭu	(over)coat	بالطو
bambi	pink	بمبي
bana, yibni	to build	بنى
banafsigi	purple	بنفسجي
bango	marijuana	بانجو
banṭalōn	trousers	بنطلون
banyu	bathtub	بنيو
banzeen	petrol	بنزين
barbireez	windscreen	بربريز
bard	a cold • cold (adj)	برد
bareed 'aadi	surface mail	بريد عادي
bareed gawwi	air mail	بريد جوّي
barghoot	flea	برغوت
barlamān	parliament	برلمان
barra	outside	بره
barṭamān	jar	برطمان
bas	only • but	بس
bās, yiboos	to kiss	باس
basboor	passport	جواز السفر
baseeṭ	simple	بسيط
baᶜsheesh	tip (gratuity)	بكشيش
baṣṣ, yibuṣṣ	to look	بص
baṭeeᶜ	slow	بطيء
baṭṭal, yibaṭṭal	to quit	بطّل
baṭṭaneeya	blanket	بطّانيّة
baṭṭariyya	battery • torch • flashlight	بطّاريّة
baṭṭeekh	watermelon	بطيخ
bawwaaba	gate	بوّابة
baybi	baby	بيبي
bayn	between	بين
bayt	house	بيت
bayt ish shabaab	youth hostel	بيت الشّباب
beeᶜa	environment	بيئة
beer	well (water)	بير
bi balaash	free (of charge)	ب بلاش
bihalwis	delirious	يهلوس
bilaazh	beach	بلاج

bil hana wa shifa! بالهناء والشّفاء!
Bon appetit!

bilaster	bandage (plaster)	بلاستر
bilastik	plastic	بلاستيك
bilyardu	pool (game)	بلياردو
bint	girl • daughter	بنت
birnaamig	program	برنامج
bishweesh	slowly	بشويش
biṭaᶜa	identification (card)	بطاقة
biyuwaga'	painful	بيوجّع
bookir	poker	بوكر
boot	boots	بوت
boozi	Buddhist	بوذي
bōsa	kiss	بوسة
buᶜ	mouth	بق
budrat baybi	baby powder	بودرة بيبي
buHeera	lake	بحيرة
bukhār	steam	بخار

DICTIONARY

bukra	tomorrow	بكرة
bukra bil layl	tomorrow afternoon/ evening	بكرة بالليل
bukra iṣ ṣubH	tomorrow morning	بكرة الصّبح
bulees	police	بوليس
buloofar	jumper • sweater	بلوفر
bunni	brown	بنّي
burg	tower	برج
burnaamig ir riHla	itinerary	برنامج الرّحلة
burtuᶜāli	orange (colour)	برتقالي
buṣla	compass	بوصلة
busta	mail	بوستة
butagaaz	stove	بوتاجاز
buṭoola	championship	بطولة

D

da (m)	this (one)	هذا (دا)
daada	babysitter	دادا
daafi/yya	warm	دافيء
daayikh/ daaykha	dizzy	دائخ
daayim/a	permanent	دائم
ḍa'eef/a	weak	ضعيف
daf'	payment	دفع
dafa', yidfa'	to pay	دفع
daffaaya	heater	دفّاية
ḍaght	pressure	ضغط
dahabi	of gold	ذهبي
dahan, yidhin	to paint (not art)	دهن
ḍahr	back (body)	ظهر
ḍaHak, yiḍHak'ala	to make fun of	ضحك على
ḍāHiyya	suburb (district)	ضاحية
dakhal, yudkhul	to enter	دخل
dakhkhan, yidakhkhan	to smoke	دخّان
daleel	guidebook	دليل
ḍalma	dark (no light)	ظلمة
dam'	tear (crying)	دمع
dammar, yidammar	to destroy	دمر
dantilla	lace	دانتيلا
ḍarab, yiḍrab	to kick	ضرب
ḍarab, yiḍrab nār	to shoot at	ضرب نار
daraga	degree (temperature)	درجة
daragit il Harāra	temperature (weather)	درجة الحرارة
ḍareeba	tax	ضريبة
ḍareeH	shrine	ضريح
dār il ubira	opera house	دار الأوبّرا
dasim	rich (food)	دسم
dasta	a dozen	دستة
dawa	pharmaceutical drugs • medicine	دواء
dawli	international	دوليّ
dawsha	noise • noisy	دوشة
dayman	always	دائماً
dayr	convent • monastery	دير
ḍayyaᶜ/a	tight	ضيّق
ḍayya', yiḍayya'	to lose	ضيع
dee (f)	this (one)	هذه (دي)
deel	tail	ذيل
deen	religion	دين
dibbaan	fly	ذباب

diblōm	degree (diploma)	دبلوم
di^{c}ee^{c}	flour	دقيق
di^{c}ee^{c}a	minute (time)	دقيقة
ḍiHik, yiḍHak	to laugh	يضحك
dilwa^{c}ti	now	الآن (دلوقتي)
ḍimn	among	ضمن
dimuqrāṭiyya	democracy	ديموقراطيّة
dira'	arm	دراع
dirāma	drama	دراما
dirāmi	dramatic	دراميّ
ḍirs	tooth (back)	ضرس
dōkha	nausea • travel sickness	دوخة
dood	worms	دود
dōr	floor (storey)	طابق (دور)
dubāra	string	دبارة
dughri	straight (ahead)	دغري
ḍuhr	noon	ظهر
dukhān	tobacco	دخان
duktōr/a	doctor	دكتور
duktōr il asnaan	dentist	دكتور الأسنان
dulaab	cupboard	دولاب
dulāb	wardrobe	دولاب
durit mayya 'āma	public toilet	دورة مياه عامة
dush	shower	دش
duwār il baHr	seasick	دوار البحر

E

'eeb	disadvantage	عيب
eed	hand	يد (أيد)
'eed	holiday • festival	عيد
'eed il qiyāma	Easter	عيد القيامة
'eed milaad	birthday	عيد ميلاد
eema	value (price)	قيمة
ey	what	إيه

F

faasid	corrupt	فاسد
faat, yifoot	to pass	فات
faatiH/a	light (colour)	فاتح
faayiz/a	winner	فايز
faḍā'	space	فضاء
fāḍi/fāḍya	empty • vacant	فاضي
faḍḍal, yifaḍḍal	to prefer	فضّل
faḍḍi	of silver	فضّي
fa^{c}eer/a	poor	فقير
fagr	dawn	فجر
fakka	loose change	فكّة
fakkar, yifakkar (fee)	to think (about)	فكّر (في)
fanaan/a	artist	فنّان
fann	art	فنّ
alfann il grafeeki	graphic art	الفنّ الجرافيكي
fār	rat • mouse	فأر
fa^{c}r	poverty	فقر
fara'	branch	فرع
faraH	wedding	فرح
faras	horse	فرس
farāsha	butterfly	فراشة
faree^{c}	team	فريق
farkha	chicken (live)	فرخة
fasaad	corruption	فساد
faṣal, yifṣil	to separate	فصل
faṣl	class (school)	فصل
fattaaHit 'ilab	can/tin opener	فتّاحة علب
fataH, yiftaH	to open	فتح
fawḍawi/yya	anarchist	فوضويّ
fayn	where	أين (فين)
faẓee'	awful • terrible	فظيع
fee daakhil	within	في داخل

fee saHitkum! في صحّتكم!
Good health! • Cheers!

feesha	plug (electricity)	فيشة
fiḍil, yifḍal	to be left (behind/over)	فضل
fihim, yifham	to understand	فهم
fikra	thought	فكرة
filfil	pepper	فلفل
film	movie	فيلم
film abyaḍ wi 'iswid	B&W (film)	فيلم أبيض وأسود
fil mi'aad	on time	في الميعاد
fil miyya	percent	في المئة
film tasgeeli	documentary	فيلم تسجيليّ
filoos	money	فلوس
fingaan	cup	فنجان
firaakh	chicken (to eat)	فراخ
fir^{c}a musiqiya	band (music)	فرقة موسيقيّة
fiṭār	breakfast	فطار
fiṭir, yifṭar	to eat breakfast	فطر
fō^c	up	فوق
fooṭa	towel	فوطة
fooṭa ṣiHHiya	sanitary napkins	فوطة صحيّة
fooṭit wishsh	wash cloth • flannel	فوطة وش
fu^c	over	فوق
fukhār	pottery	فخّار
furn	bakery	فرن
furṣa	chance	فرصة
fursha	hairbrush	فرشة
furshit sinaan	toothbrush	فرشة أسنان
fustaan	dress	فستان

G

Remember that gh appears after g.

ga, yeegi	to come	جاء
ga'aan/ a	to be hungry	جعان
gaab, yigeeb	to bring	جاب
gaab gōl	to score a goal	جاب جول
gaadil, yigaadil	to argue	جادل
gaam'a	university	جامعة
gaami'	mosque	جامع
gaamid/a	hard (surface) • solid	جامد
gabal	mountain	جبل
gadd	serious	جد
gadwal	timetable	جدول
gaahiz/a	ready (made)	جاهز
gahhiz, yigahhiz	to prepare	جهّز
gamb	next to • beside	جنب
gameel/a	beautiful	جميل
gammid, yigammid	to freeze	جامد
ganaaza	funeral	جنازة
ganoob	south	جنوب
garaayid	newspapers	جرائد
garas	ring (sound)	جرس
garazh	garage (parking)	جراج
gar'a ziyaada	overdose	جرعة زيادة
gardal	bucket	جردل
garH	wound • injury	جرح
garrab, yigarrab	to try (out)	جرّب
garsōn	waiter	جرسون
gawaab	letter	جواب
gawaab misaggil	registered letter	جواب مسجّل
gawaab mista'gil	express letter	جواب مستعجل

gawaaz	marriage	جواز
gawaz is safr	passport	جواز السّفر
gaww	weather • atmosphere	جو
gaz'a	sprain	جزع
gazeera	island	جزيرة
gazma	shoes (pair)	جزمة
geeb	pocket	جيب
gibna	cheese	جبنة
gidd	grandfather	جد
gidda	grandmother	جدّة
gideed/a	new	جديد
gild	leather • skin	جلد
gineena	garden	جنينة
gineenit il Hayawanaat	zoo	جنينة الحيوانات
gineyna	park	جنينة
gins	sex	جنس
ginsiyya	citizenship • nationality	جنسيّة
giri, yigri	to run	جرى
gism	body	جسم
gōl	goal	جول
gooda	quality	جودة
gōz	pair • couple • husband	جوز
gram	gram	غرام
gumhuriyya	republic	جمهوريّة
gumla	sentence (words)	جملة
gumruk	customs	جمرك
gurnāl	newspaper	جرنال
guwwa	inside	جوة
guz^c	part	جزء

GH

ghaaba	forest	غابة
ghaali/ghaalya	expensive	غالي

ghaali giddan — too expensive — غالي جداً

ghabi/ya	stupid	غبي
ghada	lunch	غداء
ghalaṭ	wrong	غلط
ghalṭa	mistake • fault (someone's)	غلطة
ghami^c	dark (colour)	غامق
ghani/yya	rich (wealthy)	غني
ghanna, yighanni	to sing	غنّى
gharāma	fine (money)	غرامة
gharb	west	غرب
gharee^c	deep (water)	غريق
ghareeb/a	strange	غريب
ghārib/a	stranger	غارب
ghasal, yighsil	to wash	غسل
ghashaash/a	cheat	غشّاش
ghassaala	washing machine	غسّالة
ghaṭs	diving	غطس
ghayraan/a	jealous	غيران
ghayyar, yighayyar	to change • to exchange	غيّر
ghazaal	deer (gazelle)	غزال
gheeṭ	field	غيط
gheyr mubaashir	non-direct	غير مباشر
ghinwa	song	غنوة
ghurfa	room	غرفة
ghurfa li itnayn	double room	غرفة لإتنين
ghurfa lishakhṣ waaHid	single room	غرفة لشخص واحد
ghuroor	pride	غرور

H

Remember that H appears after h.

haadi/ya	quiet	هادئ
hadiyya	gift	هديّة
haḍm	digestion	هضم
handasa	engineering	هندسة
harsh	itch	هرش

hāt/i!	هات!
Bring it!	

hawaa^{c}i/yya	trendy (person)	هوائي
hāwi	amateur	هاوي

hāyil!	هائل!
Great! • Marvellous!	

hāyil/a	wonderful	هايل
hāyil	marvellous	هايل
hidayyit il faraH	wedding present	هديّة الفرح
hidiyya	present (gift)	هديّة
higra	immigration	هجرة
hina	here	هنا
hindusi	Hindu	هندوسي
hiyya	she • they (f)	هي
hudoom	clothing	هدوم
humma	they (m)	هم
huwwa	he	هو

H (a strongly whispered 'h')

Ha^c	truth	حق
Haaga	something	حاجة
Haalan	right now	حالاً
Haami	spicy (hot)	حامي
Haamil	pregnant	حامل
Ha^{c}an, yiH^{c}in	to inject	حقن
Haaris il marma	goalkeeper	حارس المرمى

Haasib!	حاسب!
Careful!	

Haawil, yiHaawil	to try • to attempt	حاول
Habbāya	pill	حبّاية
Habb, yiHibb	to love	حبّ
Habb, yiHibb	to like	حبّ
Habeeb	lover	حبيب
Habl	rope	حبل
Haḍāna	kindergarten	حضانة

Ha^{c}ee^{c}i	حقيقي.
It's true.	

Hadd	someone	أحد (حدّ)
Hadd i sura'a	speed limit	حد السّرعة
Haḍn	cuddle	حضن
Hafeed	grandchild	حفيد
Hafla	party	حفلة
Hafla musiqiyya	concert	حفلة موسيقيّة
Hagar	stone	حجر
Hagaz, yiHgiz	to book • to reserve	حجز
Hagm	size (of objects)	حجم
Hagz	reservation	حجز
Hakam	referee	حكم
Hala^c	earrings	حلق
Hala^c, yiHla^c	to shave	حلق
Halla	pan	حلّة
Hama	mother-in-law	حماة
Hama	father-in-law	حمى
Hama, yiHmi	to protect	حمى
Hammaam	bath(room)	حمّام
Hammaam is sibaaHa	swimming pool	حمّام السّباحة
Harāmi	thief	حرامي
Harāra	heat • dial tone	حرارة
Harb	war	حرب
Haree'a	fire (accident)	حريقة
Hareer	silk	حرير

Harrān/a	to be hot	حرّان
Hasasiyya	allergy	حساسيّة
Haṣeera	mat	حصيرة
Hashara	bug	حشرة
Hass, yiHiss (bi)	to feel	حسّ (ب)
Haṭb	firewood	حطب
Haṭṭ, yiHuṭṭ	to put	حطّ
Hayaa	life	حياة
Hayawaan	wild animal • animal	حيوان
Hazeen/a	sad	حزين
Hazẓ	luck	حظّ
Hazzar, yiHazzar	to guess	حزّر

Hazẓ sa'eed! حظّ سعيد!
Good luck!

Heeṭa	wall (inside)	حيطة
Higaab	veil (head scarf)	حجاب
Hikaaya	story	حكاية
Hilim, yiHlam	to dream	حلم
Hilw	pretty	حلو
Hilw/a	sweet	حلو
Hisaab	bill (account)	حساب
Hitta	piece	حتّة
Hizam ᶜamaan	seatbelt	حزام أمان
Hizb	party (political)	حزب
Huboob il luqāH	pollen	حبوب اللقاح
Huboob muna-wwima	sleeping pills	حبوب منوّمة
Huḍn	hug	حضن
Hudood	border	حدود
Hukm	sentence (prison)	حكم
Hukooma	government	حكومة
Humma	fever	حمّى
Huᶜna	vaccination • injection	حقنة
Huᶜooᶜ il insaan	human rights	حقوق الانسان
Huᶜooᶜ madaniyya	civil rights	حقوق مدنيّة
Hurr/a	free (not bound)	حر

I

ibn	son	إبن
ibra	needle (sewing)	إبرة
ibtada, yibtidi	to begin	إبتدأ
ibtasam, yibtisim	to smile	إبتسم
idar, yiᶜdar	can (to be able)	قدر
idda, yiddi	to give	أدّى
id ḍamān il igtimā'i	social security	الضمان الإجتماعي
id dawra	menstruation	الدورة
idmān	drug addiction	إدمان
iḍrāb	strike	إضراب
iftakar, yiftikir	to think (believe) • to remember	إفتكر
iftitaaH	opening	إفتتح
igār	rent	أجار
ig-haaḍ	miscarriage	إجهاض
ightiṣāb	rape	إغتصاب
igniHa	wings	أجنحة
iHna	we	نحن (إحنا)
iHrāg	embarrassment	إحراج
iHtaag, yiHtaag	to need	إحتاج
iHtafal, yiHtifil (bi)	to celebrate	إحتفل (ب)

iHtag, yaHtag	to protest	إحتجّ

ihtamm, yihtamm bi ... إهتم ب ...
to care (about) ...

iHtigaag	protest	إحتجاج
iHtirām	respect	إحترام
iktashaf, yiktishif	to discover	إكتشف
il 'aalam	the world • Earth	العالم
i'laan wazeefa	job advertisement	إعلان وظيفة
il albaan	dairy products	الألبان
'ilāqa	relationship	علاقة
il'ārḍa	scoreboard	العارضة
'ilba	can • tin • box	علبة
'ilbit (sigayyar)	packet (of cigarettes)	علبة (سجاير)
il biṭāla	unemployment	البطالة
il busṭa	post office	البوستة
il fagr	sunrise	الفجر
il ghuroob	sunset	الغروب

ilhaᶜni! إلحقني!
Help!

il Haalaᶜ il igtima'iyya	marital status	الحالة الإجتماعيّة
il ingeel	Bible	الإنجيل
il itnayn	both	الإتنين
il khareef	autumn (fall)	الخريف
il kōn	universe	الكون
il layla dee	tonight	الليلة دي

il layla il ākheera الليلة الأخيرة
the last night

illi gayya	next	اللي جاية
'ilm	science	علم
il maṣraH il klasseeki	classical theatre	المسرح الكلاسيكي
il mawgood	present (time)	الموجود
il nifayaat is saama	toxic waste	النفايات السامّة
il reemōt	remote control	الريموت

il sana dee السّنة دي
this year

il sana illi faatit السّنة اللي فاتت
last year

il shahr illi gayy الشهر اللي جاي
next month

iltihaab fil masaana	cystitis	إلتهاب في المثانة
iltimaas	petition	إلتماس

il usboo' da الأسبوع هذا (دا)
this week

il usboo' illi faat الأسبوع إللي فات
last week

il usboo' illi gayy الأسبوع اللي جاي
next week

ilyaaf ṣinā'iyya	synthetic	ألياف صناعيّة
il yimeen	right-wing	اليمين
'imāra	building	عمارة
imbaariH	yesterday	إمبارح

imbaariH bil layl إمبارح بالليل
last night

imḍa	signature	إمضاء
imsaak	constipation	إمساك

imshi 'ala ṭool. إمشي على طول.
Go straight ahead.

I

DICTIONARY

imta	when	أي متى (إمتى)
imtiHaan	test (exam)	إمتحان
'inab	grapes	عنب
in'akaas	reflection (mirror)	إنعكاس
inbasaṭ, yinbisiṭ	to enjoy (oneself) • to have fun	إنبسط
ingileezi	English	إنكليزي
innaharda	today	النهارداً
insha'aat	construction work	إنشاءات
inta	you (m)	أنت
intaha, yintihi	to end	إنتهى
intakhab, yintikhib	to vote	إنتخب
inti	you (f)	أنت
intikhabaat	elections	إنتخابات
intu	you (pl)	إنتوا
intu il itnayn	both of you	إنتوا الإتنين
iqleemi	regional	إقليمي
iqtaraH, yaqtariH	to recommend	إقترح
iqtirāH	proposal	إقتراح
iqtiṣād	economy	إقتصاد
'ir^c	vein	عرق
'iri^c, ya'ra^c	to perspire	عرق
'irif, yi'raf	to know • to recognise	عرف
ir rabee'	spring (season)	الربيع
irtaH, yirtaH	to relax	إرتاح
irtifaa'	altitude	إرتفاع
is'aafaat uliyya	first-aid kit	إسعافات أوّليّة
is-haal	diarrhoea	إسهال
ishāra	sign • indicator (car)	إشارة
isharb	scarf (women's silk)	إشارب
ishārit muroor	traffic lights	إشارة مرور

ish shahr illi faat — الشهر اللي فات

last month

ish sharq il awsaṭ	the Middle East	الشرق الأوسط
ish shita	winter	الشّتاء
ishṭa	cool	قشطة
ishtaghal, yishtaghal	to work	إشتغل
ishtara, yishtiri	to buy	إشترى
ishtirā-ki/yya	socialist	إشتراكيّ
ism	name	إسم
ism id dala'	nickname	إسم الدلع
ism il gadd	surname	إسم الجدّ
iṣ ṣayf	summer	الصيف
istaad	stadium	الستاد
istaahil, yistaahil	worth	إستاهل
istaghlaal	exploitation	إستغلال
istalaf, yistilif	to borrow	إستلف
istalam, yistilim	to receive (something)	إستلم

istanna! — إستنّى!

Wait!

istarid, yistirid	to refund	إستردّ
istiqāla	resignation	إستقالة
istirāHa	rest (relaxation) • intermission	إستراحة
istirayyaH, yistiraayyaH	to rest	إستريّح
istirdaad	refund	إسترداد

iswid/sōda	black	أسود
itᶜaabil, yitᶜaabil (ma'a)	to meet	إتقابل (مع)
it'aasim ghurfa	to share a dorm	إتقاسم غرفة
it'abid, yit'abid	to worship	إتعبّد
it'allim, yit'allim	to learn	إتعلّم
itfarrag, yitfarrag	to watch	إتفرّج
itgawwiz, yitgawwiz	to marry	إتجوّز
itghadda, yitghadda	to eat lunch	إتغدّى
ithm	sin	إثم
i'tirāf	confession (religious)	إعتراف
itkallim, yitkallim fee tilitofōn	to telephone	إتكلّم في التليفون
itkhaaniᶜ, yitkhaaniᶜ ma'a	to fight	إتخانق مع
itmanna, yitmanna	to wish	إتمنّى
itnaffas, yitnaffis	to breathe	إتنفّس
iṭ ṭabee'a	nature	الطبيعة
it tafaawit	inequality	التفاوت
ittigaah	destination	إتّجاه

iw'a!
Get lost!
إوعى!

iza	if	إذا
izaaz	glass	قزاز
izaaza	bottle	قزازة
'izba	farm	عزبة
izn	permission	إذن
izzay	how	إزّاي

K

Remember that kh appears after k.

kaa'inaat munqarriḍa	endangered species	كائنات منقرضة
kaaᶜinat maHmiyya	protected species	كائنات محميّة
kaan, yikoon	to be	كان
kaas	cup (trophy)	كأس
kaatib/a	writer	كاتب
kaddaab	liar	كذّاب
kadma	a bruise	كدمة
kafoola	nappy • diaper	كفولة
kahf	cave	كهف
kahraba	electricity	كهرباء
kalb	dog	كلب
kalba	puppy	كلبة
kallif, yikallif	to cost	كلّف
kallim/ yikallim	to speak • to talk	كلّم
kalōn ᶜifl	lock • padlock	كالون قفل
kamaan	too • also	كمان
kamaliyyaat	luxuries	كماليّات
kameen	checkpoint	كمين
kamira	camera	كاميرا
karanteena	quarantine	كرنتينة
karrar, yikarrar	to repeat	كرّر
kart	card	كرت
kart	menu	ميني
kart bustāl	postcard	كرت بوستال
kartōna	carton	كرتونة
kārt tilifōn	phonecard	كرت تليفون
kasar, yiksar	to break	كسر
kas il 'ālam	World Cup	كأس العالم
kasitt	cassette recorder	كاسيت

kaslaan/a	lazy	كسلان
kassārit talg	ice pick	كسّارة ثلج
katab, yiktib	to write	كتب
katedriyya	cathedral	كاثدرائيّة
katoleek	Catholic	كاثوليك
kawitsh	tyres	كاوتش
kawkab	planet	كوكب
keelu	kilogram	كيلو
keelumitr	kilometre	كيلو متر
kees makhadda	pillowcase	كيس مخدّة
kibeer	old	كبير
kibeer/a	large • big	كبير
kibeer fis sinn	old person	كبير في السن
kibreet	matches	كبريت
kidib, yikdib	to lie	كذب
kifaaya	enough	كفاية
kilma	word	كلمة
kilumitr	kilometre	كيلومتر
kineesa	church	كنيسة
kireem	moisturiser	كريم

kish maat! كش مات!
Checkmate!

kisib, yiksab	to earn • to win	كسب
kitaab	book	كتاب
kiteer	often • many • too much/many • a lot • several	كتير (كتير)
kitf	shoulder	كتف
kōra	ball • soccer	كرة
kōrat qadam	football (soccer)	كرة قدم
kreym ḍid ish shams	sunblock	كريم ضدّ الشمس
kubaaya	drinking glass	كبّاية
kubri	bridge	كوبري
kufiyya	scarf (neck)	كوفيّة
kuHHa	a cough	قحّة
kukayeen	cocaine	كوكايين
kull	all • each	كلّ
kull	whole	كلّ
kulli yōm	every day	كلّ يوم
kulliyya	college	كلّيّة
kumbiyootar	computer	كمبيوتر
kumidya	comedy	كوميديا
kumsāri	ticket collector	كمساري
kurrāsa	notebook	كرّاسة
kursi	seat • chair	كرسي
kursi mutaHarrik	wheelchair	كرسي متحرك
kushk dukhān	tobacco kiosk	كشك دخّان
kutsheena	playing cards	كوتشينة

KH

khaala	aunt (maternal)	خالة
khaarigi	foreign	خارجي
khaatim	ring (on finger)	خاتم
khabar	news	خبر
khaḍār	vegetation	خضار
khaddar, yikhaddar	to drug	خدّر
khafeef	light (adj)	خفيف
khalaṣ	already	خلاص
khalaṭ, yikhliṭ	to mix	خلط

khalli baalak/ik! خلّي بالك!
Be careful!

khanzeer	pig	خنزير
kharag, yikhrag ma'a	to go out with	خرج مع
khareeṭa	map	خريطة
kharoof	sheep	خروف
khashab	wood	خشب

khashabit il masraH	stage (theatre)	خشبة المسرح
khaṣkhaṣa	privatisation	خصخصة
khāṣ lil Hafriyaat	archaeological	خاص للحفريّات
khasrān/a	loser	خسران
khāṣṣ	private	خاص
khaṭ	line • script	خطّ
khaṭeeb	fiance	خطيب
khaṭeeba	fiancee	خطيبة
khaṭeer	dangerous	خطير
khawaaga	foreigner	خواجة
khayaal	fiction	خيال
khayṭ il asnaan	dental floss	خيط الأسنان
khayyaṭ, yikhayyaṭ	to sew	خيّط
khazfi	ceramic	خزفي
khazna	safe (n) • cash register	خزنة
kheema	tent	خيمة
khidma	service (assistance)	خدمة
khidma 'askariyya	military service	خدمة عسكريّة

khilaal saa'a — خلال ساعة
within an hour

khinaa^{c}a	fight	خناقة
khōf	fear	خوف
khōza	helmet	خوذة
khuḍār	vegetables	خضار
khuḍari	greengrocer	خضري
khurm	puncture	خرم
khuroog	exit	خروج
khusāra	loss	خسارة

khush shimaal/yimeen — خشّ شمال/يمين.
Turn left/right.

khuṣooṣi	special	خصوصي
khuṭooba	engagement	خطوبة

L

la^c	no	لأ
la^{c}a, yila^{c}i	to find	لاقى
laagi^c	refugee	لاجيء
laa'ib	player (sports)	لاعب
laakin	but	لكن
laazim	necessary	لازم
laban	milk	لبن
la'bit shaṭarang	chessboard	لعبة شطرنج
la^{c}eem	creepy (slang)	لئيم
laffa	package	لفّة
lafHit shams	sunburn	لفحة شمس
lagha, yilghi	to cancel	لغى
lāma'/a	brilliant (dazzling)	لامع
lamas, yilmas	to touch	لمس
lamba	light bulb	لمبة
lansh	motorboat	لانش
laṭeef/a	nice	لطيف

la ... wala — لا ... ولا
neither ... nor

lay	why	ليه
layl/a	night	ليلة
li'ba	game	لعبة
libaan	chewing gum	لبان
libis, yilbis	to wear	لبس
lighaayit (yoonyu)	until (June)	لغاية (يونيو)
li'ib, yil'ab	to play (a game)	لعب
lil mut'a	for fun	للمتعة
lissa	not yet • yet	لسّه

lissa badri — لسّه بدري.
It's early.

li waHdo	alone	لوحده
lōn	colour	لون
loori	truck	لوري

low samaHt/i — لو سمحت.
Excuse me. (to call attention)

lugha	language	لغة
luHaat	paintings	لوحات

M

ma'a	with	مع
maᶜaas	size (clothes/shoes)	مقاس
ma'a ba'ḍ	together	مع بعض

ma'arafsh — ماعرفش.
I don't know.

maᶜaṣ	scissors	مقص

maashi — ماشي.
OK.

maashi ma'	to date (someone)	ماشي مع
maat, yimoot	to die	مات
ma'bad	temple	معبد
maᶜbara	grave	مقبرة
mablool/a	wet	مبلول

mabrook! — مبروك!
Congratulations!

mabsooṭ	happy	مبسوط
maḍa, yimḍi	to sign	مضى
ma'dan	metal	معدن
māḍi	past	ماضي
madkhal	foyer	مدخل
maḍrab	racquet	مضرب
madrasa	school	مدرسة
madrasa sanawiya	high school	مدرسة ثانويّة
mafeesh	none	مافيش
maᶜfool/a	closed	مقفول
maftooH	open	مفتوح
magalla	magazine	مجلّة
magallaat hazliyya	comics	مجلات هزليّة
maghaṣ	stomachache	مغص
maghool	passive	مغول
magnoon/a	mad • crazy	مجنون
ma'goon asnaan	toothpaste	معجون أسنان
mahragaan	festival	مهرجان
maHal il milaad	place of birth	محل الميلاد
maHall	shop	محل
maHall	department store	محل
maHall gizam	shoe shop	محل جزم
maHall malaabis	clothing store	محل ملابس
maHalli	local	محلّي
maHaṭṭa	station	محطّة
maHaṭṭit aṭr	railway station	محطّة قطر
maHaṭṭit utubees	bus stop	محطّة أوتوبيس
maHboob/a	popular	محبوب
maHkama	court (legal)	محكمة
maHmool	mobile phone	محمول
maHẓooẓ/a	lucky	محظوظ

ma'is salaama. — مع السلامة.
Goodbye.

makaan	place • location	مكان
makana/aat	machine	مكنة
makanit filoos	automatic teller (ATM)	مكنة فلوس
makhadda	pillow	مخدّة
makkār	crafty	مكّار

maksoof/a	shy	مكسوف
maksoor	broken	مكسور
maktab	office	مكتب
maktaba	library • stationers • bookshop	مكتبة
maktab is siyaaHa	tourist information office	مكتب السّياحة
maktab siyaaHa	travel agency	مكتب سياحة
makyāzh	make-up	مكياج
mala, yimla	to fill	ملى
malaabis	clothing	ملابس
mal'ab (tinis)	(tennis) court	(ملعب) تنس
malH	salt	ملح
malik	king	ملك
malika	queen	ملكة

ma'lish معليش.
Excuse me. (apology)

malyaan/a	full	مليان
mama	mum	ماما
ma'mool/a (min)	made (of) (من)	معمول
mamsha	path	ممشى
ma'mudiyya	baptism	معموديّة
manaakh	atmosphere (mood)	مناخ
mana'	prevent	منع
manadeel warac	tissues	مناديل ورق
mana' il Haml	contraception	منع الحمل
manakheer	nose	مناخير
manzar	view	منظر
ma'raḍ	exhibition	معرض
maraḍ	disease • sickness	مرض
maraḍ is sukkar	diabetes	مرض السكر
marHala	leg (in race)	مرحلة
markib	ship • boat	مركب
marra	once • one time	مرة
marratayn	twice	مرّتين
martaba	mattress	مرتبة
marwaHa	fan	مروحة

masaac il khayr مساء الخير.
Good afternoon/evening.

mas'aala	question (topic)	مسألة
masal	example	مثل

masalan ... مثلاً ...
For example ...

masāzh	massage	مسّاج
maseeHi/ya	Christian	مسيحي
masgoon	prisoner	مسجون
mashaa'ir	feelings	مشاعر
mashhoor/a	famous	مشهور
mashroob	a drink	مشروب

masmuH مسموح.
It's allowed.

maṣna'	factory	مصنع
masoora	pipe (plumbing)	ماسورة
maṣr	Egypt	مصر
masraHiyya	play (theatre)	مسرحيّة
maṣri/yya	Egyptian	مصري
maṭ'am	restaurant	مطعم
maṭār	airport	مطار
maṭar	rain	مطر
maṭbakh	kitchen	مطبخ
matHaf	museum	متحف
mawcif	stop	موقف
maw'if utubees	bus station	موقف أوتوبيس

mawwit, yimawwit	to kill (a person)	موّت
maydaan raʿeesi	main square	ميدان رئيسي
mayō	swimsuit	مايوه
mayya	water	ميّة
mayya ma'daniyya	mineral water	ميّة معدنيّة
mayya saaʿ'a	cold water	ميّة ساقعة
mayya sukhna sukhna	hot water	ميّة سخنة
mayyit/a	dead	ميّت
maẓbooṭ	right (correct)	مظبوط
medina	city	مدينة
meen	who	مين
meena	port • harbour	ميناء
mi'aad	date • appointment	ميعاد
ma'da	stomach	معدة
midalya	medal	ميداليّة
midawwar/a	round	مدوّر
migaw harāt	jewellery	مجوهرات
mighayyim	cloudy	مغيّم
mihna	profession	مهنة
mikaneeki/yya	mechanic	ميكانيكي
milaaya	sheet (bed)	ملاية
milli	millimetre	ملّي
milyōn	million	مليون
min (mayyu)	since (May)	من (مايو)
minabbih	alarm clock	منبّة
minawla	communion	مناولة
minay	menu	كرت
min ghayr	without	من غير
min ghayr filtir	without filter	من غير فلتر
minibaṣ	bus (minibus)	ميني باص
miraaya	mirror	مراية
mirāt	wife	مرات

misaa	evening	مساء

mish baṭāl
It's OK.
مش بطّال.

mishammis	sunny	مشمّس
mishi, yimshi	to depart (leave) • to walk	مشي
mishṭ	comb	مشط
mista'gil	urgent	مستعجل
mista'gil/a	in a hurry	مستعجِل
mistirayyaH/a	to feel comfortable	مستريح
mit'akhkhir/a	late	متأخّر
mit'āṭaf	sympathetic	متعاطف
mitr	metre	متر
miyya	a hundred	مئة (ميّة)
mi'za	goat	معزة
mōg	wave (sea)	موج
moogiz il anbā'	current affairs	موجز الأنباء
moos	penknife • razor • razor blades	موس
mōt	death	موت
muʿaabla	interview	مقابلة
muʿahilaat	qualifications	مؤهلات
mu'āq	disabled	معاق
mu'askar	campsite	معسكر
mubaashir/a	direct	مباشر
mudarris/a	teacher • instructor	مدرّس
mudeer/a	manager • director	مدير
mudmin/a	drug addict	مدمن
mufagʿa	surprise	مفاجأة
mufeed/a	useful	مفيد
muftaaH	key	مفتاح
mu'gab	fan (of a team)	معجب

mughanni/yya	singer	مغنّي
muhandis	engineer	مهندس
muhandis/a mi'maari	architect	مهندس معماري
muhimm	important	مهم
muHaami	lawyer	محامي
muHāfiẓ/a	conservative	محافظ
muHarrag/a	embarrassed	محرّج
muharrig	clown	مهرّج
muHarrir/a	editor	محرر
muHeeṭ	ocean	محيط
mukayyif	air-conditioned	مكيّف
mukhaḍḍarāt	drugs (recreational)	مخدّرات
mukhaṭra	risk	مخاطرة
mukhliṣ/a	loyal	مخلص
mukhtalif/a ('an)	different (from)	مختلف (عن)
mulakama	boxing	ملاكمة
mulayyin	laxatives	مليّن
mulṣaᶜa	poster	ملصقة
mumarriḍ/a	nurse	ممرّضة
mumill/a	boring	مملّ
mumkin	can (may) • possible	ممكن
mumtāz/a	excellent	ممتاز
muntagaat yadawiyya	handicrafts	منتجات يدويّة
muntakhibeen	electorate	منتخبين
munṭaliq/a	outgoing	منطلق
muntig/a	producer	منتج
muntigaat yadawiyya	crafts	منتجات يدويّة
muṣalli	prayer	مصلّي
muṣawwarāti/ya	camera operator	مصوّراتي
murabba'	square (shape)	مربّع
murag'a	review	مراجعة
murattab	salary	مرتّب
muriH/a	comfortable	مريح
muroor	traffic	مرور
murshid/a	guide (person)	مرشد
musalli/ya	entertaining	مسلّي
musalsal	series (TV)	مسلسل
musaṭṭaH	flat (land, etc)	مسطّح
musawaah	equality	مساواة
muṣawwarāti	photographer	مصوّراتي
museeqa	music	موسيقى
museeqi	musician	موسيقي
mushaa	pedestrians	مشاة
musharradeen	homeless	مشرّدين
mustaᶜbal	future	مستقبل
musta'idd/a (li)	ready (for)	مستعد (ل)
mustashfa (khāṣṣ)	(private) hospital	مستشفى (خاص)
mut'a	fun (n)	متعة
mutadayyin/a	religious (person)	متديّن
muṭahir	antiseptic	مطهّر
mutaqā'ad/a	retired	متقاعد
mutor	engine	موتور
mutusikl	motorcycle	موتوسيكل
muwaẓẓaf	office worker	موظّف
muwaẓẓaf/a	employee	موظّف
muzahra	rally (political) • demonstration (political)	مظاهرة
muzāri'	farmer	مزارع
muzdawag	double	مزدوج
muzee'	presenter (TV, etc)	مذيع
muzeel li reeHit il' araᶜ	deodorant	مزيل لريحة العرق

M

DICTIONARY

N

N

naadir	rare	نادر
naadir/a	unusual	نادر
na'al, yin'il	to ship	نقل
naam, yinaam	to sleep	نام
naas	people	ناس
nabaatee/yya	vegetarian	نباتي
naḍḍāra	glasses (for eyes)	نظّارة
naḍḍāra ma'zzama	binoculars	نظّارة معظّمة
naḍḍārit shams	sunglasses	نظّارة شمس
naḍeef/a	clean	نظيف
nafa/yinfi	to deny	نفى
nafs	same	نفس

nafs il yōm — نفس اليوم
the same day

nagaaH	success	نجاح
naghama	tune	نغمة
nahr	river	نهر
naHt	sculpture	نحت
naHya	side	ناحية
naHyit	towards	ناحية
namla	ant	نملة
namoosiyya	mosquito net	ناموسيّة
nār	fire	نار
naʿṣ	shortage	نقص
na'sān/a	sleepy	نعسان
naṣb	rip off	نصب
nasl/a	descendent	نسل
naṣya	corner (of street)	ناصية
naṭ/yinuṭ	to jump	نط
nateega	calendar	نتيجة
nayy/a	raw	نيّ
nazaf, yinzif	to bleed	نزف
naẓẓam, yinaẓẓam	to organise	نظّم
nibeet	wine	نبيد
nidim, yindam	to regret	ندم
nigeel	grass	نجيل
nigma	star	نجمة
nihaaya	end	نهاية
nihaayit il usboo'	weekend	نهاية الأسبوع
niqāb	veil (full face covering)	نقاب
niqāba	trade union	نقابة
nisbit ittaHweel	exchange rate	نسبة التحويل
nishif, yinshaf	to dry (clothes)	نشف
nisi, yinsa	to forget	نسي
nizil, yinzil (fee)	to stay (somewhere)	نزل في
nōm	sleep	نوم
noor	light (sun/lamp)	نور
nukta	joke	نكتة
nuṣ	half	نصّ

nuṣ ilitr — نصّ ليتر
half a litre

O

ōḍa	room	أوضة
ōḍit nōm	bedroom	أوضة نوم
ow	or	أو

P

pruzhektoor	projector	بروجكتور

Q

qaḍi	judge	قاضي
qāʿid	leader	قائد
qāmoos	dictionary	قاموس
qanoon	law	قانون
qarrar, yiqarrar	to decide	قرّر

DICTIONARY

qarya	village	قرية
qaṣr	palace	قصر
qawā'id	rules	قواعد
qiddees	saint (Christian)	قديس
qimma	peak	قمّة
qiṣaṣ uṣayyara	short stories	قصص قصيرة
qism il mabi'aat	sales department	قسم المبيعات
quwwa	power (strength)	قوّة

R

raagil/ riggaala	man	رجل (راجل)

raaᶜi'! — Great! • Marvellous! — رائع!

raakib/a	passenger	راكب
raakib 'agala	cyclist	راكب عجلة
raᶜaṣ, yirᶜuṣ	to dance	رقص
radd	answer	رد
radiyateer	radiator (car)	رادياتور
raᶜees	president	رئيس
raᶜees il wuzara	prime minister	رئيس الوزارة
rafaḍ, yirfuḍ	to refuse	رفض
raff	shelf	رفّ
rahaan	bet	رهان
rāhib	monk	راهب
rāhiba	nun	راهبة
rāH, yirooH	to go	راح
rakan, yirkin	to park	ركن
raml	sand	رمل
raᶜs	head	رأس (راس)
raᶜṣ	dancing	رقص

raᶜṣ shar'i — belly dancing — رقص شرقي

rasam, yirsim	to paint (artwork)	رسم
raṣeef	platform	رصيف
rasha, yirshi	to bribe	رشى
rashwa	a bribe	رشوة

rās is sana — New Year — رأس السنة

rassaam/a	painter (artist)	رسّام
raqam gawaz is safr	passport number	رقم جواز السفر
raqam il ghurfa	room number	رقم الغرفة
raqm bareed	post code	رقم بريد
raᶜy	opinion	رأي
reef	countryside	ريف
reeH	wind	ريح
reeHa	smell	رائحة (ريحة)
ribH	profit	ربح
ribHiyya	profitability	ربحيّة
rifaaha	welfare	رفاهة
rigi', yirga'	to return	رجع
rigl	foot (body) • leg	رجل
riglayn	two feet/legs	رجلين
riHla	tour • journey • flight • trip	رحلة
rikheeṣ/a	cheap	رخيص
rikib, yirkab	to board (a ship, etc) • to ride (a horse)	ركب
risaala	message	رسالة
ritm	rhythm	رتم
riwaaya	novel (book)	رواية
riyāḍa	sport	رياضة
riyāḍi/ya	sportsperson	رياضي
rub'	quarter	ربع
rufayya'/a	thin	رفيع
rukba	knee	ركبة
rukhsit 'arabiyye	car registration	رخصة عربيّة

rukhṣit siwāᶜa	driver's licence	رخصة سواقة
rukn	corner (of room)	ركن
rukoob il khayl	horse riding	ركوب الخيل
rumādi	grey	رمادي
rumansi	romance	رومانسي
ruzz	rice	رز

S

sāᶜ, yisooᶜ	to drive	ساق
saaᶜ'	cold (drinks/food)	ساقع
saa'a	clock • watch	ساعة
saada	plain (unadorned)	سادة
saafir, yisafir	to travel	سافر
ṣaaHib/ṣaHba	friend	صاحب
ṣaaHib/a	owner	صاحب
ṣaaHib/it 'amal	employer	صاحب عمل
saaHil	coast	ساحل
saaHir	magician	ساحر
saa'id, yisaa'id	to help	ساعد
saᶜal, yisᶜal	to ask (a question)	سأل
saamiH, yisaamihyH	to forgive	سامح
saayiH/sāyHa	tourist	سايح
ṣa'b/a	hard • difficult	صعب
sabaᶜ	race (sport)	سبق
sabab	reason	سبب
sabaH, yisbaH	to swim	سبح

ṣabaH il khayr. Good morning.	صباح الخير.

sabat	basket	سبت
ṣaboon/a	soap	صابون
ṣaboor	patient (adj)	صبور
ṣadaf	shell	صدف
saddaada	plug (bath)	سدّادة
ṣadeeq	boyfriend	صديق
ṣadeeqa	girlfriend	صديقة
safar	travel	سفر
safeer	ambassador	سفير
ṣafHa	page	صفحة
sagaayir	cigarettes	سجاير
sahl/a	easy	سهل
ṣaH, yiṣaH	to be right	صح
saHab, yisHab	to pull	سحب
ṣaHra	desert	صحرا
sakhkhaan	heater (hot water)	سخّان
ṣakhr	rock	صخر
sakk, yisukk	to lock	سكّ
sakrān/a	to be drunk	سكران
salaam	peace	سلام
ṣaleeb	cross (religious)	صليب
ṣālit 'arḍ il funoon	art gallery	صالة عرض الفنون
sama	sky	سماء (سما)
samaa'a	hearing aid	سمّاعة
sammaak	fish shop	سمّاك
samaH, yismaH	to allow	سمح
samak	fish	سمك
sana	year	سنة
sanawi	annual	سنوي
ṣandoo' busta	mailbox	صندوق بوستة
ṣanf	race (breed)	صنف

ṣaniyya	(at the) roundabout	صنيّة
santi (mitr)	centimetre	سنتي (متر)
sanya	second (time)	ثانية
sara^c, yisra^c	to steal	سرق
saree'	quick • express	سريع
saree'/a	fast	سريع
ṣarrāf/a	cashier	صرّاف
sawaa^c	driver	سوّاق
ṣawwar, yiSawwar	to take photographs	صور
ṣaydaliyya	chemist • pharmacy	صيدليّة
sayf	sword	سيف
sayyid/ sayyida	saint (Muslim)	سيّد
seedee	CD	سي دي
seenima	cinema	سينما
seera	biography	سيرة
shaaf, yishoof	to see	شاف
shaal, yisheel	to carry • to pick up	شال
shaamboo	shampoo	شامبو
shaamil	included	شامل
shaari'	street	شارع
shaarik, yishaarik	to share (with)	شارك
shaasha	screen (TV or film)	شاشة
shaaṭ, yishooṭ	to kick (a ball)	شاط
shaawir, yishaawir ('ala)	to point (to)	شاور (على)
shabāb	youth (collective)	شباب
shabaka	net	شبكة
shagara	tree	شجرة

shahaadit seer wi sulook	reference (letter)	شهادة سير وسلوك
shahr	month	شهر
shahr il 'asal	honeymoon	شهر العسل
shaHHaat/a	beggar	شحّاد (شحّات)
shakar, yushkur	to thank	شكر
shakhs	person	شخص
shakhṣiyya	personality	شخصيّة
shakl	shape	شكل
shakoosh	hammer	شاكوش
shalaal	waterfall	شلاّل
shama'	candle	شمعة
shambanya	champagne	شمبانيا
shamm, yishimm	to smell	شمّ
shams	sun	شمس
shamsiyya	umbrella	شمسيّة
shanṭa	handbag • bag • suitcase	شنطة
shanṭit ḍahr	backpack	شنطة ظهر
shar^c	east	شرق
sha'r	hair	شعر
shareeHa	slide (film)	شريحة
shaṭarang	chess	شطرنج
sheek siyaaHi	travellers cheques	شيك سياحي
shibaak it tazaakir	ticket office	شبّاك التذاكر
shibbaak	window	شبّاك
shideed/a	strong	شديد
shiffa	lip	شفّة
shihaadit milaad	birth certificate	شهادة ميلاد
shikōlāta	chocolate	شيكولاتة
shimaal	left (not right) • north	شمال

shi'r	poetry	شعر
shireeṭ	cassette	شريط
shireeṭvidyu	video tape	شريط فيديو
shirib, yishrab	to drink	شرب
shirka	company	شركة
shiwayya	a little (amount) • few	شويّة
shiyoo'i/yya	communist	شيوعي
shugaa'/a	brave	شجاع
shughl	work • business	شغل
shughl il bayt	housework	شغل البيت
shughl yadawi	handmade	شغل يدوي
shuhub	meteor	شهب

shukran شكراً.
Thank you.

shunat	luggage	شنط
shurt	shorts	شورت
sibaaHa	swimming	سباحة
ṣidr	chest	صدر
sifāra	embassy	سفارة
siggaada	rug	سجّادة
sigin	prison	سجن
siHaab	cloud	سحاب
ṣiHHa	health	صحّة
sikin, yuskun	to live (somewhere)	سكن
sikkina	knife	سكّينة
sikirteera	secretary	سكرتيرة
sikka	footpath • track	سكّة
sikka Hadeed	railroad	سكّة حديد
silk	wire	سلك
sillim	stairway • steps	سلّم
simi', yisma'	to listen • to hear	سمع
ṣinā'a	industry	صناعة
sinaan	teeth	أسنان (سنان)
sinn	tooth (front)	سنّ
ṣinōbar	pine	صنوبر
sintrāl	telephone office	سنترال
siqa	trust	ثقة
sireer	bed	سرير
sireer muzdawag	double bed	سرير مزدوج
sireerayn	twin beds	سريرين
siringa	syringe	سرينجة
sirk	circus	سيرك
sitt	woman	ست
siyaasa	politics	سياسة
siyaasiyiyeen	politicians	سياسيّين
soo^c	market	سوق
ṣoof	wool	صوف
soor	fence • wall (outside)	سور
ṣoora	photo	صورة
ṣōt	sound • voice • volume	صوت
su^{c}aal	question	سؤال
ṣubā'	finger	إصبع
ṣubH	morning	صبح
ṣudā'	headache	صداع
ṣudā' niṣfi	migraine	صداع نصفي
ṣughayyar/a	young • small	صغيّر
ṣuHafi/yya	journalist	صحفي
sukhn/a	hot	سخن
sukhuniyya	temperature (fever)	سخونيّة
sukkar	sugar	سكّر
sur'a	speed	سرعة
sur'at il film	film speed	سرعة فيلم
susta	spring (coil)	سستة

T

ta'aala/i! تعالى!
Come!

taalit	third	ثالث (تالت)
ṭa'amu kwayyis	tasty	طعمه كويّس
taani/tanya	other • second	ثاني
ṭaba[c]	plate	طبق
ṭaba', yiṭba'	to type	طبع
taba', yitba'	to follow	تبع
ṭaba[c]a	class (social)	طبقة
ta'baan/a	tired	تعبان
ṭabakh, yuṭbukh	to cook	طبخ
ṭabaqat il ōzōn	ozone layer	طبقة الأوزون
tabdeel	exchange	تبديل
ṭābi'	postage (stamp)	طابع
ṭabl	drums	طبل
ṭaboor	queue	طابور
ta[c]deem	presentation	تقديم
tadrees	teaching	تدريس
taḍyee[c]	harrassment	تضييق
ṭaffāya	ashtray	طفّاية
ṭafH	a rash	طفح
tafri[c]a ginsiyya	sexism	تفرقة جنسيّة
tafri[c]a 'unṣuriyya	racism	تفرقة عنصريّة
tafṣeel/a	detail	تفصيل
tagdeef	rowing	تجديف
ṭāhir	pure	طاهر
tahma	offence	تهمة
taHleel	test (medical)	تحليل
taHleel damm	blood test	تحليل دم
taHt	below	تحت
ta[c]kheer	delay	تأخير
takhfeeḍ	discount	تخفيض

ṭakhkh, yiṭukhkh	to shoot (someone)	طخّ
tal	hill	تل
ṭal'a, yiṭla'	to scale • to climb	طلعة
ṭalab, yuṭlub	to ask (for something) • to order (request)	طلب
talawwus	pollution	تلوّث
ta'leem	education	تعليم
talg	ice	ثلج (تلج)
ṭālib/a	student	طالب
tallaaga	refrigerator	تلاّجة
taman	price	ثمن (تمن)
tamboonāt	tampons	تمبونات
ta[c]meen	insurance	تأمين
tamsiliyya	soap opera	تمثيليّة
ta[c]mul	reflection (thinking)	تأمّل
tanḍeef	cleaning	تنظيف
tanturleeh	launderette	تنتورليه
tarabeeza	table	ترابيزة
tarank	long distance (phone call)	ترنك
taranseet	transit lounge	ترانزيت
ṭard	parcel	طرد
ṭaree[c]	way • road	طريق
ta[c]reeban	almost	تقريباً
tareekh	date (time)	تاريخ
tareekh il	date of	تاريخ ال
ṭaree[c] ra[c]eesi	main road	طريق رئيسي
targim, yitargim	to translate	ترجم
ṭārid namoos	mosquito coil	طارد ناموس
ṭāsa	frying pan	طاسة
tasallukh	nappy rash	تسلّخ
tasallul	offside	تسلّل

tasgeel	recording	تسجيل
taᶜsheera	visa	تأشيرة
tashree'	legislation	تشريع
taṣmeem	design	تصميم
taṣreeH	permit	تصريح
taṣreeH 'amal	work permit	تصريح عمل
taṣweer	photography	تصوير
tawᶜim	twins	توأم
tawāriᶜ	emergency	طواريء
ṭaweel	long	طويل
ṭaweel/a	tall	طويل
ṭayyāra	plane	طيارة
ṭayyib/a	kind	طيب
tazkara wāHida	one-way ticket	تذكرة واحدة
tazkara zihaab wi 'awda	return ticket	تذكرة ذهاب وعودة
ṭeen	mud	طين
tekneek	technique	تكنيك
telisköp	telescope	تليسكوب
tiᶜeel/a	heavy	ثقيل (تقيل)
tikheen/a	fat • thick	تخين
ṭili', yitla'	to climb	طلع
tilifizyōn	television	تليفزيون
tilifoon	telephone	تليفون
tillighrāf	telegram	تلّغراف
tilt	one third	ثلث (تلت)
timsaal	statue	تمثال
tinis	tennis	تنس

tiṣbaH/i 'ala khayr — تصبح على خير.
Good night.

tiruH/i wa tigi bis salaama! — تروح و تيجي بالسلامة!
Bon voyage!

titeena	dummy • pacifier	تيتّينة
tiyatru	theatre	تياترو
tizkār	souvenir	تذكار
ṭool il 'umr	forever	طول العمر
ṭool in nahār	all day	طول النهار
tōst	toast	توست
traak	track (sports)	تراك
turumaay	tram	تروماي
ṭurumba	pump	طرمبة
tuwalit	toilets	تواليت

U

uᶜaf! — أوقف!
Stop!

ubira	opera	أوبرا

udkhul! — أدخل!
Go on in!

'uᶜd	necklace	عقد
ᶜuddaam	in front of	قدّام
'uḍw/a	member	عضو
ukazyōn	(on) sale	أوكازيون
ukht	sister	أخت
uksizheen	oxygen	أوكسجين
'uloom igtima'iyya	social sciences	علوم إجتماعيّة
'umla ma'daniyya	coins	عملة مدنيّة
umm	mother	أم
'umoomi	general	أمومة
unṣul	consul	قنصل
unṣuliyya	consulate	قنصليّة
urayyib	recent	قريب
urayyib	soon	قريب
urayyib/a (min)	near	قريب (من)
urkistra	orchestra	أوركسترا
urubbi/ya	European	أوروبّي
ᶜuṣād	opposite	قصاد
uṣayyar/a	short	قصيّر

U

DICTIONARY

usboo'	week	أسبوع
usbu'ayn	fortnight	أسبوعين
'ushb	herbs	عشب
usloob	style	أسلوب
uṭn	cotton	قطن
uṭn ṭibbi	cotton wool	قطن طبّي
ʿuṭṭa	cat • kitten	قطّة
utubees	bus (large)	أوتوبيس
'uyoon	eyes	عيون

V

veerus	virus	فيروس
vitameen	vitamin	فيتامين

W

waadi	valley	وادي
waasi'/a	wide	واسع
wa'd	promise	وعد
wāḍiH	obvious	واضح
wadi il mulook	Valley of the Kings	وادي الملوك
waffar, yiwaffar	to save (time/money/etc)	وفّر
waga'	pain	وجع
waga' fil ḍirs	toothache	وجع في الضرس
waHash, yiwHash	to miss (someone)	وحش
waHeed/a	single (unique)	وحيد
walad	boy	ولد
wala Haaga	nothing	ولا حاجة
wallaʿ, yiwallaʿ	to light	ولّع
wallaa'a	lighter	ولاّعة
wara	behind • at the back	وراء
waraʿ	paper	ورق
waraʿa	sheet (of paper)	ورقة
waraʿ bafra	cigarette papers	ورق بافرا
waram	lump	ورم
waraʿ tuwalit	toilet paper	ورق تواليت
warra, yiwarri	to show	ورى
warsha	garage (repairs) • workshop	ورشة
wasaa'il mana' il Haml	contraceptives	وسائل منع الحمل
waṣal, yuwṣil	to come, to arrive	وصل
wasaq, yasiq (fee)	to trust	وثق (في)
waseem	handsome	وسيم
waṣl	receipt	وصل
waʿt	time	وقت
wāṭi	low	واطي
wazan, yiwzin	to weigh	وزن
waẓeefa	job	وظيفة
wazn	weight	وزن
wi	and	و
widn	ear	ودن
wiHish/wiHsha	bad	وحش
wiʿif, yuʿaf	to stop	وقف
wikaalat ʿanba	newsagency	وكالة أنباء
wish	face	وش
wisikh/a	dirty	وسخ
wiṣil, yiwṣil	to arrive	وصل
wuṣool	arrivals (airport)	وصول
wusṭ il balad	city centre	وسط البلد

Y

yalla beena — يالاّ بينا.
Let's go.

yasāri/ya	left-wing	يساري
yihoodi/yya	Jewish	يهودي
yila'ib kutsheena	to play cards	يلعب كوتشينة
yimeen	right (not left)	يمين
yimkin	maybe	يمكن
yōm	day	يوم
yōmi	daily	يومي
yōm ig guma'	Friday	يوم الجمعة
yōm il sabt	Saturday	يوم السبت

Z

za^c, yizu^c	to push	زقّ
za'a^c, yiza'a^c	to shout	زعق
za'laan/a	cross (angry)	زعلان
za'laan/a min	angry (at)	زعلان (من)
zabaala	rubbish	زبالة
zahr	dice • die • flower	زهر
zaki/ya giddan	brilliant (intelligent)	ذكي جداً
zameel/a	colleague	زميل
zār, yizoor	to visit	زار
zara'	plant	زرعة
zara', yizra'	to plant	زرع
ẓareef	interesting	ظريف
ẓareef/a	charming	ظريف
ẓarf	envelope	ظرف
zayt	oil (cooking & crude)	زيت
zaytoon	olives	زيتون
zayy	similar (to)	زي
zheens	jeans	جينز
zhim	gym	جيم
zhimna-asteek	gym-nastics	جمناستيك
ziboon	client(customer)	زبون
zihaab	departure	ذهاب
zihiq (min)	bored (with)	زهق (مِن)
ẓill	shade • shadow	ظل
zilzaal	earthquake	زلزال
zōr	throat	زور
zurār	buttons	زرار

INDEX

I N D E X

محتويات

FINDER

SUSTAINABLE TRAVEL

As the climate change debate heats up, the matter of sustainability becomes an important part of the travel vernacular. In practical terms, this means assessing our impact on the environment and local cultures and economies – and acting to make that impact as positive as possible. Here are some basic phrases to get you on your way …

COMMUNICATION & CULTURAL DIFFERENCES

I'd like to learn some Arabic.

'aayiz/'ayza at'alim 'arabee (m/f)	عايزة أتعلم عربي.

Would you like me to teach you some English?

'allimak/'allimik shuwayit ingileezee? (m/f)	علّمك شويّة إنجليزي؟

Is this a local or national custom?

il 'aada dee bitita'mal fil balad kullaha wala hina bas?	العادة دي بتتعمل في البلد كلّها ولاهنا بس؟

I respect your customs.

ana aHtaram 'aadatak/'aadatik (m/f)	أنا أحترم عادتك.

COMMUNITY BENEFIT & INVOLVEMENT

Does your community have problems with …?

fee mushkilat … 'andukum?	فية مشكلة ... عندكم؟

freedom of the press	Hureeyit iṣaHāfa	حرّية السحافة
human rights	huʿooʿ ilinsaan	حقوق الإنسان
illiteracy	ilumeeya	الأمّيّة
political unrest	iḍtirāb seeyaasee	إضطراب سياسي
poverty	ilfaʿr	الفقر
unemployment	ilbiṭāla	البطالة

I'd like to volunteer my skills.
mumkin aṭaww'a — ممكن أتطوّع.

Are there any volunteer programs available in the area?
fee ayy burāmig muṭaw'a fil manti'a? — فيه أيّ برامج متطوّع في المنطقة؟

ENVIRONMENT

Is there a recycling program here?
fee i'aadit tashgheel izibaala hina? — فيه إعادة تشغيل الزبالة هنا؟

TRANSPORT

Can we get there by public transport?
mumkin niruH bi na'l 'aam? — ممكن نروح بنقل عام؟

Can we get there by bike?
mumkin niruH bi 'agala? — ممكن نروح بعجلة؟

I'd prefer to walk there.
afaḍḍal aruH maashee — أفضّل أروح ماشى.

ACCOMMODATION

I'd like to stay at a locally-run hotel.
'aayiz/'ayza anzil fi fundu' maHalee (m/f) — عايزة أنزل في فندق محلي.

Are there any ecolodges here?
fee eekoolodzh hina? — فيه إيكولوج هنا؟

Can I turn the air conditioning off and open the window?
mumkin a'fil itakyeef wa aftaH ishubbaak? — ممكن أقفل التكييف وْ أفتح الشباك؟

There's no need to change my sheets.
mish laazim tighayar ilmilaya — مش لازم تغيّر الملاية.

PIRAEUS BANK
بنك پيريوس - مصر

PIRAEUS BANK EGYPT

DATE: 02/01/10   TIME   : 16:06
ATM : S6A10101   TRANS.NO: 8732
CARD NUMBER:54436**********1

W I T H D R A W A L

FROM   ******996

AMOUNT: 500,00 EGP

EGP
EGP

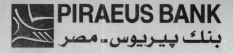

SHOPPING

Where can I buy locally produced goods/souvenirs?

alaaʿee intaag/tizkarāt baladee fayn? ألاقي إنتاج/تذكرات بلدي فين؟

Do you sell Fair Trade products?

bitbee'a intaag mubaadila 'aadila? بتبيع إنتاج مبادلة عادلة؟

Is this made from ...?	**di ma'moola min ...?**	دي معمولة من ...؟
animal skin	**gild Hayawanaat**	جلد حيوانات
crocodile skin	**gild timsaaH**	جلد تمساح
gazelle	**ghazaal**	غزال
tortoise shell	**sadafat zuHlifa**	صدفة زحلفة

FOOD

Do you sell ...?	**bitbee'a ...?**	بتبيع ...؟
locally produced food	**akl min ilmanṭiʿa di**	أكل من المنطقة دي
organic produce	**intaag bidoon mabdeeaat**	إنتاج بدون مبيدات

Can you tell me which traditional foods I should try?

ey ilaHsan akl taqleedee? إيه الأحسن أكل تقليدي؟

SIGHTSEEING

Are cultural tours available?

fee gawlaat saqafeeya? فيه جولات ثقافية؟

Does the guide speak ...?	**ilmurshid biyitkallim ...?**	المرشد بيتكلّم ...؟
Nubian	**noobee**	نوبي
Sa'idi	**sa'eedee**	سعيدي
Siwi	**seewee**	سيوي

Does your company ...?	shirkatak/ shirkatik ...? (m/f)	شركتك ...؟
donate money to charity	titbarra' bi khayreeya	بتبرّع بخيريّة
hire local guides	bitista'mil murshideen min ilmanṭi'a	بتستعمل مرشدين من المنطقة
visit local businesses	tizoor sharikat maHaleeya	تزور شركات محليّة

lonely planet
don't just stand there,
say something!
o see the full range of our language products, go to:
lonelyplanet.com

Lonely Planet Offices

Australia
90 Maribyrnong St, Footscray,
Victoria 3011
☎ 03 8379 8000
fax 03 8379 8111
✉ talk2us@lonelyplanet.com.au

USA
150 Linden St, Oakland,
CA 94607
☎ 510 893 8555
fax 510 893 8572
✉ info@lonelyplanet.com

UK
2nd floor, 186 City Rd
London EC1V 2NT
☎ 020 7106 2100
fax 020 7106 2101
✉ go@lonelyplanet.co.uk

lonelyplanet.com